G000124122

THE POWER AND THE GLORY

THE HISTORY OF THE NORTH WEST 200

This book is dedicated to my son Ben, my wife Ruth and our daughter Holly, and to the memory of William Joseph Dunlop

First published in 2002 by
Appletree Press Ltd
The Old Potato Station
14 Howard Street South
Belfast
BT7 1AP

Tel: (0) 28 90 243074
Fax: (0) 28 90 246756
E-mail: reception@appletree.ie
Web Site: www.appletree.ie

The Power and the Glory: The History of the North West 200

ISBN 0-86281-836-2

Commissioning & General Editor: Paul Harron
Designer: Wayne Matier
Editorial team: Rob Blackwell (copy editor), Jim Black & Cover to Cover
Index: Cover to Cover

THE POWER AND THE GLORY

THE HISTORY OF THE NORTH WEST 200

ALASTAIR McCOOK

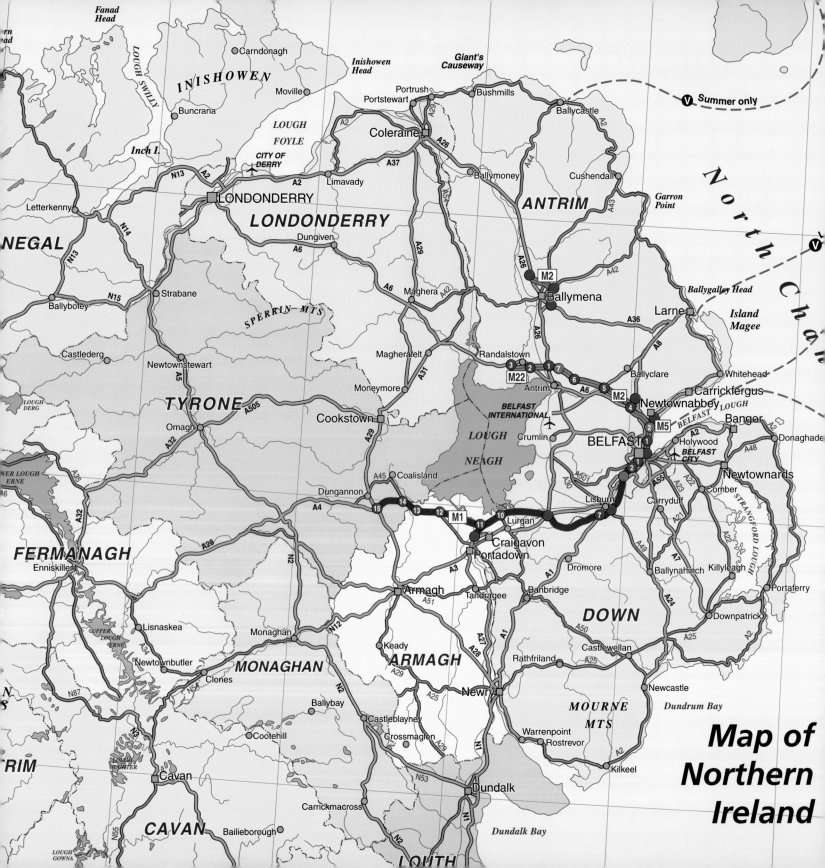

Map of Northern Ireland

Contents

Foreword

by Robert Dunlop

Throughout my career I've been privileged to compete at the top level of motorcycle racing, on some of the world's great circuits. I have many great memories of places like Macau, Dundrod, Monza and the Isle of Man, but the meeting that has given me the greatest pleasure over the years, is the North West 200. The Isle of Man TT is very special in a totally different way to the North West. The TT gives you a real buzz, but it takes up a full two weeks of the racing season and is a lot of hard work. The North West 200 is unique because it gives you all the emotion and that huge adrenaline rush in one day. Alastair McCook's timely new book, *The Power and the Glory*, records the history of this exhilarating and unique event and I am pleased to recommend it.

I remember standing at the frighteningly fast Mathers Cross, watching my brother Joey winning on the 1223cc Honda in 1981. I simply couldn't believe the corner speed he managed to carry through there. To watch was one thing, but when my debut – on a 250cc Seeley bought from Joey – came the following year, it was a real eye opener. A broken con-rod went through the crankcase, and the Seeley came to an abrupt halt going through the fast right-hander after Dhu Varren railway bridge. I'd never experienced a sudden seizure, totally without warning, like that before. It was scary, and disappointing not to finish, but the bug had bitten, and the following year I was back for more.

I had to wait until 1986 for my first win, just beating the late Gene McDonnell in a memorable 350cc battle. I didn't know it at the time but that win in 1986 was the beginning of a run of success that brought some of the crowning moments of my career. The glory days in the early 1990s riding the JPS Norton were something very special for me. The reaction of the fans that lined the course and waved me on to the chequered flag is something I'll never forget. Out of my fourteen wins, the first one, in 1986, will always be the one that means the most to me. It was my first International race win.

Over the years, Joey and I had some great battles at the North West 200. We lapped together in practice for the 2000 125cc race. The race turned into a real family affair with Joey and me battling for the lead with our nephew Paul Robinson and Ian Lougher. I really enjoyed that one.

I believe there is at least one more North West 200 win still to come for me. With the new Dunlop generation already making their mark in the sport, the task of being first past the flag on the Triangle is not going to become any easier in the years to come. I have no doubt that the young guns, William, Gary and Samuel Dunlop, will have their own North West 200 glory days to savour. The first generation has given them a lot to live up to and a hard act to follow.

The North West 200 is and will always remain my favourite day on the racing calendar. I hope it continues to go from strength to strength for many years to come, and that *The Power and the Glory* will bring the history of the event to life for every enthusiastic fan.

Introduction

I fell in love for the first time on 20th May 1967, a month short of my seventh birthday. I was seated at Metropole Corner in Portrush, on the Triangle Circuit, with my family, in the middle of the biggest crowd I'd ever witnessed. In the distance, the broad Atlantic Ocean boomed against the northern edge of Ireland; on the black ribbon of road before us that led to Church Corner and away to Portstewart, the drama of the 30th North West 200 – the first motorcycle race I'd seen – was unfolding. As they shared the spoils of victory that day, Fred Stevens and Steve Murray became – and remain – my first biking heroes. For me, they're still up there with the immortals.

That Saturday in May over thirty years ago, I fell in love for keeps. The first sight and sound of the screaming, thundering, revving massed Yamahas, Bultacos, Nortons, Matchlesses, Tritons, AJSs and Fred Stevens's Hannah Patons mesmerised me; combined with the smell of hot, sticky racing rubber and Castrol R that hung on the salty breeze that day, they made an overpowering blend. Years later, the heart beat a little faster for the female sex. The girls came and went, but that first heady intoxication lasted a lifetime.

The Power and the Glory – The History of the North West 200 is the story of Ireland's biggest sporting event. Seventy years – a lifetime if you're lucky – of racing on the world's famous Triangle Circuit has amassed a rich legacy of extraordinary achievement, human endeavour, resilience and ingenuity. This bittersweet epic of triumph and tragedy is fitting testimony to the skill and bravery of generations of the world's finest road racers, and their quest for excellence in one of sport's most unforgiving arenas.

The North West 200 has remained one of the most prestigious meetings on the road racing calendar since it first began in 1929. It continues to be a focal point in the lives of the riders and the legions of fans who make their way to the seaside circuit every year. Each year the crowds are bigger than the year before; the only bike event in Europe attracting a comparable crowd is the Spanish Grand Prix at Jerez.

Like the Isle of Man TT races, the North West 200 is held on closed public roads, but is fundamentally different from its Manx cousin. The circuit is shorter and safer, and racing is not run on a time trial basis against the clock, but with riders battling on the road, wheel to wheel. The North West 200's traditional date in May established it from the beginning as a valuable pre-TT test. Over the years, it has grown to rival the TT in terms of numbers and quality of entries, and in the sheer size of the crowd it attracts. In recent years, riders such as 1998 British 500cc Grand Prix winner Simon Crafar, Terry Rymer, Niall Mackenzie, Steve Hislop, Jamie Whitam, Carl Fogarty, Shane Norval and Carl Muggeridge have raced against TT regulars like Dunlop, Moodie, McCallan and Simpson between the walls and houses beside the seaside.

The Power and the Glory charts seven drama-filled decades, from the superiority of Norton, Velocette, Excelsior and Rudge, through the challenge of Moto Guzzi, NSU and Gilera in the 1950s, to the Japanese dominance that has been maintained for the past thirty years. To list the event's past winners is to list the sport's great riders of the last seventy years.

This book writes an important missing chapter in the rich history of motorcycle racing.

Alastair McCook

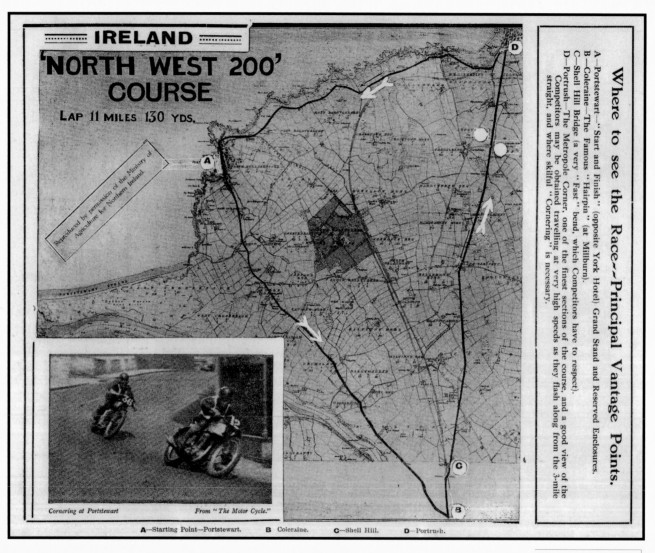

IRELAND
'NORTH WEST 200' COURSE
LAP 11 MILES 130 YDS.

Where to see the Race—Principal Vantage Points.

A—Portstewart.—"Start and Finish" (opposite York Hotel) Grand Stand and Reserved Enclosures.

B—Coleraine.—The Famous "Hairpin" (at Millburn).

C—Shell Hill Bridge (a very "Fast" bend, which Competitors have to respect).

D—Portrush.—The Metropole Corner, one of the finest sections of the course, and a good view of the Competitors may be obtained travelling at very high speeds as they flash along from the 3-mile straight, and where skilful "Cornering" is necessary.

Cornering at Portstewart.   From "The Motor Cycle."

A—Starting Point—Portstewart.   **B** Coleraine.   **C**—Shell Hill.   **D**—Portrush.

Above: map of the original Triangle Circuit.
Right: Jim Woodside (left) and Mick McSorley (right) – see p18

CHAPTER ONE

1929–50

starters set off, the "scratch men", Stanley Woods (490cc Norton) and H G Tyrell Smith (499cc Rudge-Whitworth), began their own swooping descent. The Derry and District Motor Club's long-standing dream of running a high-profile, international motor-cycle road race had finally become a reality.

All this might never have happened without the addition of the Road Races Act to the Statute Book by the Northern Ireland Government in 1922; as a consequence, the Isle of Man might have remained unchallenged as the domain of motor-cycle road racing within the British Isles. The exploits of the likes of the Collier brothers, Alec Bennett, Wal Handley and Stanley Woods at the Isle of Man TT races had been creating world headlines since 1907. The renown- ed engineer Harry Ferguson, the man who revolutionised agriculture with the Ferguson tractor,

Originally published in the Belfast News Letter

The day it all began. Riders with longer handicaps patiently await the signal to start the 1929 race as one of the shorter handicapped men roars past the pits.

The North West 200 motorcycle race was first held as a handicap event over the eleven miles of public roads – the Triangle Circuit – connecting Coleraine with the seaside towns of Portrush and Portstewart. At 1 pm on Saturday 20 April 1929, three riders pushed their machines into life from the starting-point at Magherabuoy, and began the downhill run into Portrush. These men were A McIntyre (Abingdon KD), R B Patterson (348cc OEC), and R M Osbourne (348cc Raleigh) and having received the most generous handicaps were known as the "limit men".

By 1.53 pm, having seen all but two of the thirty-one

Stanley Woods clocks up some practice miles before the 1929 meeting. In the early years competitors shared the roads with everyday traffic during practice.

Originally published in the Belfast News Letter

was quick to recognise the promotional and commercial possibilities of high-profile car and motor-cycle race meetings in Ireland. He enlisted the help of his friend Thomas Moles MP, the editor of the *Belfast Telegraph*. Together they exerted their considerable influence in an effort to bring about the necessary legislation that would allow motor sport to be promoted and developed in the province. By May 1922, county councils in Northern Ireland had the powers to close public roads for the purpose of allowing car and motor-cycle racing to take place. By October 1922, the first Ulster Grand Prix had been held on the 20.5 Clady Circuit, and declared a resounding success.

Unofficially, road racing, unheralded by the publicity that accompanied the first Ulster Grand Prix, had been taking place long before the Road Races Act came into force. One of the earliest examples was a 200-mile race, officially listed as a "reliability trial", held in July 1903.

The Ulster Centre of the Motor Cycle Union of Ireland had been founded at a meeting in Hicks Metropole Hotel, College Square North, Belfast, in January 1903. By July of that year, plans were well under way for running a road race. The organisers realised from the outset that their plans for a road race through Antrim and Derry would not receive official sanction from the authorities. Indeed, they anticipated that if made public, their plan would be quashed and so it remained a closely guarded secret.

No cheering crowds or throngs of press saw the fourteen starters on their way at 6 am on 11 July 1903 from Belfast's Donegall Street. Only five brave souls completed the bone-jarring 200-mile route from Belfast through Carrickfergus, Larne, Cushendall and Portrush, before turning inland to Derry. The route turned back from Derry to Belfast and to the finishing point at the Crown and Shamrock Inn at Glengormely, on the city's outskirts. J Burney headed the depleted field home on a Royal

Enfield to claim an historic win. His son, J G Burney, in turn, enjoyed a distinguished racing career with Stanley Woods as his mentor, business partner and, finally, father-in-law.

The 1922 Road Races Act gave rise to numerous motor-cycle road-race events. Many were short-lived, such as the Dungannon 100, 1924–27, the Ballydrain 60, 1922–32, and the Coleraine 100, held only once over five laps of a twenty-mile road circuit outside Coleraine in 1923.

The Temple Road Race, now known as the Temple 100, jumped the legislative gun and started life as the Temple 50 in 1921. The Temple meeting proudly claims to be the oldest established event in the Irish racing calendar, although it did not take place in 2000, due to serious safety concerns regarding the narrow, twisting, switch-back country roads track. It would seem unlikely, in the current climate of heightened concern for improving safety in road racing, that the Temple 100 will be held again. The Banbridge Road Race was also first held in 1921, although it only ran on three further occasions up until its eventual demise in 1930. This small, now mostly forgotten meeting, has one lasting claim to fame: it was here, in 1921, that Stanley Woods made his road-racing début.

By 1929, the Derry and District Motor Club's plans to organise and stage an event of international importance were well advanced, albeit in a somewhat modified form from what had originally been envisaged. It seemed certain that if manufacturers were given the opportunity of an early season shakedown of machinery, then star names and works' entries could be guaranteed straightaway.

A distance of 200 miles was not commonly used in 1929, and expert opinion advised that a race run over 100 miles would be more popular. In retrospect, the decision

BOWLING SEASON OPENS.—MRS. BENT (wife of the president) THROWING THE FIRS

Ir. W. Thompson's a jump in the first go on Saturday.

Originally published in the Belfast News Letter

NORTH-WEST " 200."—J. W. SHAW LEADING J. G. BURNEY AT MILLBURN CORNER, COLERAINE, IN SATURDAY'S GREAT MOTOR-CYCLE RACE.

JW Shaw leads JG Burney through Millburn Corner during the 1930 event. Shaw finished 5th, Burney settled for 6th.

machine-destroying straights, reminiscent of the Continental Grands Prix.

History reveals that although the club's original choice of name for the race remained, their original choice of venue did not. The name has continued to generate some confusion amongst those who are unaware of the event's origins. The inclusion of "200" simply indicates that the event was originally run over a distance of 200 miles. "North West" reflects the originally intended location of the race, namely on a public-roads course in the North West of Ireland.

to run the event over the longer distance made it a rigorous pre-TT test of reliability that factory teams could not ignore. Also at odds with established formats of the time was the decision to run the event on a handicap basis; the Continental Grands Prix and the Isle of Man TT races were all raced on a scratch basis.

Vindication of the organisers' choice of date and distance can be seen from the fact that by 1930 the Leinster 100 meeting had moved from its usual date in August to May, and by 1932 it had doubled in length to join its northern cousin at over 200 miles.

Whilst the Derry Club built their plans around using a public-road circuit close to the Maiden City, some of the club's members thought differently. To them it was clear that a course was required that had more to offer. The success of their meeting would, to a large extent, depend on presenting a circuit that offered many of the key elements and challenges of the TT circuit. They had become aware of one possibility that could not only do just that, but which could also incorporate long,

At the starting-point at Magherabouy, almost exactly where the chicane is now situated on the course, on the downhill run into Portrush, a grandstand had been erected on the right-hand side of the road. Directly opposite were the pits, where riders would stop to refuel throughout the race. A marquee selling refreshments was erected nearby, and a brass band entertained the gathering crowds on race day, 20 April 1929.

As Harry Ferguson left to close the roads in the official car, a strong breeze blew from the direction of Ramore Head. Consequently, many of the spectators around the start/finish area elected to stay out of the exposed, elevated positions offered in the grandstand. As the day progressed, it remained a poorly supported venture.

On race day, the Derry and District Motor Club were ably supported by officials involved in the running of the well-established Ulster Grand Prix. Their expertise was put to good use in timekeeping and general marshalling duties. As the officials took their places and the riders and machines began to file from the paddock and onto the track, it was obvious that not all of the thirty-five entrants had made it to the line.

Due to the non-arrival of his OK Supreme, Tommy Stewart was relegated to the role of marshal and Belfast riders J Carson and E Brooks also failed to take their places. J McKane, a local rider from the nearby village of Dervock, was also amongst the list of non-starters. Whilst practising on the course the previous evening, McKane was thrown from his machine after colliding with a car at Dhu Varren. He suffered a broken arm and leg, as well as serious facial injuries. As the field of thirty-one awaited the starter's flag, McKane was beginning his recovery in Portrush Hopefield Hospital.

As the Union Jack and Irish Tricolour – flown in honour of the six competitors from Eire – fluttered over the expectant gathering, the writer in the *Belfast News Letter* of 22 April 1929 commented that, "The scene at the start resembled a miniature Grand Prix."

At precisely 1 pm the starter, W Simms, sent the first three riders on their way. Belfast rider W Sullivan took over the ride on George McIntyre's 250cc New Imperial at the last minute, and he was first man through Magherabuoy at the end of lap one, closely followed by A McIntyre on the little Abingdon.

Coleraine rider Malcolm McQuigg was the first man to complete the second lap, and by that stage it looked like he had a fighting chance of making up the two laps he had conceded to McIntyre on handicap.

As the clock ran down, E G Lammey got away on his Rex Acme on 38 minutes. S A Crabtree followed on 26 minutes on his 246cc Excelsior. On 19 minutes, J W Shaw joined the fray, riding a 349cc Norton, and a minute later W H T Meagean set off down the hill on his 346cc JAP.

C W Johnston (498cc Cotton-Blackburn) started on a minute. Thirty seconds later, Percy "Tim" Hunt and Ernie Nott, both on board 490cc Nortons, left together. Another thirty seconds passed before the "scratch men", Stanley Woods (490cc Norton) and H G Tyrell Smith (499cc Rudge-Whitworth), finally took up their challenge against the clock, and the twenty-nine men on the road ahead of them. Their starts were equally poor, and they lost valuable time straight away.

Tyrell Smith was back in the pits at the end of lap one. Frantic adjustments were made to the big Rudge's steering, and over two minutes lost before Tyrell Smith changed goggles and pulled away, knowing he had a mountain ahead of him to climb.

Woods suffered an even worse fortune: after what seemed like an eternity, the Dubliner pushed home to complete his first and only lap. He retired at the pits with ignition problems.

After six laps, one-third of the total race distance, the top eight positions were as follows:

1	A McIntyre	57 min 25 sec
2	M McQuigg	1 hr 15 min 3 sec
3	J Woodside	1 hr 9 min 6 sec
4	E G Lammey	1 hr 11 min 57 sec
5	W J McCracken	1 hr 3 min 8 sec
6	S A Crabtree	1 hr 8 min 44 sec
7	W H T Meagean	1 hr 2 min 19 sec
8	J W Shaw	1 hr 4 min 35 sec

As the miles reeled by, Hunt and Tyrell Smith found their rhythm, and upped their pace with each circuit. Hunt completed his first lap in 9 min 58 sec. His time for lap four was 9 min 25 sec. The race was on.

Dublin rider T G Byrne had his handicap reduced from seventeen minutes to ten minutes as the grid assembled.

By the midway point it was irrelevant as lack of spark saw him join a list of retirements that included Chas Brockerton, whose 348cc AJS expired at Blackhill on lap one, with just over a mile of the 200 completed. Also out were Stanley Woods, F J Drummond, J Gordon, R G Corry and S A Crabtree, who for a time held a place in the top six. George Brockerton's challenge also ended on the third lap, with a broken con rod.

As the race approached half distance, it was clear that the fastest man on the road was Hunt. He was lapping at an average speed of 68.77 mph, although his handicap only allowed him to attain eighth position on the leader board. This was one place higher than J Gordon Burney, who was turning in a stunning performance on a Royal Enfield that would only select one gear from lap one. However, Burney had almost failed to make it to the start at all since he had discovered a broken clutch spring whilst completing an early-morning sighting lap. Last-minute repairs allowed him to make the start by the skin of his teeth.

By lap eleven, C W Johnston was out, sidelined with a burst oil union. By the end of the same lap, Hunt's name would also join the steadily growing list of retirements.

As the race entered its second half, an unexpected, additional hazard developed as the dry whin bushes at Blackhill caught fire. The gorse bank was quickly ablaze, and the riders had to rely on blind faith as they drove on through a pall of dense smoke that hung over the road.

The generosity of McIntyre's handicap was underlined by the fact that the little Abingdon still headed the pack as they reached two-thirds distance. By the end of twelve laps, eighteen of the original starters were out and the leader board had begun to assume a familiar look.

McIntyre valiantly held off the chasing pack for fourteen laps, but on lap fifteen he was caught and passed by Meagean, and then McCracken and McQuigg. Jim Woodside, who had held third place from the opening lap, suffered the cruellest luck: with less than a lap to go, his 346cc Calthorpe ran out of fuel. As McCracken rode home to secure an historic victory, Woodside was left to think about what might have been.

The inaugural North West 200 had been a resounding success, but there was room for improvement, especially in the areas of crowd control and insurance. It was only when the race was in progress that the organisers realised that permission should have been sought from Antrim County Council to close that part of the circuit within their jurisdiction.

Sweeping changes would take effect before the second running of the North West 200 and an acrimonious dispute would develop within the Derry and District Motor Club.

In the months after April 1929, a significant faction of the membership left and formed a new, breakaway organisation: the North of Ireland Motor Club. From the start, the newly formed club also laid claim to the right to run the prestige event. The Ulster Centre of the Motor Cycle Union of Ireland adjudicated that each of the clubs could run the race on alternative years, with the Derry club due to stage the event in 1930. Weeks before it was due to take place, the Derry club publicly conceded that they were unable to promote the meeting. The North of Ireland Club seized their opportunity and took over immediately. Their efforts were celebrated as an all-round success. A few years later, the Derry and District Motor Club ceased to exist.

With little time to prepare, the North of Ireland Club did a remarkable job. They ran the meeting as a scratch event, although prestigious handicap awards would continue to be presented for many years. It was also decided that the start/finish area would be located at

Portstewart. The new position was situated just after the fast right-hander at the York Hotel, on the short-straight charge to the treacherous, downhill, left turn onto Portstewart promenade at Henry's Corner.

To avoid congestion and the possibility of a mass pile-up at Henry's, the organisers opted to use a rolling start. The riders set off in waves, one for each class, separated by one-minute intervals. A car, driven at a stately 20 mph, preceded each class, leading them along the length of Portstewart promenade before pulling off the road, allowing the race to get underway properly.

A large crowd watched the first wave set off promptly in ideal conditions. The anticipated battle between Graham Walker and Ernie Nott began immediately. Mounted on factory-entered 499cc Rudge-Whitworths, the pair shadowed each other for the first five laps. Walker held the advantage at the end of the first and second, but by the end of the fifth lap it was Nott in front. As the team mates diced for the lead, Percy "Tim" Hunt, Belfast's Paddy Walls and Stanley Woods on the big works Norton battled to keep in contention.

H G Tyrell Smith, riding a works 350cc Rudge, had been a strongly fancied pre-race favourite, although an oiled plug on the opening lap appeared to put him out of contention before his race had properly begun. On lap two, Tyrell Smith lapped 4 mph faster than the existing lap record. A tenacious second circuit, completed at 74.1 mph, put the flying Dubliner back on terms.

The Belfast sports paper, *Ireland's Saturday Night*, published on the evening of the race, brimmed over with admiration for Tyrell Smith's heroic performance:

"This was a feat that only those who have ridden round the circuit can fully appreciate. It means that a speed of at least 100 mph must be reached on the straight portion from the Shell Hill Bridge near Coleraine until the rider turns the corner in Portrush, where he has got to come right down to about 10 mph in order to safely negotiate the sharp bend. A similar slowing down is also essential at the Coleraine end of the lap, so that with the many other less than acute bends, the absolute necessity for an open throttle on any and every opportunity becomes apparent if an average of over a mile a minute is to be maintained at all."

Ireland's Saturday Night, April 1930

Ultimately, Tyrell Smith's valiant effort was in vain. The factory Rudge had endured a punishing schedule, taking him under the existing lap record on three of his first five laps. On the sixth lap, with Tyrell Smith still pushing hard, his machine suffered a broken tappet; his heroic ride was over.

Later on, Walker completed his fourteenth lap as race leader, pitted and rejoined the fray in pursuit of victory. On the penultimate circuit, the race was decided by mechanical failure. To the surprise of the assembled crowds at the start/finish, Nott swept through to begin his last lap alone, unchallenged. Walker, his machine stricken with a broken oil pipe, was out.

Riding a 350cc factory Norton, Percy "Tim" Hunt claimed an emphatic 350cc class win, and the overall runner-up spot from Jimmy Shaw (350cc Velocette).

In the 250cc class, Ernie Fernihough's victory had upset the form book; riding a 172cc self-tuned Excelsior, Fernihough ran with the 250cc machines, and eventually ran away from them to lead Malcolm McQuigg (246cc Zenith JAP) across the line. Despite setting the fastest 250cc lap of the race at 59.25 mph, Belfast rider W A Drummond did not feature in the final placings. Along the way, he had become yet another victim of mechanical failure.

The 1930 winners table would make familiar reading over the coming two years: Graham Walker and H G Tyrell Smith would go on to score class wins, but in 1931 and 1932, the 250cc and 500cc classes would remain the undisputed territories of Fernihough and Nott.

The heavy, leaden skies of early morning had cleared by 2 pm to see the 1931 grid of twenty-seven riders get away in perfect conditions. As the pack disappeared in the direction of Portstewart, Walls and Brockerton were still struggling to get going. The smoke and noise had barely cleared before the drama began to unfold:

"All eyes turned towards the hill on the Portrush road as the distant roar of machines was borne on the still air from the east, and in a little over nine minutes, three flying figures appeared over the brow and flashed through – Nott first with Woods on his back wheel, and Meageen a second behind."

Coleraine Chronicle, 2 May 1931

Graham Walker followed the flying trio through, with H G Tyrell Smith a further second adrift. For the first five frantic laps, it was Nott leading by only feet from Woods and Meagean. Then, on the sixth circuit, the popular Cumberland rider made his move. His time for the first six laps, the opening third of the race, was 55 min 1 sec, a single second faster than Woods, and four better than Nott. As he headed Woods and Nott through the start/finish, the crowd roared their approval. Meagean defied all their efforts to overhaul him for the next twenty miles, but when Woods posted a time of 8 min 49 sec on the eighth lap, Meagean had no reply.

Woods pulled away steadily, with only Nott in contention. But as the leaders flashed through the start/finish to begin their thirteenth lap, it was Woods who trailed Nott by ten seconds. A soft rear tyre forced Woods to slow, handing the victory to Nott and third place to Meageen.

For Graham Walker, a change of class brought with it a change of fortune; Walker had been robbed of an almost certain victory in the previous year's 500cc class, but in 1931 he was entered to ride the Rudge factory's latest 350cc weapon.

On the opening lap, Walker's most serious potential rival, Percy "Tim" Hunt (348cc Norton), went out with a broken overhead rocker. Fellow 350cc competitor J R McCurdy (346cc AJS) had more serious misfortune to contend with. On the fast straight from Coleraine, approaching Portrush, he collided with L J Archer (246cc New Imperial). Both riders crashed heavily at speed and were admitted to Portrush Hopefield Hospital, McCurdy suffering a fractured leg and Archer with head injuries.

Walker was never really pushed for the win, and although he recorded the fastest lap of the race at 68.94 mph, Hunt's 1930 record of 72.48 mph remained intact.

H G Tyrell Smith on a 250cc works Rudge had torn the field apart with a new record time from a standing start. On his second circuit, he bettered his opening effort with a time of 9 min 57 sec, an average of 66.89 mph. As Tyrell Smith left the field further behind, only Sydney Gleave (SGS JAP) remained in the same race. By lap ten, Gleave was out. On lap twelve, with a comfortable lead in hand, Tyrell Smith's Rudge cried "enough", and victory was handed on a plate to Fernihough. Tyrell Smith's lead, when he had been forced to retire, was over twelve minutes. C B Taylor (245cc Excelsior) from St Anne's on Sea was the only other 250cc finisher.

The following year, the 250cc victory would again be Fernihough's. Once more, it would be shown that whilst hard riding at the limits of a machine's capabilities might please crowds, it was far from being a race-winning strategy.

For the opening six laps of the 1932 250cc event, C B Taylor and Charlie Manders fought it out, tooth and nail. After completing one-third of the total race distance, only two seconds separated them. By lap seven, Manders went out when his Rudge broke a piston rod. Soon after, Taylor joined him as a spectator when his OK Supreme cracked a crank case. Manders new lap record of 9 min 56 sec, 66.89 mph, was hollow consolation. Once again, Fernihough demonstrated the importance of consistency and reliability in taking the win. Ballymena rider R G McBurney (245cc OK Supreme), the only other 250cc machine left running, was flagged off after completing sixteen laps.

For the third year in succession, Fernihough would join Ernie Nott on the podium as a race winner. In contrast to Fernihough's win, Nott produced an emphatic tour-de-force performance that saw him storm to the front from the flag, and remain there.

Nott's first lap, from a standing start, was two seconds outside the existing record. It was a portent of what was to come. He had already established a commanding lead by the end of the first lap:

"...the roar of his exhaust had died away in the distance before Walker, his team mate, appeared over the hill, followed by the Belfast rider Walls on an AJS."

Belfast News Letter, 2 May 1932

On his second lap, Nott trimmed seven seconds off the lap record, and on the next lap, lowered it further to post a time of 8 min 33 sec, 77.71 mph. After recording an identical time on lap four, Nott completed his next circuit at an average speed of 78 mph, a time of 8 min 31 sec. After completing one-third of the total race distance, the minor placings already seemed academic. Walker, already struggling to stay on something resembling terms with his team mate, went out on lap four at

Coleraine with a seized engine. F J Drummond (Norton) moved into second place on lap five, over three-and-a-half minutes behind. At the end of six laps, Nott's advantage stretched to more than four minutes over Drummond and eleven over Stanley Woods, who held third place.

Once again bad luck dogged Woods from the start; he took 19 min 33 sec to complete his opening lap after his Norton sheared a plug. After pitting to fit a replacement, Woods set about trying to make up the time he had lost; the equivalent of one full eleven-mile lap of the circuit.

It was too much to ask, even of Stanley. Try as he might, Woods could only claim back seconds where he needed minutes. In the end he came home in third place, having completed the last seventeen laps of the race 1 min 38 seconds faster than Nott. The sheared plug had cost him dearly.

The 350cc race had been a classic battle between Wal Handley, making his North West 200 début, and H G Tyrell Smith until the latter retired on lap seven. Tyrell Smith took the lead from his Rudge team mate on the second lap, when he went round in 9 min 13 sec, a speed of 72 mph. It proved to be the fastest lap of the race, although it did not better Hunt's 1930 record of 72.48 mph. Smith's lead gradually grew from one second on lap three to three seconds on the following lap. On the fifth circuit, it was Handley who led from Smith by one second. By lap eight Smith was out, and Handley could afford to ease off, with a two-minute lead over the new second-place man, H Pinnington (AJS). Handley had more than three-and-a-half minutes in hand over Pinnington at the flag, with R J Gray a very distant third.

"On Wednesday 26 April 1933, the early morning stillness was shattered at five o'clock, when the thirty entrants set off on the closed roads for two hours of high-speed practice."

The North West 200: The First Twenty-Five Years, David Maxwell

In 1933 the format for the North West 200 underwent two major changes. Firstly, the introduction of official practice on closed public roads, despite the ungodly hour, was a major step forward. Although the second idea, running the race on a Thursday, was not. At the time there was significant opposition amongst local residents to the race being held on their doorstep and given that there was slightly less objection to the peaceful calm being shattered midweek and the obvious need for official practice, it is easy to see how some sort of compromise, or trade-off deal, might have been done. Racing would only take place on a weekday on one other occasion: when the 350cc race was also held on the Thursday of race week in 1951, the occasion coinciding with the Festival of Britain.

The distinctive figure of Ernie Nott was not amongst the twenty-three men who lined up on the grid for the 1933 meeting. With Nott, the man who had dominated the heavyweight division on the Triangle Circuit since 1929, missing, a new name would be added to the roll of honour for the Blue Riband class.

Of the thirty entrants who had shattered the early morning tranquillity in practice, seven failed to make the start. One of the missing was J H Fell of Knutsford, Cheshire. Fell, a member of a three-man team from Cambridge University, had crashed in practice at Blackhill, and was unfit to race.

By the end of the first lap, it looked as if Stanley Woods' luck had finally changed. As he began his second lap, he held a twenty-eight-second lead over a depleted field, with only five machines in the 500cc entry still running. On lap four, Belfast rider and race débutant Walter Rusk, "The Blond Bombshell", on a Sunbeam, went out. Rusk's Sunbeam also failed to last the distance in that year's Senior TT.

With his lead now extended to 7 min 27 sec over Kilkenny's Mick Mahoney, Woods looked like he had the race in the bag. Despite his works Norton developing engine trouble at three-quarters distance, Woods cruised home for his only North West 200 victory with more than twenty-seven minutes to spare over Mahoney. The winning time was just under five minutes slower than Nott's from the previous year. They were the only two finishers in the 500cc division.

Jim Woodside (left) and Mick McSorley pictured with some of the silverware they collected during their distinguished careers. The photograph shows the ex-works Rudge they shared, and which carried Woodside to victory in the 1933 250cc North West 200. McSorley used the same machine to win the 250cc class the following year.

Irene Ackerman Collection

For the first five laps of the 350cc race, it was neck and neck between Percy "Tim" Hunt (Norton) and H G Tyrell Smith (Rudge). On the third lap, Tyrell Smith went round in 9 min 8 sec, three seconds under Hunt's 1930 lap record. As the race progressed, time and again, Hunt bettered his old record. On the final lap, he carved twenty-four seconds off his 1930 time, raising the new record to 75.65 mph and coming home twelve minutes clear of H Pinnington in second place. Wesley Shaw (Norton), son of the great Jimmy Shaw, held second place until lap fourteen, when he skidded and broke a footrest. As a result, his speed dropped, allowing Pinnington to catch and pass him for the runner-up spot.

The 250cc class had a familiar tale to tell. Charlie Manders had taken his Rudge round in 9 min 37 sec to establish a new lap record of 69.09 mph. On lap eleven, with a four-minute lead over Belfast rider Jim Woodside, Manders retired with a broken rocker. Woodside, riding an ex-works Rudge, rode home for the win.

The following year brought one of the best-supported entries, spread across all three classes, since the event began. In the 500cc division, Ernie Nott was back once again to do battle, this time equipped with a privately entered Rudge. Charlie Dobson would put the New Imperial twin through its paces before taking it to the TT, whilst Tyrell Smith's chosen weapon was a 495cc OHC AJS. Amongst the private Norton runners were S B Darbishire, J H "Crasher" White and Jock Forbes, with S "Ginger" Wood riding an OK Supreme-JAP.

Making his North West 200 début as team mate to Wal Handley in the works Norton team was a quiet, unassuming Scot, whose performances were already setting the standards in motor-cycle racing. Over the next four years, Jimmie Guthrie's rides on the Triangle Circuit would set the benchmark by which others would be judged.

From a standing start, Guthrie pushed the lap record from 77.71 mph to 79.73 mph. As the laps reeled by, Guthrie continued to define new limits. At the half-way stage, he was averaging 81.44 mph and held a 4 min 20 sec advantage over Nott, with White more than a minute and a half further adrift. Handley, who held second place from the start, was out by lap four. In the end, the flying Scot carved 8 min and 52 sec off the total race time, and pushed the lap record to 82.16 mph, a time of 8 min 5 sec. Guthrie's average speed for the 200 miles was 80.37 mph.

"When spoken to after his wonderful ride, Guthrie had little to say about his achievement. His face was covered in a white froth from the sea breeze, and while wiping this off he said his ride had been uneventful. He actually did a lap more than he ought, apparently not realising that the black flag which was waved before him had, under the new international rules, been substituted for the more familiar finishing flag of black and white."

Coleraine Chronicle, 19 May 1934

In the 350cc class, Walter Rusk, riding a works Velocette at his second appearance in the race, was giving his own demonstration of how to rewrite record books and win from the front. Rusk headed the field, depleted by mechanical failures, home in a time 5 min 5 sec under the existing record. In the process, he equalled Hunt's lap record of 75.65 mph.

Along the way, Jimmy Simpson's Norton expired on lap five. Stanley Woods took over the ride on George Rowley's AJS when it was discovered, just before the start, that the petrol tank on his own machine was leaking. Consequently, Rowley was consigned to the list of non-starters. On the second lap, Woods' run of poor North West 200 luck resumed when gearbox trouble forced him out. Velocette-mounted Dublin rider J J O'Neill held second spot from the start until the eighth lap when he was overhauled by H Pinnington while he pitted, although he went on to reclaim the runner-up position and hold it to the flag. W G Wright crashed and remounted his Velocette to finish fourth behind third-place man Pinnington.

"He [Wright] was at the point of collapse at the finish, and the ambulance was called to take him to Coleraine Hospital, where he was treated for facial injuries and a gash to the leg."

Coleraine Chronicle, 19 May 1934

Wright was subsequently awarded a club medal by the organisers in recognition of his pluck and courage.

Wright's fellow competitor J H Lafone, the son of the Archdeacon of Kendal, was not so fortunate. He crashed his 350cc Rudge at the Plantation, midway between Portstewart and Coleraine. After the news of the accident was relayed to the finish by one of the dispatch riders, who were positioned at various points around the course, an ambulance was dispatched to the scene and Lafone was taken to hospital.

Riding the same 250cc Rudge that Jim Woodside had taken home for the win in 1933, Mick McSorley took the honours after long-time race leader L G Martin's Rudge failed on the final lap when he held a ten-minute lead. Gordon Burney, riding a Moto Guzzi entered by Stanley Woods, raised the lap record to 70.19 mph, but only finished in fourth place, behind McSorley, Robson and Duncan.

The winning Rudge was owned by Belfast engineer Billy Chambers, with McSorley and Woodside riding it in turn at meetings all over Ireland. While competing in Phoenix Park in Dublin the following year, McSorley's machine collided with a cow; he was badly injured and never raced again.

Stanley Woods posted his intentions for the 1935 event with an impressive display of quick laps in practice. However, on the day Woods was forced to sit out the race, reduced to the role of spectator when his Moto Guzzi broke a con rod in practice.

In the 500cc class, Jimmie Guthrie's winning average speed of 78.99 mph, slower than the previous year's, reflected the Norton star's dominance. He cruised home almost five minutes ahead of S B Darbishire, also riding as an official Bracebridge Street entry. Jock Forbes, Manliff Barrington, Ken B Leach and E C Nicholls made up the four-man Vincent HRD challenge. Forbes disputed the final podium place with H G Tyrell Smith, riding a factory-entered AJS, until his retirement on lap six. Pinnington, on board a privately entered AJS, was running in third place as the race reached the half-way point, but on lap fifteen was forced to join the list of retirees. Only fourteen of the thirty-nine riders, who had started with a minute interval between each class, completed the full distance.

Whilst Guthrie's fastest lap of 81.53 mph left his record of 82.16 mph from the previous year

The Blond Bombshell, Walter Rusk (Norton) sweeps to victory in the 1935 350cc North West 200.

Curly Richmond Collection

intact, Walter Rusk's storming 350cc ride once again redefined standards. From the off, Rusk set about a systematic demolition of lap and race records. He smashed the lap record on the third, fourth and sixth laps, finally carving twenty seconds off his best time from 1934 to set the new record at 78.63 mph, a time of 8 min 27 sec. At the flag, Rusk was almost a lap in front of runner-up, fellow Belfast rider, H Taggart. Taggart had been entered in both 250cc and 350cc classes, but had opted to ride the heavier machine. Jackie Chambers, the youngest rider in the race, and riding with an injured hand, claimed third, after works AJS-mounted Harold Daniell retired from the top-three position on lap eleven.

In the 250cc class, Chris Tattersall made the headlines for the wrong reasons. By lap twelve, a three-way battle was raging at the front between Tattersall (Python), Charlie Manders (Excelsior) and Stanley Woods' protégé, Gordon Burney (Moto Guzzi). As they crested the hill at Juniper three abreast, Tattersall was brought down when his and another machine touched:

"The spectators at the grandstand at Portstewart got the biggest thrill of the race when four hundred yards away on the Portrush road a motorcycle was seen to do a double somersault and crash into a wall. There was great anxiety for the rider, but he had parted company with his machine a second or so earlier and was unhurt except for a few bruises."

Coleraine Chronicle, 18 May 1935

Burney had seen off Mick McSorley's challenge in the early stages, and led by the half-way point. With a seemingly insurmountable advantage, Burney's Guzzi expired on the final circuit, allowing a grateful Manders to take the win. His total time was two-and-a-half minutes

faster than McSorley's winning time from the previous year. McSorley had to settle for runner-up spot, coming home ahead of L G Martin.

Of the eight starters on the grid for the 1936 500cc class, only two would finish. Once again, Guthrie was unrivalled and headed Sheffield's J W Beevers (Norton) home. At the end of 200 miles, Guthrie's works Norton had endured a rigorous test of speed and reliability. Despite the lack of opposition, Guthrie had clearly come to Portstewart with record breaking in mind. He bettered the existing lap record six times. At the end of his

Curly Richmond Collection

day's work, the new figure stood at 84.28 mph.

As the seventeen-strong 350cc field got away, Walter Rusk could only watch. An early season crash had resulted in a broken arm for the rising star and an enforced day off by the sea. As White, Thomas, and Tyrell Smith sorted out the top-

The great Jimmie Guthrie pictured with Norton team boss Joe Craig (middle) and North of Ireland Club official PJ Drummond after his 1935 500cc victory. Guthrie's four 500cc class wins between 1934 to 1937 stand testimony to one of the truly outstanding riders to have graced the Triangle circuit.

three positions, Rusk could only wait for his arm to heal and the TT to come around. White's winning average for the distance was 76.73 mph, with E R Thomas' works Velocette following the Norton home at a respectful distance. Despite taking his Excelsior round in a new lap record of 79.9 mph, H G Tyrell Smith still had to settle for the bottom step on the podium.

The dogfight of the day raged from lap two until the thirteenth in the lightweight class. Blackpool rider S V Smith (OK Supreme) and Maidenhead's Ron Harris (Rudge) were virtually locked together for 130 miles. After first-lap leader Taggart retired with a seized engine, Smith went on to hold a one-second advantage by lap three. On lap six, Smith and Harris dead-heated, although by lap nine, Smith was once again in front by a single second. Pinnington's short-lived moment of glory came on lap ten when he passed the battling Smith and Harris. Smith regained the advantage, but with two laps to go, he was forced to bow out with a seized engine. In the end, Harris came home third, behind Pinnington and a late-charging Charlie Manders (Excelsior). A new lap record of 70.31 mph saw the popular Dubliner ease home with over two minutes in hand.

Smith would wait another twelve months before returning to claim the victory that had been denied him by mechanical failure. At the flag, he took the win by twelve seconds from Belfast's George McAdam (New Imperial) after a race-long tussle. Charlie Manders (Excelsior) had once again set a new lap record although ultimate glory was denied him by a breakdown. His fastest lap of 71.5 mph, recorded before his retirement on the fourth lap, was ten seconds inside the previous record. Of the eleven lightweight starters, only two, Smith and McAdam, completed the distance.

The 1937 North West 200 is memorable as the fourth in Guthrie's quartet of 500cc wins, and his last ride on the Triangle Circuit. Riding numbers 1 and 2 in the race,

Guthrie and Frith, the official Norton entry, came home in formation, 1 min and 41 sec apart. Frith, making his début on the seaside circuit, held a top-three position throughout the race, but never seriously challenged his team mate at the front. That task had been taken up by Stanley Woods, riding the works Velocette entry. At the end of the first lap, Woods lay in third, behind Guthrie and Frith. The next time around, the flying Dubliner held a two-second advantage at the front. As Guthrie gave everything to remain in touch, he halved Woods' advantage on the next circuit, while the gap back to Frith grew steadily.

As the miles fell away, Woods' lead ebbed and grew. On lap five, it had increased to five seconds, on the sixth, one-third the total race distance, a single second separated them, and on the seventh circuit, Woods' advantage over his great friend and rival had extended to four seconds. Then on the eighth lap, at the tight left-hander at Milburn Corner, turning away from Coleraine and back onto the flat-out charge to Portrush, the front wheel of the Velocette locked. In an instant, Woods' hopes of a second North West win vanished as he crashed out of the race. He toured to the pits, where a further three minutes were lost on running repairs to his damaged front brake. Despite gamely rejoining the fray, Stanley's efforts were in vain; he retired at the end of lap ten.

Guthrie romped home for the win in 2 hr 25 min 32 sec, 1 min and 37 sec inside his race-winning time from the previous year.

Whilst Guthrie's 1936 500cc lap record remained intact, works Norton 350cc runner Jimmy "Crasher" White made his mark with an average speed of 78.94 mph, a circuit of 8 min 25 sec. White came home 2 min 48 sec ahead of factory Excelsior rider S "Ginger" Wood, with Excelsior-mounted H G Tyrell Smith holding off Jimmy Little (Velocette) for third.

Entries for the 1938 event grew to a grand total of seventy due to the forward planning of the North of Ireland Club. Cross-channel riders received three days' free accommodation, those from Eire two days' and Northern Ireland competitors one day's, all at the club's expense.

As the 1938 North West 200 got underway after a delayed start, with rain still falling steadily all around the course, it was clear that the weather would limit speeds. The record books would remain intact for another year. Police and marshals experienced difficulty preventing spectators from encroaching onto the road at a number of points around the course, and the appointed start time of 2 pm had come and gone before the starter's flag dropped.

Stanley Woods, suffering a painful kidney ailment, was a doubtful starter right up until the last minute. He made

it to the grid after being examined by a club doctor. Neither of the works Nortons, due to be ridden by Daniell and White, were ready to race so they were non-starters. Freddie Frith, the only official Norton entry to make it to the line, led from E Lambert (HRD) as the pack charged into Portstewart for the first time. At the end of the lap, Frith held a twenty-second lead. As the front men completed their second circuit, it was the orange helmet of the factory Velocette man that flashed into view, with Moore on his back wheel. As they headed for the left-hander at Henry's, Frith, his machine bearing the tell-tale signs of an excursion into the countryside, limped into the pits to retire.

A third-lap crash eliminated Lambert, Beevers and Tomlinson. As the rain fell steadily, Woods pushed on at the front of the

The start of the 1938 350cc race. From left to right: 22 S Ginger Wood, 21 G Rowley, 23 Maurice Cann, 37 C R Clarke, 36 J B Moss, 41 J Garnett, 39 R Pennycock, 30 J Cannell, and 29 H Carter.

The David Collection

field. Moore was race leader as they went through Portstewart to complete the sixth circuit, after Woods had crashed and remounted. As Woods stopped for fuel on the eighth, Moore went straight through, extending his two-second advantage to forty-eight. As Moore pitted on the next lap:

"...Woods, riding courageously in the flying spray, roared through on the tank, a mere thirty-two seconds in front."

Belfast News Letter, 16 May 1938

With four laps to go, Woods clocked two nine-minute laps to build a sixty-five-second cushion. With only twenty-two miles of the race remaining, it seemed as if Stanley's North West 200 luck had, at last, changed. As he began the final run for home onto the coast road, with one minute and seven seconds in hand, his Velocette spluttered, coughed and fell silent. Victory had been denied him, for want of the equivalent of a cupful of fuel.

"It was an unfortunate ending to a magnificent ride by a sick man on a rain-swept course, which required very careful negotiating."

Belfast News Letter, 16 May 1938

Ernie Lyons, making his North West 200 début, had held third place throughout the race. With Woods' demise, Lyons cruised home to take the runner-up spot, 4 min and 15 sec behind Moore. As Moore celebrated his win, Woods phoned his pits from Metropole Corner, requesting enough petrol to power his stricken Velocette home.

In an interview in June 2000, Lyons recalled his North West 200 début:

"I decided to be very brave and head off for the North

West 200. My brother went with me. We only just arrived in time for practice. We had no problems during practice; things went very smoothly.

We started off in the race. I was a good starter, but I soon got left behind by a few people like Stanley Woods on the Velocette, and a Norton or two. I rode my own race. Somewhere past the graveyard that used to be on the course, there was a dip down. There were three bikes in front of me and the road was wet. One of them fell off in the middle of the road. Another bike hit him, and he fell off, and the third one hit that, and down he went too. It blocked the road completely, and I took to the grass bank. The speeds would be fairly hefty there, you'd be doing about 90 mph, or around that. No chance of stopping.

"I got through on the bank, although my footrest stuck in the bank, but it didn't do any harm. I kept going. One of the riders, the first 'fella', got up and the next rider hit him with his handlebars and knocked him down. The third 'fella' hit the bike, and that brought him down. I could see all this; I was only about sixty yards behind them. Well, I usually had fairly quick reactions, I'd tend to size up the situation and decide what to do, it wasn't just involuntary."

The crash described by Lyons involved Tomlinson, Lambert and Beevers on the third lap. Lyons continued:

"I finished second in the 500cc class, only at about the same speed as Jimmy Little finished on the Velocette in the 350cc class. I was very happy to finish. I got the handicap award and the newcomers award too. That financed my racing for the rest of the year, believe it or not."

In a departure from the established format of the event, the 350cc field covered one lap less of the course than the 500cc runners. A R Foster, riding Rowley's works AJS, was a flag-to-flag winner. Brake linings had failed to arrive in time for Foster's four-cylinder 500cc machine. Not for the first time, Rowley was forced to surrender his North West 200 ride to a team mate. Foster rode the entire race without a rear brake. He slid off on lap fourteen, when caught out by the slippery conditions. Despite sustaining damage to his steering damper and front brake cable, he remounted and maintained his lead.

Leicester's Maurice Cann (Norton) remained in pursuit for over 140 miles of the total distance. With the deficit at just under five minutes, Cann crashed out of the race, allowing S "Ginger" Wood, riding the new spring-framed Excelsior, to take over second place. On the last lap, Wood also joined the list of retirements with piston trouble. Artie Bell (Norton) eventually followed Foster home, seven-and-a-half minutes adrift and six seconds ahead of third-place man J B Moss. The press hailed Bell and Lyons as "the outstanding discoveries of the meeting".

Seven of the sixteen 250cc starters completed the reduced distance of sixteen laps. Until the final circuit, H G Tyrell Smith, Wakefield's Denis Parkinson and Welsh entry J Edwards completed an Excelsior 1-2-3. On the final lap, Yorkshire's H

The streets are awash as A E Shaw trails Stanley Woods around Henry's Corner during the wet and miserable 1938 North West 200.

The David Collection

Hartley (New Imperial) edged Edwards out of third spot to prevent an Excelsior clean sweep. Tyrell Smith had originally been listed to ride the factory 500cc entry, but with the machine unwilling to start, he took over the official four-valve, quarter-litre ride from Charlie Manders, who, as a result, was a non-starter.

After losing part of his index finger in a crash on the Continent, Stanley Woods was back in the saddle for the 1939 North West 200. During practice he seized a gearbox and subsequently worked through the night in an effort to repair it, wheeling the Veloce Motors Ltd entry to the line with minutes to spare.

From the start it was Woods who led, with Lyons (Triumph) and Beevers (Norton) heading the rest of the pack. On lap one, three miles into the race, tragedy struck when Norman Wainwright lost control of his 500cc Norton at the Plantation, between Portstewart and Coleraine, after his rear tyre burst. A doctor was rushed to the scene of the accident, but Wainwright, competing in the race for the fourth time, was killed instantly.

By lap three it was the familiar story: the Woods/North West 200 jinx struck again, and Stanley went out with a seized engine. Lyons took over the lead from Beevers, with the charging Bob Foster, piloting the supercharged, liquid-cooled, four-cylinder AJS, back into contention. Foster had lost two minutes at the start with a flooding float chamber. As Foster cut his way through the slower 350c class, he locked handlebars with Portsmouth rider P T W Baker (Excelsior), who crashed out unhurt.

As Beevers and Lyons drafted through the start/finish line, Foster was right with them. On the straight drag along Portstewart promenade, he caught and passed them, but was again delayed with the flooding float chamber as he left the pits after stopping to refuel. On the thirteenth lap, Foster went out with a blown cylinder head gasket. Beevers' challenge ground to a halt on the final lap, leaving a slowing Lyons to ride home alone for his only North West 200 win.

Sixty-one years later, Lyons looked back on his celebrated victory:

"We took the Triumph up to the North West from Kill [Co Kildare] in a four-seater Clyno we had. We took the seats out and put it in. We didn't have a trailer in those times. We were there in time for scrutineering and practice. Things went so fast, you didn't have much time to look around you at all. You just got in and got the bike out. We stayed one night in a B&B, then headed home as quick as we could. I suppose it would have sunk in by the time I got home that I'd won a race.

"The bike was then a more or less standard Tiger 100 Triumph, with all the extras taken off. Racing mudguards and that sort of thing on it. It did have a TT carb. There was nothing special about the engine; the cam shafts and everything were standard. It probably could do something like 105 mph. The handling wasn't wonderful to say the least: rigid frame, and I don't think they had got the steering-head geometry quite right. On a bump or anything else, it would start to wobble. I didn't mind it, but sometimes it was so bad you thought you were going to come off.

"I always felt I had a little advantage riding in the wet on the road. I knew where to look for a bit of wheel grip and that sort of thing."

In the 350cc class, the battle had commenced, with Bell (Norton) and Rusk (Velocette) locked together at the end of lap one and Jimmy Little (Velocette) and A E Moule tight behind them. At the end of the third lap, Bell was in the pits with plug trouble. In an effort to catch the flying Rusk, he bent a valve on the following lap and his race was over. Seven miles from home, Rusk

was thrown from his Velocette at Shell Hill Bridge and although his injuries were minor, he was unable to continue. Little claimed the victory, coming home seventeen minutes clear of runner-up Louis D Gilbert (Norton).

Of the eleven riders who completed the full distance, six came from the 250cc ranks. The race brought a comfortable win for "The Pocket Marvel", Denis Parkinson, riding an Excelsior. Parkinson had shadowed Chris Tattersall, riding his own home-brewed "Special". Parkinson made his move after the opening two laps, and although Tattersall regained the advantage for one lap midway through the

Letter of congratulation sent to Ernie Lyons from the Triumph factory in recognition of his racing success.

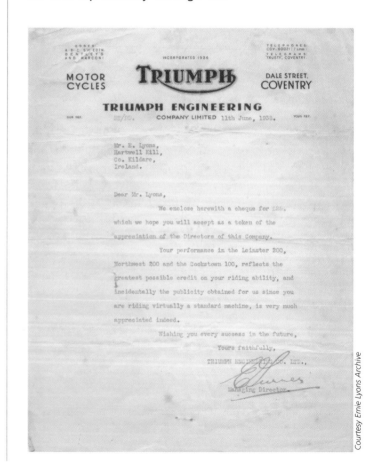

Courtesy Ernie Lyons Archive

race, it was Parkinson who came home with sixty-five seconds in hand. Excelsior-mounted Liverpudlian A Glendenning held a safe third place for the entire distance.

As the 1939 North West 200 finished, the dark clouds of war hung heavy on the horizon. Another eight years passed before the sound of tuned racing engines once again echoed above the North Antrim cliff tops. When racing returned to the Triangle in 1947, there were gaps on the grid, left by men like Wal Handley and Ted Mellors, who made the ultimate sacrifice and gave their lives during the Second World War.

966122 Airman Rusk W R, aged thirty, lost his life during a routine training flight. Rusk had flown out of No 7 Flying Training School, Westwood Farm, Peterborough, early on the morning of 8 October 1940 with co-pilot Sgt Johnston. Their Hawker Hart Special crashed near Tilton-on-the-Hill. Rusk, "The Blond Bombshell" North West 200 winner, and race and lap record holder, was buried in Peterborough's Eastfield cemetery.

Ernie Lyons returned to the seaside circuit, where he had been successful in 1939, for the 1947 North West 200 as a works Norton rider. A famous win in the Senior Manx Grand Prix in September 1946 had attracted the attention of the Norton boss, Joe Craig.

"In 1947, I rode the 350cc works Norton and Artie rode the 500. I had a tough time at the North West 200 in 1947. I didn't get the 350 until the day of the race. Artie had to ride his own Manx Norton. Would you believe, I practised on a trials bike. It was a Norton trials bike we had, a terrible camel, but it had quite a turn of speed. I had to get out on something."

Despite the failure of Bell's works Norton to arrive, 1947 would mark the beginning of his three-year dominance of the heavyweight division. Friday's early morning practice session had been delayed by poor light. When it

eventually got underway, an hour behind schedule at 6 am, Bell posted a speed of 80.05 mph; eighteen seconds faster than the best lap time he would set in the race.

Two years after war had ended, petrol was in short supply. Obtaining fuel of any type with rationing in place was a tall order and getting hold of petrol-benzol mix was simply out of the question. The combination of rain, the less potent "pool" petrol and roads in poor condition in places would limit speeds on race day.

As the 500cc pack thundered towards Henry's Corner for the first time, it was Harold Daniell who led in the treacherous conditions by twenty yards from Bell. As they streamed past the pits at the end of lap one, the positions were reversed. Bell gradually pulled away from the field, leaving Rex McCandless and Baldo Melli, who was making his North West 200 début, to dispute third place. By the end of lap three, their battle was for second place, as Daniell toured to the pits to retire after crashing near Coleraine.

Melli, responding to frantic signals from his pit, got down to the job in hand and, by the end of the fourth circuit, narrowed the gap to a mere five seconds. As the race reached half distance, McCandless responded to the mounting challenge and secured a forty-six second advantage over Melli, although he was still five minutes behind his great friend and rival.

In spite of being handicapped by a failing clutch, Bell took the chequered flag with eight minutes to spare. McCandless brought his 1939 Norton, previously owned by Bell, home with only two seconds to spare over Melli.

In the 350cc race, it would be a day of frustration for Lyons.

"I started off on the works bike and went away from the field. Then the bike stopped, well it didn't stop altogether, it got down to a tick-over coming along the coast road. With the throttle flat open it would only tick over. I had to foot-slog up the steep hill coming out of Portrush. I got back to the start and left the bike lying against a wall, and tried to tell Joe Craig what was wrong with it. Joe wasn't interested really. When I was sitting there trying to tell him that the bike wouldn't go, it started to rev itself up. I had left the throttle wide open. I got on it again and went away. I got back in the lead again I think, and a couple of laps from the finish, just after Shell Hill Bridge, the same thing happened again.

"In slowing down, or pulling into the side of the road, I got into a bit of a water-cut. The rev counter, which was terribly low on the Norton, got wiped off as I was coming to a standstill. Again the bike got going again after sitting there for a long time. I only finished fifth in the race. I think Joe was more concerned about the broken rev counter.

"He said, 'You fell off.' I said, 'I didn't fall off', which I hadn't. He was more concerned about that broken rev counter than anything else, I'm not joking."

Lyons' stop-go day of mechanical failure did not go unnoticed by the *Belfast News Letter* reporter, who noted that:

"Lyons, who had been announced as retired, arrived back at the finishing point at high speed, and gave a gesture of disgust as he received the flag."

Belfast News Letter, 19 May 1947

The race leadership see-sawed from Moule, at the end of lap one, to Chelmsford's John H Pettit, who headed the charge for two laps before surrendering his advantage to Ken Bills. The young Kent rider's challenge ended when he crashed through the hedge and out of the race at Shell Hill Bridge, allowing Pettit back in front. On the thirteenth lap, it was the Norton-mounted trio of Lyons, Malcolm Templeton and Moule in front. Lyons lost his hard-gained advantage when he was forced to pit for a plug change.

As the flag fell, Moule was briefly hailed as the winner, but his celebrations ended abruptly when it was announced that Templeton was in fact the race winner by seventy seconds. In the end, Moule was relegated to third place behind J E C Purnell (Norton).

In the lightweight class, a three-way battle was developing between the Excelsior-mounted trio of Manx challenger L G Martin, thirty-five-year-old Rochdale managing director R T B (Ben) Drinkwater, and twenty-eight-year-old Dubliner P D Gill. Martin held a one-second advantage over Drinkwater at the end of lap two, with Gill a further fourteen seconds off the pace. As Martin began his fourth lap, his engine developed a misfire, and next time round he retired at the pits. Gill steadily pulled back time on Drinkwater and on the ninth lap overtook him; he remained in front to the end. J A Dickson made it an Excelsior clean sweep when he held off L G Patterson (New Imperial) for the final podium place.

The North West 200 was not held in 1948 due to the unavailability of fuel supplies. The organisers redoubled their efforts, and the meeting was revived the following year. The response was encouraging. The largest entry in the history of the race, 113 riders, lined up at Portstewart for what would be the twentieth anniversary of the event.

The sheer size of the entry created new challenges for the organisers. The Motor Cycle Union of Ireland's guideline on the size of entry for any meeting was that no more than ten starters per mile of the course could be allowed. By this calculation, the Triangle Circuit's limit stood at 120. Although the initial entry for the 1949 event exceeded this figure, the number of non-starters maintained the numbers to just within the MCUI's ruling. The problems created by the sheer volume of the entry would prompt the MCUI to amend their guidelines, reducing the number of starters allowed to no more than seven per mile on any course.

In response to the magnitude of the challenge, eighteen timekeepers, the highest number of timekeeping staff ever deployed at any motor-cycle race in Ireland, would endeavour to translate the frantic action into meaningful speeds, times and results. Their task would prove to be a difficult one.

The grid assembled in bright sunshine:

"There was a stimulating picture of the speed game at the starting-point, where the one hundred and thirteen riders took up their starting positions in six lines. After the warming up of machines, they waited in silence, broken only by the sound of the sea, for the pistol shot which would send them on their gruelling two hundred mile ride."

Ireland's Saturday Night, 14 May 1949

It was a grid that bristled with talent. While the works 350cc Norton was entrusted to Harold Daniell, the factory's 500cc machines would be ridden by Bell and Lockett. Bill Doran and Reg Armstrong would head the AJS 350cc challenge, with Ted Frend completing the team's line-up on board the 500cc machine. Piloting a pair of Nigel Spring-entered Velocettes were Freddie Frith and Ken Bills. And at number 53 in the programme, making his North West 200 début, was a young Geoff Duke on a Manx Norton.

As the drama of the race unfolded, the debris of crashes began to litter the course. Amongst the growing list of walking wounded were T I Birrell, E Andrews, D J

Gallagher and Ken Bills, who crashed out of a 350cc fourth place in the closing stages of the race. W McVeigh sustained serious injuries after crashing at Ballysally Corner. For the second time in the history of the event, the race was blighted by tragedy: P L Phillips of Uppingham, Rutland, received fatal injuries when he crashed on the section between Portstewart and Coleraine.

For the opening six laps, Bell, Lockett and the Triumph-mounted Lyons circulated together in a high-speed display of close-formation riding. Bell led them through at the end of lap one, but it was Lockett who hit the front for the next twenty-two miles, with Lyons and Bell trading places yards from his back wheel. As the battle continued, Lyons bided his time, waiting to play his ace card when the time to stop for fuel came around. Lyons still considers the 1949 500cc race as his most memorable North West 200 ride:

"I rode an ex-Reg Armstrong Grand Prix model that I bought from Reg. It was still capable of staying with the Nortons. I was on the Triumph, sitting behind Johnny Lockett and Artie. There was a hump on the road somewhere near the cemetery. Artie and Johnny were alongside one another. There was a chap in the middle of the road they were overtaking. They went either side of him, and they were in the air at the time they passed him. When they passed him, I went through as well. He must have got a desperate fright.

"I saw Artie push Johnny just coming into Coleraine – I thought it was deliberate. There was a hedge sticking out, he pushed Johnny into it and got a wider run into the corner, although I don't think it was for that reason he did it. Johnny was up alongside him and he hit the hedge. It was fortunate there was nothing solid in it. They were certainly scrapping between themselves. Johnny got his own back at the S-bend on the straight after Shell Hill Bridge. It was taken flat out in those days, and Johnny nearly put him through the hedge. It looked bad; there was no love lost at that particular point. They did settle down afterwards. Certainly Artie wouldn't be somebody that you would try anything on. He was a tough rider.

"I tried to get in behind Artie, but I didn't have enough speed to get close enough to him. Johnny would come up and get in front of me, and then slow down to pull me away from Artie. He knew that I would be able to catch them on the twisty bits. That tactic lasted until my oil tank split on the sixth lap, and that finished it.

"I would have won that race if the bike had kept going. We had arranged for a very quick petrol filler; I think we pressurised a can or something. You wouldn't be allowed to do it now of course. There was nothing formal at that stage as regards quick fillers. Artie was filling by hand, but we had a set-up that could put enough in the tank in fifteen seconds. Artie took over a minute – there's no way he could have made that up.

"I knew that I couldn't pass them on the straights, but if I could stay with them, I knew I had them beaten. That was the tragedy: they didn't know I had the quick filler."

With Lyons sidelined, Bell set a pace at the front that no one could live with. Lockett led briefly on the eleventh lap as his team mate refuelled, but was over half a minute behind with two laps to go.

On rounding the final corner:

"Bell gave the thumbs-up signal, and was greeted by cheering crowds of thousands as he swept down the promenade."

Ireland's Saturday Night, 14 May 1949

On his way to victory, Bell carved seven seconds off Jimmie Guthrie's 1936 lap record, setting a new best speed of 85.55 mph. His total race time, 2 hr 23 min 53 sec, gave him the race record as well. Bell's record-breaking ride was further distinguished as the first post-war international motor-cycle race to be won at record speeds using "pool" petrol.

In the 350cc race, Frith and Daniell would share the honour of writing new records, with victory going to Daniell by one-fifth of a second; the closest finish recorded in the event's history.

As the field of almost eighty riders streamed away, it was Bills, Frith and Reg Armstrong who emerged to dispute the lead, with Daniell, Frith and Doran heading the high-speed train through Portstewart at the end of lap one. By the next lap, Daniell had been relegated to third place, behind Doran and Frith. So the order remained for the next two laps, as all three circulated under the lap record.

With Frith and Daniell second-guessing when the other would stop for fuel, Doran pitted first; he would crash out of the later stages of the race. With split seconds separating them lap after lap, the titanic battle raged unabated onto the coast road for the final time. Both had raced the entire distance without refuelling, and in the closing seconds, as they crossed the line virtually together, Daniell was almost taken off by an over enthusiastic official flagging them home.

"…they swept round Primrose Hill, and down round Golf Course Corner, to the finishing line, neck and neck. But in front were another pair of riders, and Daniell cut out to flash over the finishing line, one-fifth of a second ahead of Frith, after nearly one hundred and ninety miles."

The North West 200: The First Twenty-Five Years, David Maxwell

"Crasher" White's race and lap records had been obliterated. Daniell's new race average of 80.40 mph easily surpassed White's 1936 speed of 76.73 mph. Frith had the satisfaction of raising the lap record from 78.94 mph, set by White in 1937, to 81.69 mph. Duke claimed a fine third place on his début as he headed Reg Armstrong home, almost three minutes behind Daniell and Frith. The future five-times world champion would have his days of glory in the years to come.

The lightweight class had its own share of drama and

Photo originally published in the Belfast News Letter, May 1949

1949 350cc winner Harold Daniell, Norton (24), rounds Milburn hairpin ahead of R McDonald, Freddie Frith (25), and G P Ellison.

hard-fought battles. Early pacemakers L G Martin (CTS) and Ben Drinkwater (Excelsior) both went out through mechanical failure, allowing Belfast rider Joe McKimm to take over at the front. With two laps remaining, McKimm was also forced to retire when his Excelsior broke a chain. The victory appeared to be Chris Tattersall's. Riding one of his own "specials", Tattersall received the winner's plaudits, only to discover that a protest against his victory was upheld and the win awarded to Harold Kirby. W G Dehaney, the oldest competitor in the race, and J McCreadie completed the top three to give Excelsior a 250cc clean sweep.

For the privileged 100,000 who packed the vantage points and lined the black winding, eleven-mile ribbon, the 1950 North West 200 would be a memorable one – a turning point.

As the 2 pm start time approached, the sun beat down relentlessly, melting patches of tar on the roads. The fine conditions, combined with the reinstated use of 80-octane petrol, would be significant factors in the decimation of lap and race records that was to follow. The most lethal ingredient in the high-speed cocktail sat in the form of the three works Nortons on the front rows of the assembled 350cc and 500cc ranks on the grid. Bell, Lockett and Duke were the three riders on board.

As a young rising star, being part of the Featherbed Norton's first international success remains a special memory for Geoff Duke:

"I had ridden the Featherbed of course, the one that Rex McCandless actually built, at Blandford in April that year. That was the first time it was ever ridden in a race. We broke the lap record at Blandford, and won the race easily against some quite stiff opposition, the works AJS Porcupines, etc.

"Prior to that, as was almost inevitable when the bike needed testing in the first instance, it was brought over to the island, and Artie Bell and myself rushed it round Kate's Cottage, which was very bumpy in those days. The difference in the machine was just unbelievable. Then we took it to Monthlery, to the road circuit, and did about 400 miles on it. We broke the lap record by about thirteen seconds. After that, I couldn't wait to try it in a proper race. Blandford was a short circuit – a very good circuit – but I mean a Grand Prix or near to Grand Prix. Of course, the North West was always the event which Norton did as a lead-up to the TT – a test of the machines. In those days, it was much twistier than it is now. In fact, in many ways a very different circuit. In spite of having very long straights, the section along the coast road was really good, and very like a lot of the TT to be honest."

Duke had signalled his intentions, by breaking Bell's 1949 absolute course record, in practice, and was the only 350cc works entry on the grid. No other works machin-

Fr Noel Watson Collection

The McCandless brothers, Rex, and Cromie, seated with the Benial, the prototype of all modern racing motor cycles.

ery would challenge the 500cc Bracebridge Street team; with Italian-Gilera entry Dalle Fusine's non-appearance lowering the number of Senior starters to nine, Lockett and Bell, once again, ran rampage unchecked in the 500cc race.

"On the fall of the starter's flag at 2 pm, Artie Bell, as in the past two North Wests, catapulted away, with his front wheel only touching the road in spots."

On Two Wheels and Four, Basil Brindley, 1950
For the first seven laps, Bell took the race by the scruff of

the neck, and led his team mate comfortably. In the process, the lap record was raised to 87.24 mph. The only challenge to the Norton duo came, as had been expected, from the Australian pair of Harry Hinton and George Morrison, riding privately entered Nortons. As the race reached the eighth lap, Lockett took the lead for the first time in the race. Hinton, riding wildly on the ragged edge, overtook his compatriot for third place. At the last left-hander, approaching the start/finish with his sliding back wheel showering the assembled crowds with loose pebbles from the road edge, he was almost unseated several times.

Bell and Lockett now began to trade places at the front. Bell's machine had been reluctant to fire after a stop to refuel, and it was Lockett who led them through on lap thirteen with twenty seconds to spare. On the fourteenth lap, Bell pushed the lap record to 88.59 mph as he trimmed eleven seconds off Lockett's advantage. What had seemed a foregone conclusion, with Bell as the likely winner, was now shaping up to be a replay of Frith's and Daniell's blanket finish from the previous year. In the end it was almost too close to call:

"...on the final lap, as Artie came in close on the dip at the last left-hand corner, and then swept wide, Lockett, just behind, came wide at first and tried to nip inside his partner. It was a nice move, but Artie was able to squeeze out enough to drop down over the finishing line, a machine's length ahead, to win at the record speed of 85.72 mph."

On Two Wheels and Four, Basil Brindley, 1950

Fr Noel Watson Collection

Belfast's uncrowned World champion, Artie Bell, North West 500cc winner 1947, '49 and '50, hustles the Featherbed Norton around Henry's Corner, Portstewart.

lap, when he was unable to restart his machine after stopping for fuel, and he retired from the race. A J Glazebrook (AJS) completed the top three, finishing almost two minutes behind Wheeler.

Of the ten 250cc starters, Belfast's "Sparky" Cambell was first to show, leading the field on his Excelsior towards Portstewart on the first lap. Fellow Excelsior rider J Netherwood had broken the class record in practice, but could only manage second place at the end of lap one, behind the Velocette-mounted Ron Mead. Netherwood was forced to retire on the following lap. As Mead claimed a new lap record on lap three with a speed of 73.69 mph, the battle for second was coming to the boil almost a minute behind him on the road.

The Excelsior-mounted pair of Jim McKimm and J McCreadie, and A E Shaw, riding Mead's 1949 race-winning Norton, disputed the standings until the eighth lap, when McCreadie's machine failed. By lap eleven, Shaw was visibly closing on Mead and by the thirteenth lap was on level terms. Mead merely upped the pace, and the lap record to 74.23 mph, and rode away from Shaw, to win at a new race average of 72.34 mph.

Bell added success after success the following month, when he won the Junior TT and followed Duke home for runner-up in the Senior. It would be the last great ride by the smiling, gifted Irishman; his career ended after crashing with Les Graham and Carlos Bandirola at the 1950 Belgian Grand Prix.

Duke's 350cc victory was a stunning display of new levels of refinement in design, and of the St Helens rider's ample talent. As would-be challengers fell by the wayside, without ever really being in touch, Duke eased home seven minutes clear – well within the 1949 500cc record. Bob Matthews (Velocette) held second place, albeit over a minute-and-a-half adrift, before dropping to the bottom end of the top ten after a lengthy stop to change a plug. Cromie McCandless on a Beart Norton had been tipped as the man most likely to give Duke a run for his money. With Matthews out of contention, McCandless moved into second, holding off the challenge of Arthur Wheeler (Velocette) until the thirteenth

Originally published in the Belfast News Letter

George Brockerton

George Brockerton was one of Irish racing's larger-than-life characters. In a career that lasted from the mid-1920s to the early 1950s, Brockerton competed with modest reward in Ireland and the Isle of Man, although success on his home track, the North West 200 Triangle Circuit, consistently eluded him. His race results record, dominated by DNFs, does scant justice to his ability. His achievement as one of only four Irish riders to be awarded the BMCRC Brooklands Gold Star, won in 1935, is a more fitting tribute to his memory.

Nevertheless, Brockerton's name remains closely associated with his beloved North West 200 for his efforts in promoting and establishing the event in the early years. His involvement in a wide variety of colourful, short-lived careers and ventures off the track, and his disregard for officialdom, are part of Irish racing folklore.

Brockerton served as a dispatch rider in the First World War and later in the Ulster Volunteer Force. Between the wars, he performed on the "Wall of Death" at Barry's amusements in Portrush, and in the 1940s toured towns and villages, entertaining their populations with his skills as an accomplished conjurer and with his famous "mobile cinema".

A Crabtree and George Brockerton (*ht*) prepare for practice before the 1929 meeting. Neither completed the distance on race day.

After retiring from racing for several years, Brockerton returned to compete in the 1939 500cc North West 200, riding the Excalibur machine raced by his brother Chas in the 1929 event.

To commemorate the occasion, he renamed the machine "The Dart Inn", in honour of the public house he owned at the time. He was flagged off the course, two laps adrift of Ernie Lyons, the eventual winner and only 500cc entry to complete the distance.

In his career, Brockerton's scrapes with the authorities earned him a suspension from the Motor Cycle Union of Ireland on more than one occasion. He once famously toured the course at the North West 200 in a van covered with placards proclaiming the message to the assembled crowds, "If you want to see a real motor-cycle race, come to the Cookstown 100 next Wednesday."

George Brockerton died on 30 April 1965 at his home in Bellaghy, Co Derry. The George Brockerton Memorial Trophy is presented in his honour at the North West 200 every year.

Curly Richmond Collection

Jimmie Guthrie

Jimmie Guthrie, one of the true giants of motor-cycle racing, was born in Hawick, Scotland, on 23 May 1897. His father, Jimmie Senior, was a keen amateur cyclist who owned a variety of motor cycles at the beginning of the twentieth century.

Guthrie fought in the Great War as a private in the King's Own Scottish Borders. Wounded twice in action, in Gallipoli and later in Egypt, he completed his military service as a dispatch rider. He bought his first motor cycle, an army surplus model, in 1919 on re-entering civilian life.

Jimmie Guthrie with Joe Craig (middle) and P J Drummond in 1935 – see p 21

The road to the very peak of achievement in motor-cycle competition began with successes in local hill climbs. He won his first sand race at Saltburn near Redcar in 1924. In an impressive TT début, he rode a New Hudson to runner-up spot behind the Norton-mounted Alec Bennett in the 1927 Senior TT. The following year he joined the Norton team as a works rider.

The unreliability of the 1928 Norton bikes made his début year as a works rider a disappointing one. Guthrie's second year with the Bracebridge Street outfit was overshadowed by a major crash at Greeba in practice for the 1929 TT. At the end of two years with Norton, Guthrie had little to show for his efforts on the track.

For his assault on the 1930 season, Jimmie switched to AJS machinery provided by wealthy sponsor Nigel Spring. His fortunes changed and he scored his maiden TT win; the 1930 Lightweight on board a 250cc AJS, as well as claiming a 350cc victory at the German Grand Prix.

Jimmie returned to the Norton team in 1931. It was a partnership that delivered twenty-six TT and Grand Prix victories, and four consecutive 500cc North West 200 wins, in the years that followed.

"He was a quiet and retiring chap with a gentle sense of humour, but never used two words where one would suffice.

"In the 1933 Junior TT he came third, had clouted the bank at Hillberry, bending a footrest, and had come off at Quarter Bridge, bending some more bits of the bike and skinning his hand and arm. Interviewed afterwards he said, 'I found the flies troublesome'."

Gordon Small, *Hawick's Racing Legend*, 1997

While interviewing Ernie Lyons for this book in June 2000, Ernie recalled a brief meeting with Jimmie Guthrie.

"Well, I only saw Jimmie Guthrie riding a few times. He was a terrific rider. I think himself and Joey Dunlop would be very similar.

"I happened to be alongside Jimmie on an AJS at the start of practice for the 1936 Leinster 200. He said to me, 'That's the sort of bike I started on, one just like that.' That made my day, to meet the great Jimmie Guthrie."

At forty years of age Guthrie, still at the top in his sport, made the decision to retire at the end of the 1937 season. On 8 August 1937, with a two-minute lead in hand, Guthrie began the final lap of the German Grand Prix at Sachsenring. Norton boss Joe Craig signalled his rider to ease off on his final circuit, victory seemed assured.

But on a flat-out downhill, right-hand bend Jimmie Guthrie crashed and later died from his injuries.

Some attributed the accident to mechanical failure, but Stanley Woods, out of the race and touring with a broken fuel pipe, saw what happened. According to Woods, Kurt Mansfield, the German BMW works rider, drifted off line, causing Guthrie to crash through a row of saplings and into a ditch.

Woods accompanied his great friend to hospital in the ambulance, but the roads were choked with traffic and spectators returning home. The journey took two hours. Speaking in 1992, Woods said, "We'd been friends, team mates, and rivals for ten years. I was shattered."

The saplings Jimmie Guthrie hit that day are tall trees now, and a memorial plaque, The Guthrie Stone, stands at the spot where his final race ended.

At The Cutting, the place where he stopped and retired from his last TT, the 1937 Senior, stands the Guthrie Memorial. From there you can see his native Scotland on a clear day.

The Londonderry Trophy, presented to the winner of the 500cc Scratch Open class at the North West 200 each year, was renamed the Jimmie Guthrie Memorial Trophy in honour of one of motor cycling's greats.

In 1967 his son, Jimmie Guthrie Junior, riding a Frances Beart Norton, won the Senior Manx Grand Prix.

Fr Noel Watson Collection

Artie Bell

The tall, dark-haired figure, impeccably suited with cigarette in hand, dwarfs the Featherbed Norton beside him, as he smiles across the years from the monochrome photograph. The instantly recognisable style of Artie Bell, shamrock emblazoned across the front of the helmet, huge frame wrapped gracefully, almost lovingly, along the exquisite lines of the Norton in full cry, is an image that tells a different story. Contrast the man relaxed, at ease with the world, with the study of raw, naked aggression, deeply etched on the lines of the face, the gritted teeth, the set of the jaw. Fifty years after his final race, all we have left of the greatness that once produced such a frightening turn of speed on a racing motor cycle are photographs, enduring icons of Artie Bell's contribution to motor-cycle racing's rich past.

Born in Belfast in 1915, Artie Bell began his distinguished racing career in the early 1930s riding a 350cc Triumph Tiger 80 in trials competitions. His relationship with Rex McCandless saw them embark on a variety of ventures as business partners and collaborators in refining the fundamental design of racing motor cycles, the ultimate expression of which was manifest in the legendary Featherbed Norton. Throughout it all they remained close friends.

Bell's name is primarily remembered for his rides as a member of the works Norton team, which he joined in 1947. Despite the fact that Bell had only once previously visited the Isle of Man TT, as a spectator in 1935, Norton team boss Joe Craig signed Bell to ride for the team in the 1947 TT, after seeing him win the 500cc race at the 1947 North West 200. Bell upset the form

Artie Bell hustles the Featherbed Norton around Henry's Corner, Portstewart – see p 33

book by leading his more experienced team mate, Harold Daniell, until, responding to team orders, he slowed to allow Daniell through to take the win.

Victories at Assen and Dundrod made his rookie year as a works rider a memorable one. A maiden TT win in the 1948 Senior, with over ten minutes to spare over runner-up Bill Doran, was followed with a 350cc victory at the Swiss Grand Prix. He virtually made the Dutch TT his own with a famous victory in the wet in 1949, giving him his third win there in three years.

Until 1950, success had been achieved riding the cumbersome, and largely outdated, Garden Gate Norton. With Norton's latest weapon at his disposal, Bell gave the Featherbed design its first international win at the North West 200 in 1950. A win in the Junior TT seemed to indicate world dominance for the Bell/Norton combination, with world titles an inevitability.

Sadly, it was not to be. Artie Bell's racing ended as the result of injuries he received after crashing with Carlos Bandirola and Les Graham at the Belgian Grand Prix at Spa in 1950. Belgian doctors wanted to amputate his left arm, but eventually saved the badly injured limb.

Artie Bell survived to pursue a successful business career, as well as retaining an involvement in racing as mentor and sponsor to a crop of promising young riders. Belfast's uncrowned World Champion died aged fifty-seven in 1972, after suffering a heart attack.

Fr Noel Watson Collection

The McCandless brothers, Rex, and Cromie, seated with the Benial, the prototype of all modern racing motor cycles – see p 32

Rex McCandless

Stanley Woods once said that the average motor cyclist had no idea of the debt owed to Rex McCandless. He also summed up the personal experience of many of McCandless' contemporaries when he described him as "a very difficult man to get on with".

Rex McCandless, a self-taught engineer with a genius mind, bequeathed his greatest gift, the Featherbed Frame, to Norton and changed the world of motor cycling forever.

He was born the son of a farmer in Hillsborough, Co Down, in 1915. His father, a small-time player on the stock market, gambled and lost heavily in the 1928 crash. Facing financial ruin, he abandoned his family and fled. At thirteen years of age, Rex left school with very little formal education and became the family provider.

"I always seemed to have an instinctive ability to know what was wrong, and to find a very simple way out of what appeared to be an obscure problem. I can't account for it, I'm just very lucky."

(Rex McCandless attempting to explain his extraordinary talents on the BBC Northern Ireland radio documentary *From Featherbed to Fairway*.)

With his great friend Artie Bell, Rex had devoted much thought and discussion to what they saw as an inherent weakness in the design of racing machines. They agreed that instabilities manifest in the front end at speed stemmed from design faults at the rear. In other words, "the tail was prone to wag the dog".

"First of all," explained McCandless, "a tube could only be strong in tension or compression. Therefore you had to try and design a frame where the stresses would not be where the bends were, but where the straight tubes were, and as such I never had a failure."

The application of these principles produced a one-off machine, "The Benial" (Latin for "Beast"). The Benial, "the best handling bicycle I ever made", was raced by Rex's younger brother, Cromie, at Bangor Castle in July 1945, the first post-war race meeting in Ireland. It was in effect the working blueprint for what would later become the Featherbed.

Ernie Lyons remembers racing against the McCandless home-built special that summer's day:

"It was the prototype of all modern racers. Rex wasn't a graduate engineer, he learned the hard way. He was tremendously logical. He'd argue something and go back to basics and start building up from there. He realised at a very early stage that the bicycle-type frame was never rigid enough with the weight of the engine swinging out of it on fast bends."

The well-known, Belfast-based sponsor and tuner, the late Terry Hill, recalled McCandless first offering Triumph his new frame. Rex outlined his ideas as he dined with a senior engineer at a prestigious motor-cycling dinner. When his proposal was dismissed, McCandless' annoyance boiled over, and he upended the table, food and all, around the unfortunate man.

By 1947 Norton's managing and technical directors, Gilbert Smith and Joe Craig respectively, had recognised the world-beating talent of the Belfast rider Artie Bell, and had signed him to ride for the works team. The potential of McCandless' work was not lost on Smith and Craig, and before too long his designs were incorporated into the Bracebridge Street factory's designs for racing machines.

The new Norton racer was demonstrated before the factory's assembled top brass on the Isle of Man mountain course in the autumn of 1949. By the winter of 1949, Bell, Duke and Eric Oliver embarked on an intensive testing programme at Monthlery. In the process they covered hundreds of miles at racing speed and set twenty-one world records.

Norton's new secret weapon was first raced at Blanford on 29 April 1950. With Geoff Duke aboard the victory seemed effortless.

"After that," said Duke, "I couldn't wait to try it in a proper race. Blanford was a short circuit, a very good circuit, but I mean a Grand Prix or near a Grand Prix."

As the year wore on, success followed success for the Norton team. Bell had claimed the Senior class at the Leinster 200 before laying waste to the opposition on the Triangle Circuit. In the 500cc North West 200, Bell and Lockett claimed a Norton 1-2, and Duke took the 350cc honours. At the TT, Norton swept all before them and filled the top three places in both the Junior and Senior races. At the TT prize presentation, Harold Daniell quipped that Norton's new, all-conquering racer was as comfortable as a featherbed; the rest, as they say, is history.

Looking back on his career, Duke paid tribute to McCandless' contribution: "As a comparative newcomer to racing, I had a terrific amount of success, which to a very large degree could be attributed to the McCandless machine."

In his lifetime, Rex McCandless applied his God-given ability to designing trials and sports cars, the McCandless Autogyro and other inventions too numerous to mention. The Mule, designed in conjunction with Harry Ferguson, outpaced Jeep and Landrover in field tests, but despite intense interest from the military never went into production.

In his latter years, McCandless took up golf, and quickly produced a home-made putter, which he designed and put to use on the golf course with deadly efficiency. It was soon banned by the sport's authorities. Rex McCandless lived out the final years of his life in an old converted railway station with a sea view at Killough, Co Down. He died on 8 June 1992, aged seventy-eight.

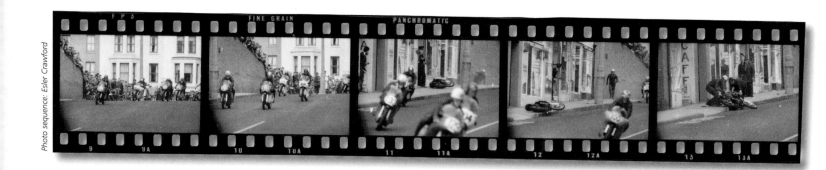

Photo sequence: Esler Crawford

South African Andreas Georgeades' crash approaching Portstewart harbour during the early stages of the 1965 500cc race. The bike was destroyed in the fire but Georgeades walked away unscathed.

Arthur Whee
– see p

1951-71

CHAPTER TWO

1951–71

The 1951 North West 200 ran over an extended two-day programme as part of local celebrations for the Festival of Britain.

On the hottest day of the year so far, fifty-one riders lined up for the start of the Junior 350cc held on the Thursday. Sharing the front row of the grid with Armstrong's works AJS were the Norton partnership of Duke, Dale and Lockett. Lockett, a last-minute replacement in the team for Harry Hinton, whose arrival from Australia had been delayed, would ride a 1950 model, whilst Duke would be equipped with a 1951 engine housed in a 1950 frame.

As the flag dropped, J S Slater's AJS rocketed to the front. His moment of glory would be short-lived, however. Duke led Lockett, Dale, Armstrong and the private AJS of Robin Sherry through at the end of lap one. His time of 7 min 58 sec lowered the lap record by three seconds from a standing start. It was, however, still short of his best time of 7 min 37 sec from the previous morning's practice.

Another new record of 7 min 45 sec (85.73 mph) on the following circuit took the St Helens rider twenty-six seconds clear of Lockett, with Dale a further two seconds adrift. With newcomer Sherry closing rapidly on Armstrong's misfiring factory machine, news began to circulate around the course of a major accident at Drumslade, three miles from the start/finish.

On a practically straight stretch of road, one machine had wobbled at speed, struck the grass bank on the left of the circuit and rebounded into the road, bringing down nine other competitors. Thirty-five-year-old William Bennison from Sableford, Staffs, was rushed to hospital, but died shortly afterwards from his injuries.

On his début on the Triangle Circuit, Les Parry's Velocette oiled a plug on the line; after changing it he set off in pursuit of the fifty riders before him. Cresting a rise at Drumslade, Parry came upon the accident and hit the strewn wreckage flat out in third gear. He recalls the scene, "like something from a L S Lowry painting, there were riders and bikes everywhere. I woke up in a field, my helmet cracked and my Velo in pieces."

On his fourth lap, Duke recorded a time of 7 min 27 sec, a speed of 89.19 mph, to better Artie Bell's 1950 500cc record by three seconds. He pitted leisurely on the eighth lap and rejoined the fray. By the end of his eleventh circuit, Duke led Lockett by 4 min 15 sec and had lapped all up to fifth place on the road.

Lockett caused the sensation of the race when he led Dale through at the end of lap twelve. To keep weight to a minimum, Duke opted to carry neither a plug spanner nor spare plug. When lack of spark brought his

Norton to a standstill at Shell Hill, Duke could only park his stricken machine and watch a titanic, all-Norton battle develop between Dale and Lockett.

At the end of the sixteenth lap, Dale led by a single second. As the pair thundered through Portstewart and onto their final frantic eleven-mile dash, Dale's lead remained unchanged. He held the slender advantage at Coleraine, but Lockett was in front at Portrush. On the coast road, with a last supreme effort, Dale whipped past his team mate to head him home by two bike lengths. After an eternity in the pits whilst his team worked on the factory AJS' defective rear brake, Armstrong followed Sherry home in fourth place.

Left pushing at the start when his all-new 1951 model refused to fire, it was Duke who led the high-speed Norton train through at the end of the first lap of Saturday's eighteen-lap Senior race. At the fast right-hander leading onto the start/finish, his machine snaked wildly after hitting orange peel thrown onto the road by spectators. It would be Duke's only troubled moment; for the next seventeen laps, he set about systematically destroying the record books and the opposition.

Lap after lap Duke upped the pace, until on his seventh circuit, in a time of 7 min 22 sec, Geoff Duke became the first rider to lap the Triangle Circuit at over 90 mph. On lap ten, Duke raised the tempo and went around in 7 min 12 sec – a speed of 92.27 mph – and for the next eight laps, his pace never dropped below 90 mph, despite the frantic signals from the Norton pits to slow down. At the end of Duke's 200-mile tour de force, Lockett was the only rider still on the same lap, albeit five minutes behind in second place.

On the penultimate lap, Dale slowed at the pits for running repairs, but was waved through by team manager Joe Craig. Riding one-handed while holding a loose carburettor in place, Dale limped home in a distant third

place, eleven minutes after Duke had taken the chequered flag.

Arthur Wheeler's Moto Guzzi leapt to the front of the fourteen 250cc contenders that started one minute after their 500cc counterparts. For the next sixteen laps, Wheeler pulled away from the bickering pack behind him. On the ninth lap, he broke Ron Mead's 1950 lap record of 74.23 mph with a speed of 74.53 mph. At the flag, Wheeler had almost seven minutes to spare before David Andrews completed the distance to claim the runner-up spot.

The punishing demands of the course exacted a heavy toll on the lightweight runners. W J Netherwood's campaign was over on the second lap, and Maurice Acheson's serious challenge for a top-three finish ended when his Excelsior failed on the eighth lap. At the half-way point in the race, David Andrews held a safe but distant third place, over four minutes behind second-place runner Fron Purslow. On the final lap at Portrush, Purslow's Norton ran out of petrol; he coaxed the last dregs from the tank and restarted. Running on fumes, two-and-a-half miles from home on the coast road, his engine died. Purslow pushed home to a standing ovation to claim the final place on the podium behind Andrews.

The 500cc Manx Norton, on loan to Reg Armstrong from the factory, would be the closest the 1952 event would come to boasting an official manufacturer's entry. After three laps of shadowing Cromie McCandless, Armstrong hit the front when McCandless made an unscheduled pit stop. The four minutes lost, as his mechanics tightened loose tank bolts on the Francis Beart-tuned Norton, cost McCandless the race.

Despite returning the fastest lap of the day at 88.78 mph, McCandless could not get near the dogfight that was developing at the front between Armstrong and

Ivor Arber (Norton). For four laps, Arber – an ex-fighter pilot and holder of the Air Force Cross – traded places at the front with Armstrong, until the Dubliner's chain broke. Early leader Harold Clark made it a Norton clean sweep, coming home six-and-a-half minutes behind McCandless.

It would be Arber's only North West 200 victory; the Kettering rider lost his life after crashing his 499cc Beart Norton at Hillberry later that year in practice for the Manx Grand Prix.

For the opening laps of the 350cc race, Rex McCandless matched his younger brother by leading the field. McCandless held an eight-second lead over D C Birrell (Norton), with A C Taylor (Norton) giving chase. On the eighth circuit, whilst overtaking Dickie Carter, McCandless tangled with the 500c runner at Dhu Varren, causing both riders to crash out of the race.

Louis Carter recalled the incident on the BBC Northern Ireland radio documentary *From Featherbed to Fairway*:

"At that time, my brother was riding in the 500cc class and Rex in the 350 on a very quick Norton. He made up the minute on my brother, and coming up out of Portrush around a bend that doesn't exist anymore, they came together and both came off. They weren't satisfied with that, they had to get involved in a bit of fisticuffs. Motor Cycle said

the only place it could happen was in Ireland – a boxing match in the road while an international motor-cycle race was taking place. Rex could get a bit worked up over certain things, especially if he thought he was right."

With McCandless out and otherwise engaged, the order at the front after half-way saw newcomer H A Pearce (Velocette) ahead of the Nortons of veteran Albert Moule and Taylor. Moule lost the lead when he stopped to refuel, whilst Pearce completed the full distance without stopping. On lap thirteen, he set the fastest lap of the race at 83.753 mph to take the victory by 1 min 39 sec.

For the second year in succession, the bright-red Guzzi of Arthur Wheeler

The 1952 class winners receive their laurels from Mrs McQuigg, wife of Malcolm McQuigg, runner-up in the 1929 North West 200. They are from left to right, Harry Pearce, 350cc winner, Ivor Arber, 500cc winner and Arthur Wheeler, 250cc winner

Howard McQuigg Collection

led the 250cc field through Henry's Corner on the opening lap. With expected challengers Wilf Billington and Ron Mead both retiring, Wheeler was never pushed over the sixteen laps, but still carved seventeen seconds off his 1951 lap record to raise the new standard to 76.96 mph on his way to a second lightweight win. Once again, David Andrews followed Wheeler home to claim the runner-up spot.

The much-anticipated appearance of the ultra-fast works Gileras with Dickie Dale and Reg Armstrong on board fell far short of expectations. Instead, the performances of Ken Kavanagh and newcomer Syd Lawton on the works 500cc Nortons stole the 1953 headlines.

As the temperatures soared, melting patches of tar around the course, Armstrong led the twelve-strong Senior field away. By the end of the lap, both Nortons had posted speeds of 90 mph from a standing start, with Kavanagh leading his team mate by twenty-five yards. Already, Armstrong was losing touch back in third, with Dale completing the top four.

Dickie Dale (3) and Reg Armstrong line up on the works Gileras for practice before the 1953 North West 200.

Lawton and Kavanagh traded record lap times as the miles fell away, and the gap between the Nortons and the Italian thoroughbreds grew.

Fr Noel Watson Collection

Kavanagh began by bettering Duke's standing record by five seconds, with a speed of 93.71 mph. On lap seven, Lawton put two seconds of daylight between himself and Kavanagh, going around in seven minutes exactly to raise the record to 94.82 mph.

As the midway point came and went, Dale's race was

Fr Noel Watson Collection

over; a flying stone shattered his goggles. As Dale made his way to hospital, Armstrong struggled on, by now a minute-and-a-half adrift of the flying Norton pair in front. With the first sub-seven-minute lap seen on the course, Kavanagh

Armstrong and Dale round York Corner in formation during the 1953 500cc race. The Gileras much anticipated début ended in disappointment. Dale retired after a stone shattered his goggles, Armstrong struggled home in third place, almost four minutes behind Syd Lawton and Ken Kavanagh.

reclaimed the record with a time of 6 min 58 sec, a speed of 95.25 mph. It was to no avail. The tenacious Lawton hit the front on the final lap, and with a new record of 96.2 mph headed Kavanagh home by eight seconds. Lawton's last lap had earned the North West 200 the rightful claim to the title of "fastest race in Britain and Ireland" for the first time in its history. One hard-earned third place, finishing over four minutes behind the winner, had not been the result the Italian factory had hoped for.

The talking point of the 1953 meeting was the first public appearance of the Kneeler Norton, due to be ridden in the 350cc event by the Rhodesian Ray Amm. The machine, fitted with pannier tanks almost totally enclosed within its silver streamlining, and with the rider in a virtually prone position, was a head turner. Despite the level of public anticipation, no one was more excited about the machine's début appearance than Amm.

David Maxwell, author of *The North West 200: The First Twenty-Five Years*, recalls Amm's joy when his ride on the revolutionary machine was confirmed. Whilst Kavanagh and Amm familiarised themselves with the course hours before official practice was due to get underway, Maxwell received the news that the Silver Bullet was on its way to Portstewart from Belfast, ridden by its designer, Rex McCandless. He flagged the Norton teamsters down on the road and informed Amm of the news:

"Amm nearly waltzed with his machine in the road when I told him the news. At no time before or since have I ever seen such an outstanding manifestation of sheer joy and enthusiasm."

Before getting clearance to race, Amm was required to demonstrate the Norton's stability. After convincing the officials, his race would be short-lived and an anticlimax. 1952 Senior Manx Grand Prix winner Bob McIntyre (AJS) led them out of Portstewart for the first time, with Amm in last place, struggling with fuel starvation problems. Eddie Cambell, flag marshal at Henry's that day, watched the pack through with Stanley Woods spectating close by and showing a keen interest in the design direction his former team had taken. Woods was clearly unimpressed and commented dryly, "It doesn't look much like a Norton to me."

Even a stiff breeze, just enough to catch the Kneeler side-on, would have been enough to have made life very difficult for Amm. But with the still conditions suiting him, the Rhodesian set about the task of reeling in the entire field. By the third lap, he held fourth and had set what would stand as the fastest lap of the race at 88.5mph.

Fr Noel Watson Collection

Ray Amm on the Kneeler Norton pictured with mechanic Arthur Edwards (centre) and the Silver Bullet's inventor Rex McCandless. Amm set the fastest lap before retiring from the 1953 350cc North West 200 on the fourth lap. It was the machine's only full race appearance.

Early leader Jack Brett retired his factory Norton at the pits at the end of lap two, after crashing out of the lead. On lap four, Amm joined his team mate as a spectator when the fuel pump broke on his futuristic mount. By the half-way stage, McIntyre led Pearce (Velocette) by a minute and by five from Albert Moule (Norton) in third. Pearce's determination saw him claw back thirteen seconds from McIntyre's lead, but at the finish the twenty-four-year-old Scot was untroubled by any challenger. His fellow Scot J L Patterson completed the top three on his AJS.

Once again in the 250cc division, Arthur Wheeler came, saw and conquered, setting the seemingly obligatory lap record at 78.2 mph and winning at a new race record speed of 76.23 mph. Behind him, David Andrews completed his own hat-trick of runner-up awards, with Velocette-mounted Bill Webster in third.

The works Gileras returned to Portstewart the following year, for what would be the event's Silver Jubilee. The team was now comprised of Armstrong, with Duke replacing Dale. A young Tommy Robb, five-times North West 200 winner (1959–65), recalls the awe-inspiring sight of the Gileras at full cry, kindling his desire to compete in the event:

"The first year that Duke and Armstrong rode the Gileras, I raced in a grasstrack meeting on the Friday evening in Portstewart. I watched the race the next day, and it was exhilarating to watch the Gileras with nose fairings fitted on the coast road. The sound of those eight cylinders together was just superb."

McIntyre and Ken Swallow mounted on a pair of G45 Matchlesses, and George Costain (Grand Prix Triumph) were the only other non-Norton entries in the fifteen-strong field. Behind with their machine preparations for the TT and under increasing pressure, Norton withdrew their entries the week before the meeting.

After four laps, Armstrong led with Duke close behind and McIntyre already thirty-six seconds adrift. At half distance they were dead-heating, but an extended pit stop by Armstrong gave Duke the advantage. An oil plug in the frame of the Gilera had worked loose, spraying a fine oily mist around Armstrong for the entire first half of the race. He rejoined after a change of helmet and goggles, and gave chase with a mountain to climb.

Next time around, Duke refuelled and was away before Armstrong appeared. On the next three laps, Duke

returned the identical times of 6 min 49 sec, a new lap record of 97.37 mph, and pulled out a thirty-five-second lead. With a lap and a half remaining, his race ended at Milburn, after the gear-timing failure, experienced in early season testing at Imola, recurred. With Duke out, Armstrong eased the pace, coming home over two minutes clear of McIntyre, with Jackie Wood (Norton) a further six minutes behind in third.

For the 350cc race, Derek Farrant took over Bob McIntyre's ride on a 7R, and headed the practice times with a speed of 88.58 mph, ahead of Derek Ennett (AJS) and the 1954 South African 500cc champion, Rudy Allison (Norton). Farrant led from the start, but went out on lap three. For the opening thirty-three miles, Ennett and Allison were locked together as they disputed second. With Farrant out, the stakes were raised; for sixteen laps they raced shoulder to shoulder, with the lead changing on every lap. At half distance the timekeepers could not split them, and after fifteen laps both Allison and Ennett were credited with an identical race average speed of 86.94 mph.

As the Manx rider stormed through Portstewart and onto his final lap, it was the Velocette of Harry Pearce that followed through in second. His petrol tank split, Allison pushed the mile to the pits, took on fuel and rejoined the race to finish third to a standing ovation. Ennett had his own drama on the final lap, limping home with only the lower gears available.

From a standing start, Wheeler lowered the 250cc lap record by three seconds. With his main challenger David Andrews out on the third lap, Wheeler maintained a race-long assault on the record books. By the end of the day, Wheeler had hoisted the lap record to 81.94 mph and lopped twenty-three seconds off the race average. Finishing four minutes behind Wheeler, Bill Maddrick (Moto Guzzi) edged out Wilson Ferguson (Excelsior) from the runner-up spot by a single second.

Morton's Motorcycle Media Archive

Duke and Armstrong returned in 1955 to finally score an emphatic Gilera North West 200 "1–2" at the factory's third attempt. Jack Brett and Belfast's Willie Spence were Norton's official entries. In accordance with Norton's recently adopted policy to only race machines which could be purchased by private owners, Brett and Spence were provided with production-based 500s.

In truth, the British manufacturers were no longer prepared to shoulder the cost of developing machinery capable of taking on the challenge emerging from continental Europe. The decision would ultimately contribute to the decline and eventual demise of the British motor-cycle industry.

Ideal conditions and the Gilera's proven speed, combined with course improvements that straightened the section between Portstewart and Coleraine, raised anticipation amongst the 80,00-strong crowd of the first 100-mph lap.

At the end of the first lap, Brett was still in touch with

the leading pair, six seconds behind Armstrong, with Duke sandwiched in the middle. Next time around, both Gileras recorded identical speeds of 98.58 mph, five seconds under the old lap record, and broke away from the field. On lap five, Duke took the wide line around the fast right-hander leading onto the start/finish to ride around Armstrong and into the lead; as he passed his pits, a clearly unhappy Armstrong pointed to the rear of his machine.

With Spence crashing out at Portrush on lap seven, and Brett forced to pit three times during the race with clutch trouble, Duke and Armstrong were left to race each other. By lap eight, Duke commanded a thirty-three-second lead, and on the next lap upped the pace again to record a time of 6 min 39 sec, a speed of 99.98 mph. It was the fastest lap of the race, but Duke had been denied the elusive "ton" by a mere second. At the end of 200 racing miles, Duke, who had noticeably eased off in the later quarter of the race, led his team mate home by over two minutes. Kiwi newcomer Maurice Low's (BSA) riding on the ragged edge had come close to relegating Brett to fourth place.

Duke's contribution to the Italian factory's success on the seaside circuit reflected his technical understanding of design as well as his skill on the track:

"I'm glad I didn't ride the 1953 Gilera at the North West. The handling was terrible, it was quite a pig. At the end of that year, they literally redesigned it – a lot of it around suggestions I put to them. From the end of 1953 onwards, the Gilera was absolutely fantastic, and of course with all that power you're talking about at least 10 mph more than the Nortons had. It was a very nice bike to ride, very smooth.

"I got them to copy the Norton geometry, the engine was lowered in the frame, and that made a big difference. The weight distribution was different though. The Norton was about 50/50, whereas the Gilera was 60% on the front wheel, and that kept it more or less glued to the ground. You didn't need a steering damper, even at the TT, the North West or the Ulster, which was quite remarkable.

"The Gilera with its sheer speed and superb handling was an absolute dream to ride at the North West in 1955. It was really flying on the long straights there. Even without streamlining on it, it was still doing

Below: Geoff Duke rounds Henry's Corner on the works Gilera en route to victory in the 1955 500cc race. The five-times World Champion's final North West 200 win brought his tally to three after his 1950 350cc and 1951 500cc victories. Bottom: The 1955 class winners receive their silverware. From left to right, Alan Lyons, 250cc winner, Geoff Duke, 500cc winner, and Jackie Wood, 350cc winner.

Fr Noel Watson Collection

Steven Wilson Collection

about 150 mph, 20 mph more than the Nortons, which was quick in those days."

Former Clerk of the Isle of Man TT course Jack Wood first competed in the North West 200 in 1953. His finest moment came in 1955 when he won the 350cc race:

"They put the regulation out for 1953 saying that people would get free entry and three nights' accommodation if they lived outside England, Ireland, Scotland or Wales. So we phoned up and said, 'Look, we come from the Isle of Man, can we have free entries and accommodation, the same as Europeans?' and they said, 'yes'. That's how people like Derek Ennett, Denis Christian, George Costain and Sid Mizen, the Manx contingent, started to go over to the North West.

"I think I got a third in the 500cc race one year, and then in 1955, riding Geoff Duke's 350cc BSA, I won. The BSA was going very well, and I settled quickly into first place. It was revving in whatever gear we were pulling down into Coleraine at 8,000, which was exceptional for a pushrod engine at that time. It went beautifully.

"Geoff was on the 500cc Gilera, and he caught me up going up from Shell Hill Bridge, heading for Portrush. I was all tucked in, trying to get another hundred revs. He came up beside me and signed over, 'Are you all right? What are you revving at?' Then he just waved, changed down a gear and went. I thought I was going like hell until we had that little moment together and he left me sitting.

"Towards the end of the race, the clutch started slipping and I had to be a bit cautious of opening her up. The clutch was pretty hot when I finished, but that was the only problem I had. It was a beautiful ride."

Wood led the race from the second lap after posting a speed of 86.95 mph. Last-minute entry and first-lap leader Willie Gibson battled in the chasing pack for the minor places, with his entrant Les Cooper, Malcolm Templeton and the Australian Bob Brown. Cresting the brow of the hill on the sixth lap at Drumslade, Cooper was temporarily unsighted and touched John Horne's 250cc Rudge. Out of control, his AJS mounted the kerb and collided with a telegraph pole.

Portrush rider Don May recalls seeing the stricken Cooper prostrate on the grass bank on three consecutive laps, before an ambulance took him to hospital where he later had a leg amputated. Templeton, detuned after witnessing the accident, continued until the tenth lap before pulling in.

With Cooper out, Bob Brown moved into third place behind Gibson, until the Scot went out with a seized engine, with two laps remaining. Wilfie Herron (BSA) passed Brown's fellow countryman Alan Burt (AJS) on the final lap to complete the top three.

The 250cc class saw the first appearance at an Irish meeting of a privately entered NSU, entrusted to the capable hands of Alan Lyons. Lyons led from start to finish, sharing the unique distinction with his older brother, Ernie, winner of the 1939 500cc class, of being the first brothers to win on the Triangle Circuit.

Despite a lengthy pit stop at the end of the thirteenth lap, Lyons cruised home with three minutes to spare over Velocette-mounted Harold Kirby. Early top-three runner David Andrews retired on lap two, and as the race progressed, machine failure saw the challenges of Fron Purslow and Wilf Billington fall by the wayside. On the final circuit, R D McCutcheon's Norvel fell victim to mechanical problems, allowing Jimmy Herron (BSA) onto the bottom step of the podium.

For the 1956 500cc event, Bob McIntyre, riding Joe Potts' Norton, fitted with pannier tanks, planned to go the full race distance without stopping. The race was packed with drama from the flag. Denis Christian dropped his Matchless at the start, and as Wilfie Herron's Norton went broadside off the line, the pack roared past him and towards Portstewart.

Louis Carter's race was over on the first lap when he crashed out at Agherton Cemetery, the streamlining on his fallen Norton saving him from more serious injury than a fractured kneecap. On the first circuit, Kiwi Bill Aislabie lay ahead of 1955 double Manx Grand Prix winner Geoff Tanner and ten seconds behind McIntyre. Tricky conditions second time through Ballysally Corner, where a brief shower had made the surface treacherous, almost caught Jackie Wood out. A very slight spray thrown up from the machine in front was Wood's only warning of rain. Aislabie was not so lucky: he crashed out, sustaining what would prove to be fatal injuries.

As Paul Fahey slid out of the top six at Metropole on lap four, Jimmy Drysdale and then Bob Anderson set about giving chase. Anderson refuelled in under twenty seconds on lap nine, and resumed still in second place. On the next lap, McIntyre was forced to pit with fuel feed problems. He rejoined the race and set about regaining the forty seconds that Anderson had on him. With two laps remaining, McIntyre had halved the deficit, and at Metropole on the penultimate lap, he had cut it back to fifteen seconds. With Anderson in his sights, McIntyre approached Portstewart to begin what promised to be a tense last lap.

As McIntyre approached the start/finish, with the fleeing Anderson already tucked in and at full cry on the promenade, the Scot was shown the chequered flag. He pulled in only to learn that a staggering miscalculation had been made. The flag had been intended for Sammy Millar, coming through seventeen seconds behind to win the lightweight class. A disgusted McIntyre refused to resume, and Anderson eased home with minutes to spare from Tanner, with D G Chapman in third.

Race day dawned with Geoff Duke's 350cc Velocette failing to arrive on time. Before proceedings got underway, Duke explained the circumstances of his non-appearance over the public address system to the disappointed 80,000 crowd. At the front, Jimmy Buchan and Ralph Rensen harried early leader Alastair King. Jackie Wood, riding a Velocette entered by Duke, had pulled ahead of fellow Manx rider Derek Ennett:

"In 1956, Derek Ennett (we called him 'Chunky'), got ahead of me early in the race. Going round Henry's Corner onto Portstewart promenade, there was a lamp-post with a bale on it on the right-hand side. He caught it with his shoulder, and it really detuned him for a while. I was surprised because he was a very courageous rider. I passed him, but didn't stay in front of him for long. He regained his confidence and went on to win the race."[1]

With Buchan crashing out at Shell Hill on lap two as he tried to avoid the fallen Norton of Canadian Gerald Robarts, Rensen moved ahead of King by lap three, with Ennett now third. As the factory AJS hit the front on the sixth circuit, King gave chase setting a new lap record on the final lap of 90.72 mph. His efforts were in vain, as Rensen shaded the runner-up spot by a second at the flag.

In an eventful practice, Australian Eric Hinton lapped twice inside Arthur Wheeler's 1954 lap record. Derek Minter would play no part in the proceedings after crashing his MV Agusta in practice at Blackhill. Sammy Millar's performance on the Thursday evening was decidedly low-key as he struggled with carburettor settings on his NSU. There was little indication of his blistering performance to come in the race.

As Hinton took the lead, Millar locked onto the Australian's back wheel. Third time around, they shared a new joint lap record; but with five laps to go, travelling marshal Malcolm Templeton reported Hinton having stopped at Coleraine to examine his rear tyre after a big slide. Millar took the win by thirty-one seconds, after crashing and remounting at Dhu Varren on lap thirteen. Despite a new lap record of 91.13 mph in the closing stages, Hinton could not deny Millar the glory of being the first Irish winner of the 250cc class since 1934. Jimmy Herron on a sleeved-down Norton came home in third, over a lap behind.

Millar dominated the class with three consecutive wins between 1956 and 1958, but was denied the chance of four on the trot by circumstances beyond his control:

"The previous year (1955), the NSU had arrived but was stuck in customs, and Terry Hill couldn't get it released in time. We were at the North West with an entry waiting for the bike to come. Customs could be very difficult in those days, and the bike didn't arrive until the week after the race. Alan Lyons won it, but I think I could have had four wins in a row if the bike hadn't been impounded by customs.

"The NSU was a good bike in its day: we led the TT until the big end gave up and Monza until it developed electrical problems, where we finished third in the end. We were really on our way with that bike.

"With a full fairing it was quick, but using full streamlining at the North West was dangerous in places. They gave you an extra 15 to 20 mph, but they definitely made things very exciting. On the straight from Coleraine to Portrush you might be hitting 130 mph, but the wind could catch you and blow you off the road. That's why they were banned in 1957. You had the thing literally at full lock on the straight against the wind.

"At the North West in 1956, we had a lot of trouble starting the NSU because we were pulling such a high gear and I was a bit inexperienced. The field was well away before I got it fired up. I caught them up, but Eric

Hinton was hard to beat. I had a bit of a problem navigating after I crashed. When I hit the road, I cracked my goggles. I was lucky not to get glass in my eyes, but had to finish the race looking through one lens."

The long-anticipated first 100-mph lap of the Triangle Circuit was finally achieved on lap eleven of the 1957 500cc race by Jack Brett, riding Lord Montagu's Norton. At the beginning of 1957, RAC officials inspected the course with a view to deciding if the circuit was suitable to host the TT car races. The course was found to fall short of the minimum width requirement of thirty feet in places. Local council officials gave assurances that the necessary work would be completed. No cars ever raced on the Triangle, but by the time May came around, the difficult, winding Larkhill section at Portstewart had been transformed into virtually a fast straight. The plan to race cars on the Triangle was not a new idea; the North of Ireland Club had planned to stage the Ireland (North West) Trophy Car Race on 28 September 1935. With plans for the event well advanced, the RAC decided the circuit was not suitable and refused to issue a permit. The decision was endorsed by the Ministry of Home Affairs, who sealed the fate of the never-to-be motorsport spectacular by withholding the obligatory Roads Closing Order.

With no official Norton entry, thirty-nine-year-old Brett and Alan Trow, Lord Montagu's Norton-mounted entries, were free to race with their choice of streamlining. The factory had scorned the use of streamlining, but on race day, Brett's 1956 model was fitted with a long-nosed or bullet-nosed cowl.

In practice, Geoff Tanner had been unable to prevent the wind from lifting his goggles at full bore on the straights. Unable to find a suitable replacement pair before race day, Tanner set off on the 200 miles with the securing strap fastened as tight as he could bear. This seemingly minor detail would eventually cost him the

Esler Crawford

race and, arguably, a place in history as the Triangle's first "ton-up man".

Fastest man in practice Brett led at Metropole on the opening lap, but shadowed Tanner and John Clark at the end of the lap. With a stiff breeze on the Coleraine to Portrush straight playing havoc with the streamlined machines, Brett took over second place as Trow retired at the pits, and Clark's single-cylinder Guzzi hit the bank at Dhu Varren and crashed out. Tanner led Brett, Ken Patrick and Wilfie Herron, but surrendered the lead to Brett when he stopped for fuel on lap eight. The magic ton seemed to be a certainty as Tanner gave chase, lapping at 99.79 mph. But it was Brett who made history, finally posting a time of 6 min 37 sec, 100.03 mph on lap

eleven, as Tanner retired at Mathers Cross. The tightness of the helmet's securing strap had, as the race progressed, given Tanner a headache, which became a migraine and, in turn, impaired his vision.

History in the making as Jack Brett rounds Metropole Corner on his way to winning the 1957 500cc race. In the process Brett became the first rider to lap the Triangle Circuit at over 100 mph.

As rain began to fall around the circuit, causing a number of minor tumbles at Milburn, Brett romped home with seven minutes to spare over Patrick, with Jackie Wood in third.

"I remember at the end of the race we went into some pub on the sea front in Portstewart. I left and went back to the hotel, got showered, changed and went back out.

ett was still sitting there with a band of enthusi-rinking and telling yarns. He was exceptionally good at that, he was a comedian. That always sticks in my mind: Jack sitting there after he won the race, setting the first 100-mph lap and still in his leathers, enjoying the pints and keeping the boys entertained well into the night." [2]

From the off, Bob Anderson was in a different class in the 350cc race. He held a twenty-second lead over Arthur Wheeler at the end of lap one, lapping at 90.95 mph from a standing start. Behind Wheeler the express train of Bob Brown, Ralph Rensen, Bernard Codd, Alan Holmes and Jimmy Buchan thundered through, with no more than ten seconds separating them.

As the battle for second developed into a three-way dice between Brown, Rensen and Wheeler, Anderson disappeared into the far distance, raising the lap record to 95.96 mph in the process. On lap eight, Brown's shamrock-green streamlined Velocette was out with clutch trouble at Shell Hill, and as Wheeler dropped off the pace, Holmes went clear in second place. After two more frantic laps, Holmes was again in a ferocious three-cornered scrap, with Rensen and Buchan on his shoulder. Almost immediately his troubles eased, as Rensen retired and Buchan was forced to settle for third after an unscheduled pit stop when the streamlining on his Norton began to work loose.

With only ten riders contesting the 250cc class, the result seemed a foregone conclusion, with Sammy Millar red-hot favourite to take the win. A last-minute delivery of spare parts was rushed from Belfast, when Millar's NSU developed trouble on race day morning. As the field tucked in and headed towards Portstewart, Millar was still pushing. By Coleraine he was in the lead, heading Dave Chadwick and Velocette-mounted Harold Kirby. As Sam Hodgin retired from the fray with engine trouble, Dave Chadwick's challenge ended when he dropped his

MV at Metropole. He remounted only to retire at the pits, as Millar's relentless charge took him four minutes clear at the half-way stage. Fron Purslow (NSU) held Kirby off for the runner-up spot, while Millar coasted home for his second successive lightweight success.

Brett returned to the 1958 meeting to repeat his 500cc victory. Mechanical failure in the form of McIntyre's Norton dropping a valve made it more of a case of defeat snatched from the jaws of victory for the gritty Scot. By Milburn on the first lap, McIntyre had taken over at the front from newcomer Bruce Daniels, and for the next fifteen laps he dominated the race.

Brett, riding the Slazenger-entered Norton, had no answer as McIntyre on the Joe Potts' Norton pushed the lap record to 102.04 mph, and opened a twenty-one-second lead after six laps. Geoff Tanner retired on the fifth lap, leaving Brett alone to take on the task of reeling in McIntyre. Behind Brett, Daniels and Bob Brown (Norton) were locked together in the dispute for third.

With a forty-second lead in hand, McIntyre's race was suddenly over, and as he completed the sixteenth lap on foot, Brett, with five minutes to spare over the duelling Daniels and Brown, could afford an extra stop to check he had enough in the tank to take him home.

Ken Patrick and Alan Holmes started together, sharing an all-Norton 350cc front row with Dave Chadwick and Alastair King. King broke clear of a chasing pack that included Patrick, Holmes, Ralph Rensen and Jimmy Buchan, with late-starting 500cc runner Bill Smith in the thick of it. As Rensen retired after six laps, and Buchan lost ground after refuelling, Patrick and Holmes remained locked together, both lapping in 6 min 59 sec on lap thirteen to set the joint fastest lap of the race. King was never headed or seriously challenged, winning with ease, with Patrick following him home, four seconds ahead of Holmes.

Fresh from winning the 200cc class at the Cookstown 100 the previous week, one S M B Hailwood lined up on the second row of the 250cc grid, well aware of the threat posed by Terry Hill's NSU-mounted trio of Millar, Robb and Andrews. It would be Hailwood's only North West 200 appearance, and it proved to be a memorable one.

Fastest man in practice Bob Anderson took the BSA-powered Geoff Monty Special into an early lead, followed by Fron Purslow and Hailwood coming off the second row. On the long run into Portrush, Anderson's "Special" broke a con rod, and at the end of the lap Robb streaked through, with Hailwood and Millar already losing the tow. Robb steadily pulled away from the battle for second, but on the fifth lap, everything changed in an instant:

"The 1958 250cc North West 200 against Hailwood and Millar was probably one of my best ever rides. I'd managed to break clear by about eight or nine seconds, when I hit a patch of oil, just after cresting Black Hill, and came off. The bike slid up the road, Mike just managed to avoid me and Sammy went past on the inside.

I picked the bike up. The screen was broken, so I ripped it off and kicked the footrest straight. I was a bit annoyed to say the least. I bumped the bike down the hill, and set off after them. I'd lost about thirty seconds by that stage. I broke the lap record on each lap after that, trying to get back with the boys. In the end I finished about ten seconds behind them."[3]

With Robb gaining on the pair of NSUs in front by almost four seconds per lap, the epic Hailwood/Millar duel entered its last eleven miles, with Hailwood still leading. With the exhaust

Tommy Robb leads Mike Hailwood and eventual winner Sammy Millar as the 1958 250cc battle rounds Metropole. Robb crashed out at Blackhill but remounted to obliterate the lap record on every circuit in his efforts to reel in the NSUs of the leading pair.

Esler Crawford

beginning to come adrift on Hailwood's Sportsmax, he still held the advantage onto the coast road, but with the chequered flag in sight, Millar pulled from his slipstream and draughted across the line to take his third North West 200 win by two bike lengths.

"I was riding for Terry Hill, with Artie Bell helping out. Artie was my hero, he pointed me in the right direction in lots of ways. Look at the photographs from those days, streamlined shoulder pads, one-piece leathers, even the back of my helmet was streamlined. Those were all Artie's ideas.

"Mike was always a very, very, strong rider, and with Tommy there as well, I knew it was going to be a hard one to win. We all fired off together. I always liked to win at the slowest speed possible, and I sat behind Hailwood right until the last lap. Coming into Portstewart, I saw a bit of an opening. I never looked up, head down and gave it everything I'd got. I didn't even look over my shoulder when I went over the line. If you'd have given Hailwood half a chance, he'd been back through again.

"After I'd won he didn't say much, but I know his old man tried to buy my bike off Terry Hill. They always liked the best equipment, the Hailwood camp. Terry, Artie, and I were happy men that day."[4]

Only weeks before the 1959 North West 200 was due to take place, the North of Ireland Club dropped the bombshell that they were in no position to run the event because of financial problems. At the eleventh hour, the Ulster Centre of the MCUI, in conjunction with the Coleraine and District Motor Club, stepped in and saved the day.

With the organisers opting for a radical change in format, the North West 200 became a 200-mile event in name only. The new race programme provided four separate races, run in classes over shorter distances. It was a formula that would allow Tommy Robb to claim the distinction of being the first rider to write his name twice in the record books as a race winner on the same day.

Robb, married only the previous week, had interrupted his honeymoon to win the first race of the day: the five-lap 125cc race.

"The 125cc had only five entries. It was the only 125cc race that was held there until the 1990s; Robert Dunlop was the next rider after me to win the class at the North West.

"That year, Fron Purslow was riding the Desmodromic Ducati and I was riding Geoff Monty's standard Ducati. The Desmo should have romped off into the distance, but Fron became complacent. He started taking it easy half-way through the race. Every lap I was getting a little bit quicker. I managed to scoop him up at the last corner and win the race."[5]

Fresh from his hard-fought victory over Fron Purslow by 0.6 seconds, Robb, on the Geoff Monty Special,[6] led for the entire seven laps of the 250cc event, heading Noel Orr's NSU home by 1 min and 42 sec.

Geoff Duke had entered the 250cc class, but the World Champion opted to go instead in the nine-lap 350cc class, run concurrently with the 500cc field. Duke's race lasted just 400 yards, after his Norton ground to a halt on Portstewart promenade. As Duke made the short walk back to his pit, Alastair King set about notching up his second consecutive 350cc win.

King's Norton headed AJS-mounted Alan Shepherd by yards at the end of the first lap. Clawing hard-earned seconds from his rival as the miles fell away, the Glaswegian upped the pace to push the lap record to 98.26 mph on the fifth circuit. His effort saw him break

Victor Freeman Collection

After setting the fastest 500cc lap, mechanical failure robbed Bob McIntyre of victory in 1958. He returned to complete the job the following year, pictured here in typical style at Portstewart on the Joe Potts Norton.

McIntyre's AJS spluttered on the grid for an eternity as Tommy Robb (AJS) and Jack Ahearn (Norton) led the 350cc field into the bottleneck at Henry's Corner for the first time. By Coleraine, McIntyre led from the AJS-mounted quartet of Robb, Ron Langston, Tom Thorp and Alan Shepherd. By Metropole, the high-speed game of catch-up chased a new leader, in the shape of Derek Minter's silver Norton. At the end of the lap, Shepherd pulled clear by fifty yards, but at the end of the second, Minter, McIntyre and Thorp were only inches from his back wheel. As Minter and Thorp retired at Metropole on lap three, the Shepherd/McIntyre battle raged on unabated. On the last corner of the last lap, Shepherd saw his chance and clung to the tighter line at the fast right-hander to head McIntyre across the line by one-fifth of a second.

clear at the front by over twenty seconds. Shepherd had no reply, and with four laps remaining, the race was effectively over.

The main drama in the 500cc race focused on the race-long scrap for second place between Peter Middleton and John Holder. McIntyre led from the start, and as the race unfolded, the popular Scot equalled and then raised the lap record to 102.56 mph. At the end of nine laps, McIntyre cruised home with over two minutes in hand, with Holder finishing a single second behind Middleton.

Bob McIntyre would end the 1960 event with only the 350cc runner-up plaque to show for his efforts, despite being in the thick of memorable 350cc and 500cc battles.

With the non-appearance of the much-anticipated Terry Hill-entered Bianchi twins – due to be ridden by Minter, Millar and Noel Orr – Robb led the depleted 250cc field on his Geoff Monty Special by half a minute at the end of the first lap. In driving rain, Robb made his second lightweight win look easy, as he lapped the entire field with the exception of runner-up Tom Thorp's BSA Goldstar-based TTS.

Robb's run in the 500cc class would prove to be a different story. On wet roads, McIntyre led Langston (Matchless) by seven seconds at the end of the opening circuit, with Minter a further ten seconds behind. As Minter moved ahead of the silver Matchless of Langston, top-three challengers Terry Shepherd (loose streamlining) and Tom Thorp (clutch) retired at the pits. Minter was the quickest man on the circuit on laps four and five, and moved into the lead on lap six when the Scot stopped to refuel. On lap seven, McIntyre was out when the oil tank that had leaked onto his wheel since the second circuit finally split.

With Minter in a clear lead, the 60,000-strong crowd's attention now focused on the tooth-and-nail scrap between Geoff Monty's Matchless-mounted team mates, Robb and Alan Shepherd.

"We were hitting each other on the downhill straight to Metropole, bouncing off each other's fairings. Alan was a very good rider, but a very hard rider."[7]

On the final lap, it was Robb who responded to the go-faster signals from the pits to equal Minter's fastest lap of the race at 102.30 mph and squeeze home just in front of Shepherd.

With the maple leaf proudly emblazoned on his helmet, a young, unknown Canadian started his first pure road race from the back of the grid. The 1960 North West 200 was Mike Duff's first race in Europe.

"It was for me, very intimidating. It was a great prelude to the TT. I'd never raced at over 120 mph – never raced on a proper road course before. I could have really hurt myself on that type of course without the experience. In the race, the fairing bracket on my Norton broke after two or three laps. I was lying really close to last place. The fairing floated back and jammed the handlebars, and I retired at the pits to watch Minter win the race. I was really overwhelmed by the class of rider I was com-

peting against. I realised very quickly that if I was going to succeed in any way, I was going to have to beat these people.

"The North West 200 was perfect preparation for the TT. The Isle of Man was overwhelming enough, but seeing it after I'd been to the North West made it much easier to accept.

"Without question, road racing is very dangerous; you have to leave a certain amount of room, it's a different style of riding. I took that attitude, especially in the Isle of Man. The TT was a necessary school to teach you consistency, to teach you how to race against yourself. I always left a third of the road everywhere. You don't make mistakes on the island, and the Irish road circuits are the same. There are houses, telephone boxes and gates to run into, and they really hurt."[8]

By 1961, further improvements to the circuit had straightened out the approach to Milburn, and removed the more severe kinks from the coast road. Although speeds would rise as a result, the overall opinion amongst competitors was that the course was losing its pure road-racing character.

The opening race – the 350cc – would prove to be McIntyre's hardest fought victory of a famous record-breaking 350/500cc double. On the opening lap, Neville had taken over at the front from McIntyre, but it was Shepherd, making his comeback after a big "off" at Imola the previous month, who was first through Metropole. A mile into the second circuit, Shepherd went down at Primrose, leaving McIntyre clear from Neville by thirteen seconds, with Minter and King disputing the last place on the podium.

Phil Read, missing most of practice due to the late arrival of his Norton and forced to start from the back of the grid, gained twenty-nine places on the opening lap. On lap four, Read moved into second place, pushing the lap record to 101.78 mph in the process. In response, McIntyre upped the tempo to win by thirteen seconds, at a race average of 100.18 mph, the first time a 350cc race had been won at an average of over 100 mph in the British Isles.

After five miles, McIntyre had compensated for a poor 500cc start and moved into the lead at Shell Hill. On drying roads, McIntyre showed scant regard for the troublesome cross-winds that buffeted the machines on the long straights, as he opened the taps to hoist the lap record to 106.12 mph on the second circuit. As his challengers fell by the way, Robb out with a broken piston and Minter riding pillion back to the pits with a travelling marshal after crashing out on the fast S-bend approaching Milburn, McIntyre pulled away. As Fred Neville fought back from an excursion up a slip road early in the race to eventually claim third place, McIntyre coasted into the final eleven miles with over seventy seconds to spare, with Phil Read again finishing second.

As the 250cc field pushed away, Tommy Robb was already flat on the tank of his Geoff Monty Special and well on his way towards Henry's Corner. Shepherd had caught him by Portrush, but was already losing ground when his Aermacchi ground to a standstill with big-end failure at Milburn on lap three.

Lacking in practice and riding an over-geared NSU, Dickie Carter was on Robb's case by the fourth lap. Moving into second place ahead of Arthur Wheeler, he carved twelve seconds off Robb's lead on his penultimate circuit. Robb responded with a record final lap of 92.98 mph to seal his third consecutive lightweight victory.

The organisers had struggled against a combination of factors to attract an entry that came close to the depth of quality that was, by 1962, expected. The withdrawal of trade support had made life difficult for race officials, who had already been forced to compete for entries with national meetings at Brands and Aberdare. With Derek Minter opting to ride at Brands where he scored a 250/350/500cc hat-trick, and Robb and McIntyre on international duty at the French Grand Prix, a new hero would emerge in the absence of so many past winners.

Twenty-six-year-old Alan Shepherd emulated McIntyre's 1961 achievement by scoring his own 350/500cc double. Only an emphatic 250cc winning ride by Arthur Wheeler, eleven years after his first win on the Triangle Circuit, denied Shepherd a history-making hat-trick.

By lap three, Shepherd had recovered from a poor start, hoisted the lap record to 103.63 mph and steered his bright red AJS ahead of Peter Middleton's Norton. Next time around, Shepherd was clear of Middleton by eight seconds, and in the end made winning the 350cc programme opener look easy. The battle of the race was unfolding behind Middleton, as newcomer Ralph Bryans and Freddie Fischer slugged it out for third place.

"To be frank, the only time I had to race hard against anyone at the North West was my first one in 1962 against Freddie Fischer, when he rode the 350cc Deardon Norton. I rode Jim Wilson's 350cc Norton. That was a very, very, tight race. I just pipped him on the last lap and managed to grab third place by a bike's length. I never had any hard battles except in my first one. In the rest, I just managed to clear off."[9]

The main threat to Shepherd's 500cc victory disappeared as Middleton's engine seized and Fischer retired at the pits. Shepherd wrestled the big Matchless round at a consistent 103 mph, out of sight of the tussle for second between local riders Bill McCosh and Ray Spence. In the end, Spence won the battle, finishing well adrift of Shepherd.

In the 250cc race, experience would count for everything. As Stu Graham's engine hesitated on the line, Shepherd and Dickie Carter gave chase to a rapidly disappearing Wheeler. Wheeler lapped at 91.90 mph from a standing start, and then broke the lap record next time around. Wheeler completed the fifth and final lap, in 6 min 58 sec, pushing the record to 95.20 mph and sealing his fifth North West 200 lightweight win.

The logistics and financial strain of running the annual international event finally proved too much for the North of Ireland Club, resulting in the cancellation of the 1963 event. The withdrawal of trade support had made the task of attracting a quality entry a difficult one, to the point that the organisers felt that the crowds would stay at home to watch live television coverage of the FA Cup Final.

Racing resumed in 1964 with the responsibility of running the event being taken on by the Coleraine and District Motor Club. Despite only attracting an "entry poor by past standards",[10] a crowd of over 50,000 returned to watch Ralph Bryans and local hero Dick Creith carry off an Irish clean sweep.

In the 250cc five lapper, Bryans began by breaking Arthur Wheeler's lap record by almost 2 mph, before demoralising the opposition with a new record of 97.83 mph. At the end of the first lap, the tiny Belfast rider had taken the Glen Henderson-entered Honda almost a minute clear, as his team mate Jack

Isherwood languished in the pack, after his Honda was delayed by ignition trouble at the start.

Trevor Barnes dropped out of second place when his Guzzi broke an oil pipe on the second lap, leaving George Purvis, riding an ex-works Mondial, to head a charging Isherwood home behind Bryans.

As Bryans repeated his disappearing act and ran away with the 350cc race, a monumental battle for the minor placings raged behind him. Two seconds separated Bill McCosh (AJS), Jack Wilmott (Norton), Len Ireland (Norton) and Jack Findlay. The Australian's Tom Kirby-tuned AJS performed poorly in practice, and desperate last-minute repairs were still being carried out as the grid lined up.

On lap four, Wilmott retired at the

Ralph Bryans' 250cc/350cc doubl[e] made it a clean sweep for the Irish i[n] 1964. The diminutive Hond[a] teamster sweeps onto Portstewar[t] promenade on the 350cc Honda t[o] deliver the first of the Japanes[e] giant's sixty-two North West victorie[s]

Esler Crawford

pits with a sick engine. As Bryans extended his lead to over a minute with a lap of 102.14 mph, just a second outside Shepherd's 1961 record, Findlay was on the back wheel of McCosh's scarlett AJS. On the penultimate lap, Findlay moved ahead and still held the advantage for the final run along the coast road. As they flashed through the final right-hander onto the start/finish, McCosh pulled out of Findlay's slipstream to head him across the line by twenty yards.

"There was nothing really outstanding about it at all. I just cleared off and led every lap in both races. With a 350 twin against boys on Nortons and 7Rs, they were completely and totally outclassed, the Honda was so much quicker. You could have won it as you pleased really."[11]

While Bryans' classy double brought the first victory by a Japanese manufacturer on the seaside course, the 500cc race was a triumph for a decidedly home-brewed combination. It is no exaggeration that the exploits of local rider Dick Creith, a farmer from the nearby town of Bushmills, riding the Joe Ryan "Fireplace" Norton, are something of Irish racing folklore. In an era when the Irish had come to accept that in the big events on home soil, race winners would invariably come from the ranks of the established big names from overseas, Creith would upset the form book with international wins at the North West and the Ulster.

Joe Ryan had raced with modest success. He was a fireplace manufacturer from Ballyclare, who had no training as an engineer whatsoever, but who had the innate ability to take a standard Norton and make it faster than virtually anything else on the track. Renowned for their grubby appearance in the 1960s, the Ryan "Fireplace" Nortons were formidable opposition.

"The first time I ever set eyes on the Ryan Nortons, I thought they'd been kept in a hen house all year. But

Esler Crawford

when I saw how they went, I just shut my mouth after that. All that glitters isn't gold. They certainly were some performers."[12]

Bushmills farmer Dick Creith flicks the Ryan Norton through the Shell Hill S-bend during the 1964 500cc race, the first of his two back-to-back senior wins on his local circuit.

As the 500cc field pushed away, McCosh's G50 Matchless fired a second before the Ryan Norton coughed into life, and only a second separated the pair as they flashed through Portstewart after the first eleven miles. At the end of three laps, Creith was ahead by ten yards, with Findlay in third and a chasing pack of Wilmott, John Wilkinson and Swiss visitor Roland Foell in pursuit.

On his fifth circuit, Finlay set the fastest lap of the race at 103.53 mph to move onto McCosh's back wheel. By Milburn, only 200 yards of empty road separated the Australian from Creith after McCosh pulled out. By the penultimate lap, Findlay was clearly closing in on the leader, but without warning his engine cut out at Dhu Varren, and then restarted before the hard-chasing Wilkinson and Michael Bancroft appeared.

With Creith in an unassailable lead, Findlay settled for second. However, further drama was yet to unfold on the coast road. As Bancroft and Wilkinson went through Juniper Hill, neither giving an inch in the battle for third place, Bancroft lost control, smashing into the grass bank and breaking his thigh. Wilkinson struck the bank in his efforts to avoid the fallen Bancroft, but limped home in third with a badly buckled front wheel and the rear brake rod of his Norton trailing on the road.

Joe Ryan returned in 1965 with a brace of Nortons to surpass his 1964 result. The opening race of the day, won by Ian McGregor on Ryan's 350cc grubby Norton, was overshadowed by a serious crash involving the young American Tony Woodman.

"…as the riders lined up on the starting grid, all eyes were on number 76, the lanky, long-haired American Tony Woodman (AJS), who had electrified the crowd during practice by his unorthodox style."

Belfast News Letter, 24 May 1965

John Cooper was one of many who had witnessed Woodman's riding on the ragged edge during practice. The two ate together on the morning of the race, and Cooper offered his own words of advice to the newcomer, urging him to show caution on the unforgiving public-roads circuit.

From the start, the two were together in an uncompromising three-way duel with Irish rider Len Ireland. Ireland, the first-lap leader, was sandwiched between Cooper and Woodman, who both recorded an identical second lap time of 98.60 mph. As they flashed through the start/finish to

begin their third circuit, Woodman made his move and took the lead as the trio approached the short, downhill descent to Henry's Corner.

As Cooper and Ireland watched the rapidly disappearing No 76 AJS, it was clear that Woodman had seriously mis-judged his braking. In an instant, the race leader crashed heavily, leaving the course and ending up on the cement apron above Portstewart harbour, sustaining serious injuries.

By the fourth lap, McGregor's bright red Norton had caught the clearly detuned Cooper and Ireland. Next time around, McGregor was in front, but as the leaders set out on their final circuit, he had been relegated to fourth, behind Cooper, Ireland and Robin Fitton, riding in close formation. Over the next eleven miles, McGregor set about the task of picking off his

With the crowd only feet from the action, Tommy Robb nips round Henry's during his winning ride in 1965 on the 250cc Bultaco.

Esler Crawford

rivals. In so doing, he clocked the fastest lap of the race at 100.65 mph to head Cooper home by two seconds, with fifty yards covering the top four.

For Ireland, riding the Honda that had carried Bryans to victory in the previous year's 250cc race, it was a day when victory would always remain just tantalisingly out of reach.

Robb's works Bultaco had proved troublesome in practice. In response, mechanics flew in from the Spanish factory on the day before the race to sort out the problems. At the end of lap one, Robb led Ray McCullough (Greeves) by six seconds, but with a lap of 95.98 mph as the race reached its midpoint, Ireland began to close dramatically on the race leader. On the last lap, Ireland moved into the lead, but rounding Church Corner as he headed onto the coast road for the final time, the front wheel of his Honda began to slide away on an isolated damp patch on the road. In the belief that his front forks were leaking oil onto the tyre, Ireland eased off and the race was lost.

Before lining up for the 500cc race, Creith had a brush with officialdom that almost saw him sidelined as a non-starter:

"Nortons at that time were all the same in that they would have leaked a lot of oil in a long race; it couldn't be avoided. Joe [Ryan] used to sprinkle cement dust round the wheels before we went to a race to soak up the oil. It might not have looked good but it did the job.

When I went in to get the bike scrutineered, there was a whole row of other riders with their bikes waiting, the

Esler Crawford

place was full. When it came to my turn, they refused to even look at the bike until I took it away and washed it. I was kinda' cut you know, because they were all laughing. Joe said we'll just put it back in the van and go home. At the finish up they were glad to get us back."[13]

Dick Creith's 500cc class win in 1965 was followed with victory later that year in a downpour at the Ulster Grand Prix. It was his last and most successful season in the sport. With the offer of works rides on the table, Creith quit at the top and retired at the end of the '65 season.

The relationship between Creith and his sponsor was based on a close mutual respect. The man who Creith describes as having "got on with extra well" and who shared the same dry sense of humour never missed a chance to wind his rider up. As the signal to clear the grid before the start of the 1965 500cc race was given, Ryan's parting words were, "Dick, if you saw the state of the big end in that thing you'd be scared to start her."

Creith, a notoriously slow starter, was still pushing the

ILFORD   F P 3

19A   20   2 4   21   21A

dark blue Norton as the field streamed into Henry's for the first time. At the end of the lap, he had passed over twenty other riders and lay in fourth position behind Fitton, Cooper and George Buchan. On his third circuit, Creith moved into the lead with a lap of 103.91 mph. On each lap, the flying farmer increased the pace, posting the fastest lap of the race at 106.23 mph on his sixth time around. With Cooper retiring at the pits and Fitton going out at Shell Hill, Creith cruised home with more than a minute to spare over Buchan, with Dan Shorey holding off Chris Conn for third place.

"More than half of the overseas riders managed to cross St George's Channel to fight out the international classes in the Irish classic."

Motor Cycling, 28 May 1965

The 1966 seamen's strike that had caused the postponement of the TT came close to forcing the cancellation of the North West 200. In the face of adversity, the organisers persevered. Their efforts paid off, and the meeting went ahead. Peter Williams, a twenty-six-year-old engine designer from Kent, had good reason to be grateful. Riding Tom Arter's G50 Matchless, Williams claimed victory from Scot George Buchan by three seconds, the largest margin that had separated the pair throughout a race-long duel.

Ian McGregor had set the fastest lap of the race at 101.52 mph, but retired after five laps at Metropole with rain falling all around the course. As Buchan moved into what would be a short-lived lead at Metropole on lap five, Selwyn Griffiths slid off in the treacherous conditions. Williams regained the advantage on the fast sweeping coast-road section, but neither could break clear of the other, with the lead see-sawing to and fro.

Buchan was in front by two yards, barely a bike's length, as the big 500s skittered and weaved on the skating rink surface and into lap seven. Next time round Metropole, Williams made his move and edged ahead, pulling clear of his rival to win by one hundred yards.

Williams' mastery of the treacherous conditions denied Buchan a dramatic 350/500cc double. The Scot had led from start to finish to win the 350cc race, before the rain came down. For the first five laps, Buchan's task had not been an easy one, with Len Ireland's tenacious ride in pursuit coming to an abrupt end when he hit oil dropped on the coast road where South African Ray Flack had crashed earlier. Ireland suffered a similar fate, but the hard luck story of the race belonged to Tommy Robb.

Robb's Bultaco had coughed badly on the grid before eventually spluttering into life at the back of the forty-

strong field. The Belfast Grand Prix regular refused to concede that the race was a lost cause. His perseverance seemed about to be rewarded when, with a lap to go, he lay second, visibly closing on Buchan. On the final lap, Robb was freewheeling on the fast straight between Coleraine and Portrush after his chain broke, leaving John Blanchard to hold off Bob Steele for second spot. As Buchan celebrated, few would have anticipated that the victory would be Norton's last on the circuit until Robert Dunlop's double super-bike win on the JPS Wankel-engined Norton in 1990.

Peter Williams peels into Church Corner on the Arter Matchless during the 1966 500cc race. 350cc winner George Buchan gives chase through the rain.

On a day when luck deserted the

Esler Crawford

Irish, a broken chain again cheated Robb of a possible 250cc victory. Until the fourth lap, Robb and Bultaco-mounted John Blanchard had been virtually inseparable. Robb had broken the lap record on the second and third laps, before Blanchard had the final say, raising it to 99.29 mph. While Blanchard crossed the line with a comfortable advantage over Peter Williams' Reg Orpin's Greeves, his rivals were unaware that his race had almost ended in Portrush on the last lap:

As Buchan chases Williams through Metropole in the 1966 500cc race, Selwyn Griffiths' challenge ends as he slides out of third place in the greasy conditions. Williams and Buchan take turns in front on the following laps.

"Coming down the long drop to Metropole on the last lap, the engine died. I freewheeled towards the corner, almost in tears, changing down gears all the way. As I tipped into the corner I decided to take the chance and let the clutch out in first, and the engine freed itself and fired. I used the kill button to change gear along the coast road; I never closed the throttle the whole way to the finish. The engine virtually exploded as I crossed the finish line."[14]

The 1967 North West 200 would prove to be one to remember for Italian designer Guiseppi Paton and his collaborator Bill Hannah. On a day when blustery winds sent showers scudding across the course, Fred Stevens gave the small Hannah-Paton factory their finest hour, delivering 350cc and 500cc victories with consummate style and ease.

Esler Crawford

1966 250cc winner John Blanchard steers the Bultaco between the crowd and the manhole covers on Portstewart prom.

The meeting had opened with Ken Daniels dropping his 350cc Norton on the start line, forcing starter Stanley Woods to take evasive action from the riderless machine. Stevens first-lap lead of nine seconds became eighteen a lap further into the race. Mechanical breakdowns halted the progress of slow-starting Ian McGregor and then ended Peter Williams' steady run in second place, allowing Stevens to win by minutes from Malcolm Uphill, with a hard-charging Len Ireland passing Rob Fitton, Tom Dickie and Chris Conn on the last lap to take third.

Percy Tait's factory Triumph refused to start and remained stranded on the line as the 500cc pack thundered into life. A lap into the headline race of the day and Stevens clearly had a fight on his hands as the massed 500s of Fitton, Uphill and Blanchard thundered through Portstewart, a second behind the rear wheel of

the green Hannah-Paton. As the race progressed, a familiar story unfolded as Stevens inched away to lead by ten seconds after two laps and seventeen after four laps.

Stevens maintained his relentless pace, lapping within 0.63 mph of Bob McIntyre's outright lap record, and as the race reached midway the chasing pack were already out of touch and disputing second place. Ian McGregor was out with a broken rear brake linkage after coming off the back of the grid to hold fourth by lap four. Robin Fitton had recovered from an excursion up the slip road at Metropole to lie just outside the top three, only to crash out at Juniper on the fifth lap. With the intense battle for the minor placings going off the boil, it was a distant, strung-out procession headed by Blanchard and Uphill that followed Stevens home.

Steve Murray's years of trying for an elusive win on the Triangle Circuit were finally rewarded when he headed the 250cc field home:

"After the first race of the day – the 350cc – Len Ireland came up to warn me about the conditions. He said, 'Going past the Plantation, I was sitting on the white line in the middle of the road, and the wind caught me and blew me right across to the grass on the left-hand side,

Clifford McLean

1967 350cc and 500cc winner Fred Stevens on the Hannah Paton at Metropole.

"When I arrived at Milburn, Bill Smith had dropped his Kawasaki and was sliding up the road. At Ballysally, I could see Patsy McGarrity on his ex-works Honda and his brother Michael on a Bultaco, as well as Brian Steenson and Ray McCullough. I got past Derek Chatterton at Blackhill and then passed Tommy Robb on another Bultaco.

"Tony Wilmott had a 'helluva' fast Royal Enfield, but he went up the slip road at Milburn when he had the lead. I just got away from everybody and won. I couldn't believe it. I first went to the North West with my father when he rode in the 250cc race in 1949, and there I was winning it twenty-five years later."[15]

be careful Steve.'

"In practice, I had ridden a Rickman G50 borrowed from John Williams, but it broke a crank pin and I only made it to Mathers Cross on my first lap. Bill Smith was out on Gerald Brown's twin-cylinder Kawasaki, and he stopped and gave me a lift back to the pits. After warming up the Bultaco, they took forever to warm up, I only had time to get a couple of laps in. It broke a primary chain at Blackhill, and I ended up with no 500cc ride, and starting from the back row in the 250cc race.

"When the flag dropped, the Bultaco did what the darned things were famous for: it gassed up, and when I finally got it going, and went round Henry's in last place, it started to rain. When I got to the Plantation, it was so dark you could hardly see a thing. I'm in the right-hand gutter and everyone else in the middle of the road with the throttle rolled off, because the rain was so heavy.

Robb's race was over before he completed a lap when his Bultaco's engine broke a crank a mile from the start/finish, allowing Wilmott to take over at the front. With Wilmott losing the advantage on lap two, Murray got his head down to win by fourteen seconds, while Patsy McGarrity set the fastest lap of the race to head Derek Chatterton and his brother Michael home.

By 1968 the tireless efforts of Coleraine and District Motor Club stalwarts Ossie McChesney, Jubilee Maxwell and Bertie Anderson were paying dividends. Since the club had taken over the task of running the event, they had endeavoured to restore it from the early 1960s' doldrums to its rightful place as one of the prestige events on the motor-sport calendar. By any definition, the 1968 meeting would prove to be a classic in the North West 200's distinguished history. Stanley Woods, present at every race on the Triangle Circuit since racing began there in 1929, declared the meeting the best he had ever seen.

Despite Bill Smith and John Cooper setting new lap records on their way to hotly disputed 350cc and 500cc wins, the task of reinstating the circuit as the fastest in the British Isles fell to little Ralph Bryans on his 250cc Honda. On his way through the *Motor Cycle News* speed trap, Bryans was clocked at 138.5 mph – 4 mph faster than the best 500cc machine. Even Bryans had not anticipated riding at the pace that developed as he fought to get back amongst the leaders after an unscheduled pit stop on lap two.

Bryans leads Gould, Steenson and Findlay into Henry's Corner, 250cc race, 1968. Gould won, Bryans set an absolute course record of 109.23 mph but had to settle for fourth place.

From the off, the game plan had been simple: a first-lap blast to Coleraine should have allowed Bryans to open enough of a lead to ease off and win from the front at his own pace. By the end of the lap, Bryans had pulled well clear of the pack but so too had Yamaha-mounted Rod Gould.

"Honda stopped Grand Prix racing at the end of 1967, and I had on loan from them a 250-6 and a 125-5. I went back to the North West with the 250-6 in 1968. I had a fairly healthy lead, but unfortunately those little rubbers that go between the cylinder head and the carburettors went a bit soft. The whole bank of carbs worked loose and dropped off around Coleraine somewhere. As soon as it stopped, I could see immediately what was wrong, so I popped them back on again and held them with one hand and rode back to the pits. We tied them on with a bit of locking wire and I set off in pursuit.

"Coming down into Portrush on the last lap, I could see Findlay and Steenson, and I had a real go to try and catch them on the coast road before the line. I closed ground on them but didn't catch them. Once you're in a race it's never over until the flag drops. The other guys might have all broken down on the last lap, you just don't know. You're never there unless you finish. To be frank, if the carbs hadn't fallen off the thing, I'd never have lapped at 109 mph."[16]

With Bryans temporarily sidelined, Gould, riding a five-port, Yamaha-powered, Bultaco-framed "Special", never looked

Clifford McLean

like being caught. At the end, he had more than a minute to spare over the titanic battle that raged between Steenson and Findlay since the third lap. Last-lap heroics from Steenson decided the dispute for second place, but at the end of the five lapper, the centre of attention was undoubtedly Bryans. On his penultimate lap, he had shattered the absolute course record, going round at 107.69 mph. As he completed what will long be remembered as one of the great, big-hearted rides, his rear tyre covered in oil, Bryan's meagre reward for a record-shattering last lap of 109.23 mph was fourth place, three seconds behind the Bultaco of Findlay.

The 350cc curtain-raiser saw the Aermacchis of Kel Carruthers and Brian Steenson head Peter Williams, Bill Smith, Billie Nelson on the Hannah-Patoni, and Rob Fitton through at the end of lap one. As John Cooper retired from the fray, Smith clocked 103.22 mph next time round to hit the front. It was not enough to break the resolve of the determined Carruthers who headed the frantic dash towards Henry's and into the fourth circuit. At the end of the lap, the Australian clung to Smith's tail, while Williams' challenge ended at the pits with big-end failure. As Steenson pushed the lap record to 104.23 mph next time round, Carruthers coasted into the pits and out of the race with a broken crankshaft. Well clear of John Hartle in third, Smith, riding the ex-Patsy McGarrity Honda, made experience count, leading the young Queen's University student across the line by four seconds for his only North West 200 win.

Fastest man in 500cc practice, Rob Fitton "led off what many described as the finest race ever seen on the North West course."[17] Fitton lay in the midst of a ten-man bunch, with Carruthers leading from Cooper at the end of the lap. As the mayhem continued on the next, Fitton retired at the pits. By lap three, Gould had joined Cooper, Findlay, Nelson, Carruthers, Hartle and Ron Chandler, all bent on overtaking new leader Williams. A record lap at 107.45 mph by Cooper was only enough to move him into second behind Findlay.

A broken con rod ensured that Findlay's lead was short-lived, allowing Williams to regain the advantage from Chandler and Cooper. After six laps in the supporting cast, Nelson made his move, only to take to a slip road at the Boulevard almost immediately. He rejoined the fray in fourth, with the original ten-strong leading bunch now reduced to Cooper, Chandler and Williams.

The trio rounded Church for the seventh time with nothing between them. As they thundered under the railway bridge at Dhu Varren, a back marker loomed ahead. Cooper and Williams went safely past on the outside, but as Chandler tried to squeeze through on the inside, his front wheel was taken away and he crashed out of the race.

As Williams trailed Cooper through the start/finish to begin the final lap, he gave the thumbs down to his pit. Four miles later, he had joined the list of retirees, allowing Nelson and Gould to complete the rostrum. Malcolm Uphill freewheeled across the line in fifth after his engine seized on the coast road.

The race remains prominent in the mind of fourth-place finisher Denis Gallagher:

"I enjoyed that race immensely. I was dicing for the lead early on. I had never ridden on any circuit near the speeds we were getting to that day. It highlighted to me that if you're going to be riding at high speeds on a circuit like that, you need to learn the routine for it. You can't do what you do on short circuits, it's a different way of approaching the thing altogether. It was certainly an eye-opener for me.

"I remember Cooper coming up alongside me coming out of Portstewart by the graveyard. He actually hit me, clattered me with his fairing. He'd never seen or heard of me, and he probably thought, what's this whipper-snapper doing here.

"I was very annoyed and I spoke to him about it after the race. I said, "Take your glasses off because I've got something to say." I wasn't disappointed by the result, it was an enjoyable day's racing, and I think I

One of the finest races ever seen on the Triangle Circuit, the 1968 500cc race. Billie Nelson leads Cooper, Chandler and Hartle at the height of the frantic battle. Cooper took the win from Nelson, Chandler crashed out of the top three.

surprised a lot of them as well as myself that day. I've always gone racing to enjoy myself, to go as fast as I can, get as good a result as I can, but at the end of the day to come home in one piece if that's possible."[18]

Rod Gould brought the curtain down on a memorable decade of racing on the Triangle Circuit with Yamaha's first double victory. By 1969, the Japanese manufacturers had achieved the unthinkable, and replaced the British

Rowland White

factories as the dominant force in motor-cycle racing.

Gould hustled a 350cc evil-handling Daytona Yamaha around at 110.17 mph in practice – an unofficial absolute course record. Before the race, his mechanics took 20cc of oil from each of the front fork legs in an attempt to rectify the handling problem. Four miles into the race, Gould had already pulled clear of the chasing pack by 200 yards.

At the end of the second lap, a new record of 108.61 mph put Gould out of reach, as Phil Read, making his first appearance of the year on home soil, Carruthers, Stastny, on the works Jawa, Smith, Crawford and Steenson gave chase. As Stastny struggled in the closing stages with electrical problems, eventually limping home in ninth, Cooper (oiled plugs) and Smith (ignition coil) were forced from the action.

Jack Findlay finished third, after riding for most of the seven laps with his boot jammed against a split in the base of the tank of his Yamaha. An exhaust that had threatened to come adrift completely in the last two laps had not made Findlay's top-three finish easy, after a gallant fight back from twelfth place on lap one.

Despite adding a 250cc record race average, and fastest lap to his earlier 350cc lap and race records, Gould's thoughts were on the 112-mph lap that might have been if the Japanese twin had handled more sweetly in the opening race. Lack of fourth gear from lap one made little difference to Gould in his demolition of the 250cc opposition.

The Banbury rider led on every lap to finish over a minute and a half clear of what had amounted to open war between Robb and Uphill for the entire five laps. There was nothing to separate Robb's Yamaha and the Crooks' Suzuki on performance as they battled grimly through every corner. Robb edged ahead as they went through the Boulevard for the final time to head Uphill across the line by five seconds. Behind Billy Guthries' lonely ride in fourth place, Tom Herron pulled from Stastny's slipstream to push the Czech star back to sixth, just ahead of Steve Murray.

Jack Findlay's Linto and the Weslake twin, due to make its much publicised racing début in the hands of Phil Read, were not on the grid as the 500s lined up. The press had elevated the Weslake to a British "world beater" before it had turned a wheel in anger. In practice, the twin had made the 500 yards to Henry's Corner, before spluttering to a halt; it would be its only "competitive" racing appearance. Years later Read reflected:

"That was a disaster wasn't it, that was a big mistake. I wish I had never wasted my time with it, it was totally uncompetitive."

The epic all-Seeley, John Blanchard/Brian Steenson battle over the opening seven laps of the 500cc race would be decided when Steenson took to a slip road. Both Blanchard's Chuck Seeley and the Queen's University machine had taken turns at the front on the opening lap. Kel Carruthers ground to a halt on lap two with a broken valve spring, and as the quartet of Tait (Triumph), Gallagher (Matchless), Robb riding the Ryan Norton and Ron Chandler (Seeley) scrapped for third, Blanchard and Steenson broke clear at the front.

By lap five, Tait was out with a seized engine, and Steenson and Blanchard had recorded an identical race average of 105.64 mph.

"In the race on every lap, Steenson was outbraking me into Metropole. I had disc brakes, he was using drum. I kept thinking, this shouldn't be happening, he shouldn't be able to do what he was doing. Eventually, I thought if he's going past it'll have to be on the footpath, and I moved from the middle of the road to my left. He had to

Photo sequence: Rowland White

Ray McCullough (162) nips through as Brian Steenson drops his Aeramacchi at the Boulevard, Coleraine. 350cc race, 1969.

Clifford McLean

The only racing appearance for the infamous Weslake-twin. The "Great British Worldbeater" with Phil Read aboard lasted only 400 yards in practice in 1969.

road, cutting out the slow left-hander at Metropole. With the cost of running the event ever increasing and little sponsorship forthcoming from local government, race officials announced their intentions to abandon the Triangle Circuit. Plans to implement a £100,000 road improvement scheme posed a serious question mark over the availability of the coast road section anyhow, and the organisers decided to move the North West 200 over the border and into Donegal. The deciding factor would be the size of the anticipated cheque Bord Fáilte would offer in sponsorship. When May came around again in 1970, the grids lined up where they nearly always had done.

The meeting would see the end of an era with Ralph Bryans' farewell ride and the beginning of a new one with Tom Herron's 350cc victory. For the first time since 1959, the organisers diversified from the standard three-race format and added a production class. Despite attracting a quality entry, the class was dropped the following year, only being reinstated for 750cc and 1300cc machines in 1987.

shut the throttle off, and I got away from him for a bit. That was a tight race." [19]

By the time Bill Smith dropped the Hannah-Patoni, its rear tyre covered in oil, in spectacular style at Henry's on the final lap, Steenson had already settled for second, after his Seeley began to lose power. Unsure whether his problems stemmed from fuel starvation or faulty ignition, the young Queen's University student rode the closing stages with the petrol cap open in case the fuel lines were blocked. A place on the bottom step of the podium showed that Robb, a specialist on the smaller-capacity machines, had lost none of his touch on a 500.

By 1969 the organisers had made further changes to the course, running the race between the houses through the Boulevard, just before the old Milburn Hairpin, and turning at Portrush into Glenvale, and onto the coast

In a 350cc race marred by the fatal injuries sustained by Andrew Manship in a first-lap crash at Juniper Hill, twenty-one-year-old Herron made an electrifying start and was well clear of Robb and Cooper at the end of the opening lap. Robb gave chase, equalling the class record and then moving into the lead on lap four. The confrontation between youth and experience rapidly shaped up to be compulsive watching, as Herron squeezed ahead at the Boulevard only to be playing catch-up again by Metropole. Then the Yamaha sucked a stone into the carburrettor at Juniper, and as Herron's TR2 roared through alone, the white-leathered figure of Robb cut a disconsolate figure as he coasted to the pits to retire.

North West 200 débutant Tony Rutter retired from fourth just after midway, leaving John Cooper on an over-geared Yamaha to take second, forty-two seconds behind Herron. Aermacchis filled the remainder of the top six, with Cecil Crawford claiming a safe third place, well clear of the dog-fight between Roy Graham, Peter Berwick and Denis Gallagher behind him.

Three classes ran concurrently in the production race, with the 250cc machines covering seven laps, the 500s eight laps and the 750s nine. For the first half of the 750cc race, Percy Tait's factory Triumph Trident had the edge on straight-line speed, but the superior handling of Malcolm Uphill's Bonneville made for an even match. On the last lap, Uphill clocked a speed of 107.87 mph to pull clear and win by fifty yards, with the Norton Commando of Peter Williams a further hundred yards behind in third.

Stuart Graham's win came after a poor start and a brief mid-race battle with John Williams. His 500cc Suzuki whispered into life unheard by Graham, who kick-start-

Rowland White

ed twice and was left sitting. By lap three, he had caught and passed the Honda of early leader John Williams. Williams immediately regained the advantage, only for Graham to make the decisive move on the penultimate lap.

He started and finished his career as a winner. Ralph Bryans winning his last race, the 1970 350cc on Luigi Taveri's ex-works Honda.

The focus of attention in the 250cc class fell on the seven-lap battle for second place between the Crooks' Suzuki-mounted pair of Stan Woods and Ralph Bryans. Bryans' T20 had already 26,000 miles on the clock, but proved to be more than a match for Woods. Cliff Carr, riding Eric Housley's Ossa, took the lead on the approach to Coleraine on the opening lap and stayed there. At the flag, Carr was over a minute in front of the squabbling Suzukis.

With the non-appearance of Santiago Herrero's works Ossa, the story of the 250cc race was Ralph Bryans' final, glorious competitive ride. On an eight-year-old, ex-works, 250cc Honda-4, the pint-sized Grand Prix hero devastated the entire field before making the unexpected announcement that he was calling it a day. No one was more surprised by the news than Honda, who immediately began the desperate search to find a last-minute replacement to join Cooper and Robb, entered on factory-prepared, four-cylinder CB750s in the Production TT.

As "...the crowds all around the circuit could hear the banshee wail of Bryans' Honda echoing across the green fields of Ulster,"[20] the sight and sound of Bryans' last hurrah amounted to near sensory overload.

"In 1970 I borrowed an old 250-Four from Luigi Taveri, a friend of mine living in Switzerland. Unfortunately, it burned a hole right through the piston in practice, so I had to rebuild the engine overnight. It was just the wrong choice of spark plugs.

"I had to start from the back of the grid. I had it in my own mind that I was going to stop, win or lose, after that race. I didn't tell anybody but I had my mind made up.

"I managed to be in fourth by the first corner, and I passed two more of them coming out of Portstewart. Leaving Portstewart, you used to go up a hill, then there's a downhill left-hander, before it goes uphill again. Well, I passed one on the outside there, and got the other one up the inside, and just cleared off and won it.

"I was very pleased with that result. I had the distinction of winning the first road race that I ever competed in, and winning my last one. I started as a winner, and I finished as a winner, so I can't complain I suppose."[21]

Malcolm Uphill held a 1.8-second advantage over Tony Rutter after a race-long duel for the runner-up spot, after Alex George was forced to retire and mechanical problems dropped Stan Woods and Peter Berwick out of contention.

Queen's University's 500cc Seeley two-stroke made its first, eagerly awaited appearance in practice, taking Brian Steenson around at 102 mph before breaking a primary chain. In the race, Steenson opted to ride the four-stroke version, only to suffer the same problem while leading on the last lap.

Bill Smith's Kawasaki-3 was unmatched on straight-line speed, but did not last a lap after the front brake nipple snapped off. John Blanchard's race plan was to break clear from the pack early on. As Blanchard tipped his Chuck Seeley into the frightening right-hander at Mathers Cross, flat on the tank ("That corner nearly killed me in 1970"[22]), the back let go. He awoke in hospital the following day, and began counting his blessings.

The 500cc race quickly became a thriller as Steenson pushed the lap record to 107.69 mph on lap two, and then to 108.73 mph on his next circuit to lead from Peter Williams (Arter Matchless) and Tommy Robb. On lap eight, with Robb already out with a broken primary chain, Williams went through Glenvale well clear of Cooper, and with no sign of Steenson. The Belfast student's race had ended on the run from Portstewart to Coleraine, allowing Williams to cruise to his second victory on the course.

Two weeks later, Steenson lost his life after crashing in the Senior TT.

Malcolm Carling

Peter Williams crests Black Hill on his way to his second North West 200 win, the 1970 500cc race.

a sad and dismal farewell to the "old" course. At the end of the day, Smart, Rutter, Robb and Herron lay in hospital, all crashing out in the freezing, slippery conditions.

Despite all the heavens could send down, the 350cc race quickly developed into a classic encounter. As a light drizzle rapidly became a downpour – pronounced "the worst conditions I've ever raced in," by Paul Smart – Robb, wearing a Barbour jacket over his distinctive white leathers, pulled clear by 200 yards after two laps. By then, Herron was already en route to hospital after crashing into spectators at Juniper Hill on lap one. Read set the fastest lap of the race fourth time round to move into the lead, after Robb clipped Smart's rear wheel and went down heavily at Juniper. Robb had asked the organisers for extra baling at the exact spot where he crashed. Cooper continued, clearly detuned after flying debris smashed the screen of his Yamsel. He quickly regained his focus to take over from Smart at the front after water in the ignition sidelined Read's Yamaha. As Rutter struggled with a misting visor, just holding off the challenge from Alan Barnett for third, Smart disappeared into the spray to win from Cooper.

On a day when driving rain and blinding spray swirled off the cliff tops, John Cooper, Paul Smart and Derek Chatterton became the last men to record wins on the original Triangle Circuit. In future years, massed packs would no longer surge around Henry's Corner and through Portstewart on their way to Milburn Hairpin via McHugh's Plantation and Drumslade. From 1973, the course would swing left at York Hotel, onto Cromore Road and through the country towards Shell Hill. The 1971 North West 200 was

"It was raining heavily as the 250cc field formed up, with a front row that would have done justice to a Grand Prix: Gould, Smart, Sweden's Kent Anderson and Read."

Motor Cycle, 26 May 1971

Once again, water in the ignition ended Read's chal-

Rowland White

The mighty Grand Prix works Yamaha team, Gould (1) and Anderson (5), line up in the evening sunshine for practice in 1971. On race day the heavens opened.

lenge five miles into the first lap. Rutter, Smart and Gould were already well clear of Cooper by Portrush, but as Gould retired at the pits, they began the second circuit out on their own. On lap three, at Crannagh, a fast left-hand sweep approaching Coleraine, the leaders touched, with Rutter hitting a concrete post as they crashed out together. New leader Cooper was not without his own worries, but still led on the final lap, despite a steadily worsening crack in an expansion cham-

Rowland White

ber. He nursed the sick Yamaha home in second, as a relieved Chatterton tiptoed to the flag for his first North West 200 victory, surviving numerous scares on the way, after aquaplaning on standing water that lay on all parts of the course.

As the heavens opened, the 500cc race, shortened from nine laps to six, finally got underway. In the truly treacherous conditions, John Cooper and his close friend and travelling companion Geoff Barry were well clear of the field by the end of the opening lap. As the race reached the half-way point, Barry Kemp was forced to relinquish a place on the leader board due to a misted visor. He rejoined in twelfth place, and fought his way back to fourth, behind Peter Williams' Arter Matchless, and ahead of the Irish challenge of Gerry Mateer and Abe Alexander.

For six laps, the Seeleys of Cooper and Barry skated on the edge of adhesion with never more than split seconds between them. As they began their fourth lap, Cooper led by 0.4 of a second. On the fifth,

The last men to win on the original "old" course. 1971 500cc winner John Cooper (21) follows 350cc winner Paul Smart around Henry's Corner.

81

Malcolm Carling

Derek Chatterton crests Portstewart prom with the harbour and a wall of spray behind him. 1971 250cc winner.

Barry was fractionally ahead, but the pair set out on their final lap, side by side. Cooper had inched ahead by the Boulevard, and held just enough in hand to remain there to the flag. As the sodden crowd dwindled away and started for home, Cooper uncorked a bottle of Bushmills and began his celebrations.

The political situation in Northern Ireland spiralled on a downward curve of self-destruction into 1972. Under pressure from the Northern Ireland Government, who considered any sizeable public gathering a potential flashpoint for trouble, the organisers had no option but to cancel the 1972 meeting.

NOTES

1 From an interview with Jackie Wood, August 2000.
2 Jackie Wood, August 2000.
3 From an interview with Tommy Robb, Belfast, August 2000.
4 From an interview with Sammy Millar, Belfast, August 2000.
5 Tommy Robb, August 2000.
6 Tommy Robb: "It was a wonderful bike. Basically, it was a BSA, Geoff having extensively modified the engine, crank, piston, bore, etc. It was a really good starting bike, a real flyer, especially on high-speed circuits with long straights, ideal for the North West."
7 Tommy Robb, August 2000.
8 Michelle Duff, February 2000.
9 From an interview with Ralph Bryans, August 2000.
10 *Motor Cycling*, 30 May 1964.
11 Ralph Bryans, August 2000.
12 From an interview with Denis Gallagher, August 2000.
13 From an interview with Dick Creith, April 1996.
14 From an interview with John Blanchard, February 2001.
15 From an interview with Steve Murray, 1999.
16 Ralph Bryans, August 2000.
17 *Motor Cycle News*, 22 May 1968.
18 Denis Gallagher, August 2000.
19 John Blanchard, February 2001.
20 *Motor Cycle News*, 27 May 1970.
21 Ralph Bryans, August 2000.
22 John Blanchard, February 2001.

Esler Crawford

Ralph Bryans

Ireland's only Grand Prix World Champion was born in Belfast on 7 March 1941. Ralph Bryans caught the racing bug after attending his first meeting as a spectator, the 1957 Ulster Grand Prix. He began his own racing career by winning the 200cc class at the Tandragee 100 in 1959, riding a 197cc Ambassador. The following year, Bryans won the 200cc Irish championship, and then moved up to campaign a 350cc Norton, supplied by sponsor Jim Wilson.

1962 brought TT début rides on the 350cc Norton and a 50cc Benelli, supplied by Fron Purslow. Bryans joined forces in 1963 with Joe Ryan, and returned to the island with a CR93 Honda twin, and an ex-works Benelli single, supplied by Fron Purslow. By the end of the year, Bryans' natural ability and tenacious riding had brought him to the attention of the factory teams. After signing a contract to ride with the Spanish Bultaco team for the 1964 season, Honda offered works rides on their 50cc twin and the four-cylinder 125.

With Mr Bulto suitably compensated by Honda, Bryans began a career as a works rider for the Japanese factory that would see him crowned 50cc World Champion in 1965, and finish third in the 1966 125cc title race. At the end of the 1967 season, Honda withdrew from Grand Prix racing. With championships being decided on points scored from half of the season's rounds plus one, Bryans could only reflect on what might have been if all rounds had counted. If all results had counted, Bryans would have added the 250cc title to his 50cc crown.

Other highlights of a career that earned him the distinction of scoring points in all five solo Grand Prix classes included finishing third in the 1967 350cc table, despite only riding in three of the eight rounds, and a 1966 50cc TT win ahead of Taveri and Anderson.

At the age of twenty-nine, Ralph Bryans ended his racing career as he began it, a winner. He moved to live in Scotland where he began a successful car parts business, continuing to compete in trials competitions until 1990.

Clifford McLean

photos

Massed start of the 350 c.c. class.

Above: The start of the 350cc race, 1937. From left to right: 19 J R Dulson, 21 J W Beevers, 16 J H White (Works Norton), 36 H G Tyrell Smith (Works Excelsior), 26 Claude Clark, 33 W L Dawson, 18 Herbert Tomlinson, 35 S Ginger Wood (Works Excelsior), 24 C Gauterin, 31 John Hayes, 34 John Dunne, 34 T McEwan, 37 E A Mellors (Works Velocette), 20 Charles B Sutherland.

Right: Jimmy Guthrie takes the chequered for his fourth and final North West 200 win, the 1937 500cc.

Previous page: Dick Creith awaits the start of the 1964 500cc on the Joe Ryan Norton. It was the first of the two famous back-to-back victories for the Bushmills star.

Left: Charlie Manders gives chase on the Works Excelsior out of Shell Hill Bridge during the 250cc 1937 meeting.

Below: 1939 500cc winner Ernie Lyons in action at the Belfast Millennium Motorsport Festival, Stormont, August 2000. Ernie's son Richard is in the chair.

Alastair McCook

Fr Noel Watson Collection

Above: Ray Amm at full cry on the Kneeler Norton. 350cc race 1953, York Corner.

Right: 1953 prize presentation, from left to right: Reg Armstrong 3rd in the 500cc race, Bob McIntyre 350cc winner, Syd Lawton 500cc winner, and Arthur Wheeler 250cc winner.

Howard McQuigg Collection

Fr Noel Watson Collection

Esler Crawford

Above: With sailors in the crowd from the Royal Navy destroyer at anchor in Portstewart bay, Willie Baird cranks his 350cc AJS into Henry's Corner, North West 200 1955.

Left: Geoff Tanner led the 1957 500cc race and looked to be on course to set the first 100 mph lap until a splitting headache forced his retirement. Pictured rounding Metropole Corner on his 500cc Norton.

Above: Bob McIntyre on the 500cc Norton at Portstewart, 1960.

Right: The 1964 battle for runner-up. AJS-mounted Bill McCosh just holds off Jack Findlay (Norton) at the flag.

Esler Crawford

Esler Crawford

Left: Tommy Robb leads the 1965 250cc race onto Portstewart prom.

Below: 1966 350cc winner George Buchan shows style and speed.

Esler Crawford

Esler Crawford

Left: Peter Williams (60), Brian Steenson (58), Kel Carruthers (54), chase Bill Smith on the 350cc Honda (62) through the downhill sweep through the old York Corner, 350cc race, 1968.

Below: 1968 250cc winner Rod Gould on his way to third place in the 500c race at Henry's Corner.

Bottom left: Kel Carruthers on his way to 4th place in the 1969 350cc race. Carruthers ended the '69 season as 250cc World Champion riding the works Bennelli.

Clifford McLean

Rowland White

Rowland White

Above: The famous North West 200 atmosphere perfectly encapsulated as the thronged spectators look on from the packed railway embankment and bridge at Dhu Varren, North West 200, 1970.

Right: Czech Grand Prix star Frantisek Stastny rode 250cc and 350cc works Jawas on the Triangle Circuit in 1970.

Rowland White

Pictured on the grid by Clifford McLean

95

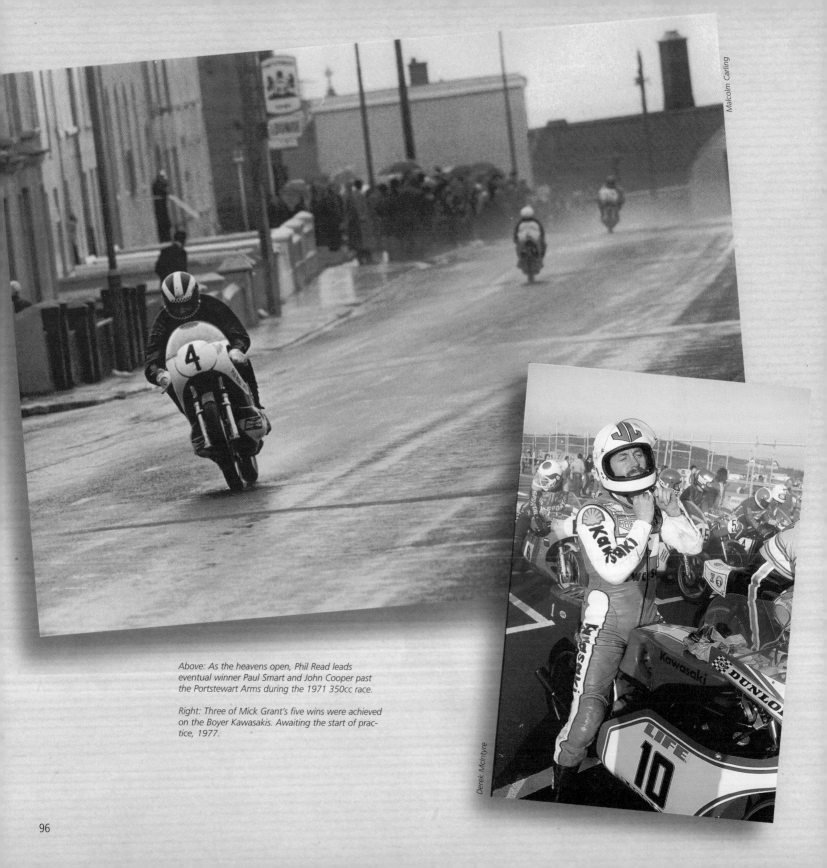

Above: As the heavens open, Phil Read leads eventual winner Paul Smart and John Cooper past the Portstewart Arms during the 1971 350cc race.

Right: Three of Mick Grant's five wins were achieved on the Boyer Kawasakis. Awaiting the start of practice, 1977.

Left: John Newbold won the 500cc race in 1978 and was just beaten to the flag in the sensational 1980 superbike race by Keith Heuwen. Sadly he lost his life in a crash at Juniper Hill in 1982.

Below: With 1978 250cc winner Tom Herron out of sight, Ray McCullough gets down to the task of holding off Chas Mortimer's challenge. McCullough and Mortimer came home second and third.

Derek McIntyre

Clifford McLean

Jim McBride

Above: Ten times winner between 1973 to 1982 Tony Rutter in the pits awaiting the start of practice in 1979.

Right: Brian Reid's only win came in the 1989 600cc race. The ex Formula Two World Champion is pictured here at Black Hill during the 1986 350cc race.

Alastair McCook

Left: Newton, Coulter and McCallan at Juniper Hill in the opening 250cc race in 1994.

Below: Woolsey Coulter beat Newton by a hair's breadth in the opening 250cc race in 1994. Ian Newton made up for the disappointment in race two. The celebrations tell the story.

Alastair McCook

Left: Nick Jeffries with the New Zealand designed and built Britten, 1994.

Below: Mark Farmer rode for the Britten team in 1994. Two weeks after the North West 200, Farmer lost his life in a practice crash in the Isle of Man.

Alastair McCook

Left: 1996 double 250cc winner Woolsey Coulter sweeps into the start/finish chicane.

Below: New Zealand newcomer Chris Haldane drifts through Primrose Hill. 1996 superbike race.

Alastair McCook

Alastair McCook

Alastair McCook

Above: 1997 Superbike winner Michael Rutter at
Metropole.

Right: In space no one can hear you scream.
McGuinness follows Ramsey under the railway
bridge in the 1997 250cc race.

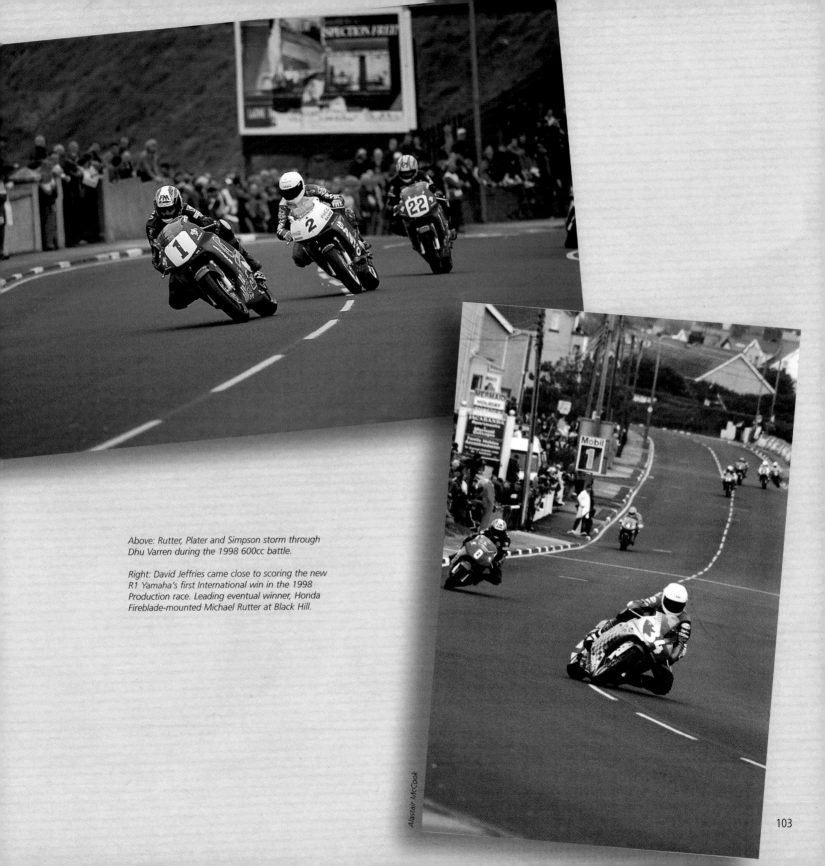

Above: Rutter, Plater and Simpson storm through
Dhu Varren during the 1998 600cc battle.

Right: David Jeffries came close to scoring the new
R1 Yamaha's first International win in the 1998
Production race. Leading eventual winner, Honda
Fireblade-mounted Michael Rutter at Black Hill.

Above: 1999 hat-trick hero David Jeffries under pressure from Honda teamster Jim Moodie.

Right: Race morning 1999. David Jeffries tries his new V&M leathers for size.

Above: The Demon Vimto SP1s of Joey Dunlop and John McGuinness lead Adrian Archibald out of York Corner in the 2000 opening Superbike race.

Above right: The V&M R6 Yamahas of Jeffries (1), Rutter (60) and Lougher (5) outnumber Jim Moodie's Honda. 600cc race, 2000.

Right: Michael Rutter enjoys the spoils of victory on the rostrum after his 2000 treble.

Alastair McCook

Alastair McCook

Alastair McCook

Photo sequence: Graham Ward's battle with Brian Gardiner for a top six finish in the 2000 Production race ends in disaster on the final corner. Ward walked away unscathed.

Ireland's SATURDAY Night

NORTH-WEST 200 REPORT AND PICTURES TO-DAY

Ireland's SATURDAY Night
The 'All-Sports' Paper

Price 24p (33p in Eire)

SATURDAY, MAY 13, 1989

91st YEAR

70,000 crowd applaud a Scots first-timer

SCORCHER STEVE

... as Dubliner Laycock breaks course record

Hislop crowned King of th[e]

SALUTE Steve Hislop. The 26-year-old rider from the Scottish Border country scored his first Irish road race win when he shattered the field to take the King of the Road Superbike race before a sunburned 70,000 crowd at today's international North West 200 over the Portstewart-Coleraine-Portrush circuit.

Hislop who led for most of the race ended up with a record race average of 117.26 mph to finish ahead of Dublin rider Eddie Laycock with Robert Dunlop holding onto a tenacious third place. Laycock, however, had the satisfaction of breaking the absolute course record with a speed of 118.33 on lap five of the six lap racer.

Although Hislop's win looked easy from the stands he had problems which only became apparent after he had finished. The sweat from his face he said: "I nearly ran out of petrol. The engine began to splutter and I thought that Rob [...] me at that stage, would catch up on [...] was delighted to get to the flag first [...]

Hislop who is no stra[...] added that alth[...] reckon [...]

1973–01

CHAPTER THREE

1973–01

Tony Rutter's breathtaking 1973 250/350cc double victories established the diminutive Midlands rider as a firm favourite with the Irish fans. The return of the North West 200 to the road-racing calendar, albeit as a national event, produced "some of the best road racing ever seen in this country".[1]

The meeting, run on a course shortened to 9 miles 1,257 yards, got off to the worst possible start when thirty-one-year-old Graham Fish lost his life after crashing in practice. Saturday's five-race programme began in subdued style with Jackie Robinson leading a

One of the North West 200's most successful and popular riders, Tony Rutter in 1974 at Black Hill.

Clifford McLean

well strung-out field home at the end of the low-key, three-lap, 200cc opener. A first lap of 88.53 mph pulled Robinson six seconds clear of nearest rival Courtney Junk, and from there he simply cruised home to win the only 200cc race ever seen on the Triangle Circuit.

In contrast, the 250cc race quickly developed into a classic, as Tony Rutter and John Williams swapped places at the front for the entire five laps. With Ray McCullough's Yamsel refusing to fire on the line, the task of upholding Irish honour fell to Tom Herron, who held off the attentions of Rutter's close friend and travelling companion, Barry Randle, to finish third, well behind the two-way dice at the front.

With the advantage see-sawing between Williams and Rutter, new records were inevitable. On the third circuit, Rutter edged in front, lapping at 105.05 mph. Williams stayed with him, and as the high-speed duel crested Quarry Hill for the final time it was the red and blue figure in front. But the glory would be Rutter's, as he pulled from his rival's slipstream to set the fastest lap of the race at 105.97 mph, and cross the line a bike's length in front.

Rutter opened 350cc proceedings with a lap of 106.48 mph, and then upped the pace with successive laps of 111.37 mph and then 112.44 mph to build an unassailable lead. The expected challenge from John Cooper evaporated when his Yamsel expired on lap four. The leader board saw little change as the race progressed, and Rutter freewheeled across the line, well clear of Williams who claimed the runner-up spot by 0.2 seconds from Randle.

The 500cc and 750cc races, run concurrently, produced victories for Billy Guthrie and Geoff Barry, after the early front-runners in both classes were forced out through mechanical failure. After three laps, John "Moon eyes" Cooper held a commanding lead over the 750cc field, but over the next two circuits, Seeley-Norton-mounted Geoff Barry caught and passed the slowing BSA. Hampered by fuel starvation problems, Cooper fought back, and held a four-yard lead as they began the final lap. In the end, it was all in vain for Cooper as Barry romped home well clear of the Norton of Wilfie Herron, with Cooper trailing home in third.

For the opening three laps of the 500cc race, it looked as if the North West 200 victory that had proved so elusive over the years was at last within the grasp of Billy McCosh. A worsening misfire in his Suzuki proved terminal on lap four, and with fancied-runner Ray McCullough's QUB2 Seeley already sidelined, Billy Guthrie (Yamaha) took the win from Sam McClements and Manx-rider Danny Shimmin.

On Saturday 18 May 1974, John Williams became the first rider in the history of the North West 200 to score a hat-trick when he rode to three wins in one day. Williams' day's work also included a new absolute course record and second place in the 250cc race.

Derek McIntyre

John Williams, the first man to score a hat-trick of North West 200 wins on one day, crests Black Hill, 18th May 1974.

Williams began the day with a start-to-finish 350cc win, which left the opposition floundering in a wall of spray and thrilled the sodden crowd that thronged the length of the waterlogged course. On roads made treacherous as the rain came down in stair rods, Williams led by the proverbial mile at the end of lap one, peering in vain into the gloom behind him in search of opposition who were nowhere in sight as he set out on his second circuit. Down the field, the atrocious conditions wreaked havoc.

"When I started racing, the Manx Grand Prix was the pinnacle, I didn't even think about the TT in those days, it was too far in the distance. I eventually rode at the TT and won my first one in 1973. I got an offer to ride at the North West 200 in 1974. I was very excited about it, and was there with my new-found friend, John Williams. We'd ridden together in the factory-Honda team at the 24-hour race in Belgium. We won there and became great friends after that.

"The weather for practice in 1974 was glorious, and I remember having a sort of workshop down by the Sea Splash Hotel (Portstewart) and working down on the rocks on the bikes with Phil Haslam. We were in our shorts because the weather was so nice, but how it changed for that Saturday.

"It poured down with rain, and Phil crashed right in front of me at Mathers Cross. I'd led the race from the start, but between Shell Hill [there was no roundabout then] and Mathers, first John [Williams] and then Phil came by me. As he came past there was an unbelievable wall of spray, and coming out of Mathers there was no sign of him at all. It was just as if he'd been plucked into the air by the hand of God. Phil broke his hip and was out of racing after that for some time.

"Mathers Cross saw the demise of many riders prior to my time racing there and since. Wayne Gardner almost crashed in front of me there. I was following him and Rob McIlnea around there, and Wayne hit the bank on the inside and was very lucky to stay on.

"I remember Tom Herron crashing in that race as well, after Mathers on the run into Portrush near to where the chicane [Magherabuoy] is now. I was talking to him after the race finished in the pits and his oversuit was ripped to shreds. I asked him what had happened and he said he had been following me when just where the road drops down over a slight rise, his bike aquaplaned, turned 180 degrees and Tom ended up following me

Derek McIntyre

down the road on his back. I remember the expression he used; he said 'I was fit to touch your back wheel for 50 yards.' We were doing the same speed except Tom was on his back and I was on my bike."[3]

Charlie Williams' first win on the Triangle came in the 1975 350cc race. He won the class again in 1980, followed by a 500cc victory the following year.

Williams mastered the conditions to head Tony Rutter home by almost two minutes; with Billy Guthrie completing the top three a further minute clear of Mick Grant, another North West 200 débutant.

On drying roads, part two of Williams' history-making hat trick came in style, with a 500cc victory at a winning average of 105.33 mph, and over one-and-a-half minutes in hand over namesake, newcomer and runner-up Charlie Williams. Starting the final lap, Billy Guthrie held a clear seventeen-second advantage over the third-place man, but a broken crankshaft relegated him to fifth place in the end.

As the 250cc grid lined up, the sense of expectation – of history about to be made – hung heavy in the air. It was not to be as Williams fought back from fourth place on lap one, moving ahead of Grant and Charlie Williams by lap three, only to be denied by "The Dromara Destroyer", Ray McCullough. McCullough's ride completed a record of winning at every race meeting in Northern Ireland, including a celebrated Ulster Grand Prix win in the rain around a slippery Dundrod in 1971 over a world-class field that included Phil Read and Jarno Sarrinen.

"I remember in that race looking round as I was going out of York Hairpin and John was just coming into it, lap after lap, the distance always the same. Near the end, I think he decided he wasn't going to do any better, and he eased off a bit.

"John Williams was a real decent character, he just said he had tried his hardest and wished me good luck."[4]

Williams secured his place in the record books, setting a new absolute course record of 115.80 mph on the way to an emphatic 750cc victory. Mick Grant had bettered the old course record with a lap of 113.32 mph to emerge as the early race leader, but Williams was quick to reply with a lap of 114.81 mph. As speeds rose, Grant's lead was cut to just three seconds on lap four. Next time around, it was Williams in front, and as Grant retired on the sixth lap, Williams could afford to ease off, still finishing over a minute and a half ahead of Barry Randle and Billy Guthrie. Suzuki-mounted Roger Sutcliffe's fifth place was the only top-six finish for a non-Yamaha-mounted rider all day.

In contrast to the previous year's dismal conditions, 1975 will long be remembered as a vintage year, when temperatures soared and a young rising star from Yorkshire, resplendent in the green livery of the Boyer Kawasaki Team, pushed the lap record to an astonishing 122.62 mph as he romped to a 500/750cc double.

The headlines announced, "Grant smashes two-miles-a-minute barrier."[5] Mick Grant's blitz on the record books raised the winning race average speed to 119.96 mph, 4 mph more than the previous lap record, and on a course lengthened by five hundred yards with the reintroduction of the Metropole section.

"We were brought up on short circuits in England, and in my early career I'd been weaned on diving up the inside. You didn't bother so much about the racing line; you just had to pass people. The technique in Grands Prix then and now is to take a nice smooth line, because generally the circuits are a lot quicker. I'd never seen anything like the North West 200. Silverstone was perhaps the quickest circuit I ever raced on, and although there were very fast corners on it, the North West was just a different ball game. I'd raced a fair bit of my career up to then on circuits that weren't so fast. It was a different technique to learn, a bit of an eye-opener. I definitely struggled a wee bit when I went there first in 1974.

"The 500cc Kawasaki was not a good package in 1975. I remember having to dice with Tony Rutter, who was on a 350cc Yamaha. The Kawasaki was quite a bit heavier than the Yamaha and it didn't really have more horsepower, so it wasn't really the ideal tool. I remember going down towards Shell Hill Bridge side by side with Tony, and there was nothing between the two bikes. I thought, I've got my work cut out here.

"The 750cc was a different kettle of fish. On the 500cc, the handling was OK, but it didn't have a lot of horsepower, about the same as the 350cc Yamaha of the time. In fairness, if somebody had offered me a 350cc Yamaha, I would have preferred it to the Kawasaki. The 750cc was a better package altogether, unbelievably quick. I think they were one of the nicest looking motorbikes that's ever been designed, so neat and clean in the design, fabulous. Not only did they give good hp, they only weighed 130kg, which is about the weight of a modern

Grand Prix bike, and no matter what people think about their reputation, they actually handled well.

"On the Kawasaki, I was very, very lucky to be the right man in the right place to get the machinery. Maybe I worked hard enough to get it. On fast circuits like the North West they made life a lot easier."[6]

For one glorious lap, Percy Tait not only challenged the

place behind Ditchburn. Grant regained the lead as Ditchburn pitted on lap five, and as his fuel load lightened, recorded a lightning-fast 122.62 mph on his final circuit, with Ditchburn completing the "1-2" for the team, finishing out of sight of South African newcomer Alan North, riding the Hailwood Yamaha.

With Ditchburn a non-starter in the 500cc event, Grant's main challenge came from Tony Rutter, who was tucked

Clifford McLean

mighty Kawasakis of Grant and team mate Barry Ditchburn, but led briefly before running wide at Metropole. By the end of the opening lap, the veteran's TZ750 Yamaha was back in touch with the leading duo, but seized at Portstewart, leaving Grant with all the time in the world to refuel on lap four and resume in second

in three yards behind Grant's back wheel as they completed lap one. Whilst Rutter could match the charging Grant on

The all-conquering Boyer Kawasakis of Ditchburn (8) and Grant (7) in formation at Metropole in 1975.

straight-line speed, the superior handling of the Kawasaki-3 proved decisive. Rutter held second place throughout the race to finish twenty-five seconds adrift and claim his only podium finish of the day. Despite setting another lap record of 117.49 mph on the penultimate lap of the three-cylinder, factory machine's world début, Grant complained of under gearing, but already had high hopes of what the flying "Green Meanie" could be capable of at the following month's TT.

In the seven-lap 350cc opening race of the day, Charlie Williams took the win after resigning himself to finishing second to Martin Sharpe who led for the first five laps.

"Martin Sharpe and I broke clear of the field, but Martin had a very fast bike and was riding it very well and he started to pull away from me. I was well ahead of everyone else, and had a look over my shoulder and thought, you'll just have to settle for second place here Charlie.

"We came out of York Hairpin and accelerated up the hill, Martin was probably twenty or thirty yards ahead of me, and suddenly I saw something drop on the floor. All of a sudden, Martin came to an abrupt halt; his gear lever had broken off. I went on to win the race from Bob Heath and Neil Tuxworth."[7]

The 250cc grid lined up without the Harley Davidson of Ray McCullough. The quietly spoken Queen's University technician had been refused permission to practice after arriving at the circuit without an international licence, and faced with the option of starting from the last row, McCullough withdrew his entry. Derek Chatterton emerged in front, after an early close battle with Martin Sharpe and Cliff Carr to pull clear by the midway stage. Chatterton's win, with a new lap record of 111.66 mph into the bargain, saw him become the first rider to win on both the "old" and "new" courses.

Further changes saw the newly built roundabout at Ballysally on the outskirts of Coleraine introduced to the circuit in 1976. As the heavens opened, Charlie Williams led the opening 350cc race from the fall of the starter's flag. Buffeted by strong cross-winds on flooded roads, Ray McCullough on the Irish Racing Motorcycle's Yamaha headed the pack by Shell Hill. As Joey Dunlop's challenge ended on lap two, and Williams' on lap four, McCullough gave a master class in wet-weather riding, leading the bedraggled field home, with a late-charging Tony Rutter filling the runner-up spot.

McCullough's fortunes changed dramatically in the 250cc race, run in the worst conditions of the day.

"I'd won the 350cc race, but got a really bad start in the 250cc. I was in something like twenty-eighth place going into the first corner. At the roundabout, I could count only six in front of me, and I thought to myself, if I can keep this up, I'll catch them by Metropole. Going over the rise as you start the descent into Portrush, I'd had a couple of wee slides on the 350cc, but I thought the 250 wouldn't be going as quick, will I keep it flat out or ease it a wee bit. I made my mind up to ease off, but the throttle stuck open, and then I hit a patch of shiny tar, the bike turned right round and pitched me off. I slid about three hundred yards, the whole way down the hill, and ended up past the school.

"I got up and there wasn't a mark on me, not even a scratch. I looked round and the bike was on fire, burning in the hedge. I pulled the tank off it and threw it into the field, but the fuel spilled out and set the field on fire. A marshal arrived with a fire extinguisher and put it out in the end. I raced the bike the following week at the Cookstown 100."[8]

After a race-long battle that saw the lead ebb and flow between Ian Richards and Tony Rutter, Richards splashed his way to the win, six seconds clear of Rutter, with one W J Dunlop making the first of many North West 200 podium appearances in third place.

Bertie Martin

The 1976 350cc race gets underway. Nos 19 Ian Richards, 27 Richard Nott, 2 Geoff Barry, 26 Graham Waring, 22 Derek Huxley, 16 Joey Dunlop, and 12 1974 winner Phil Carpenter, are still pushing as 5 Charlie Williams gets down on the tank. Williams retired on lap five, while Ray McCullough revelled in the atrocious conditions to win from Tony Rutter and Sam McClements.

For the sodden crowds, the high-light of the day was the sight of Martin Sharpe and Frank Kennedy heading the 500cc race home on the British-built Spartans. The prospect of a win for local favourite Kennedy seemed a distinct possibility, as he led them out to begin the final lap. Kennedy had taken over at the front after Stan Woods retired at Metropole after leading for the opening four laps.

Pre-race favourite Percy Tait started from the back of the grid after sitting out most of practice when his Suzuki-4 seized on the front, offside cylinder. Running deliberately rich as a precautionary measure, Tait made an atrocious start on a machine that was over jetted, and was never in the hunt. As the laps fell away, other challengers fell by the wayside. Phil Carpenter exited fourth place with an oil leak on lap two, and Steve Parrish went out at Shell Hill when his Suzuki seized, just as it had done in practice.

Despite a race-long misfire that grew steadily worse by the mile, Kennedy still led on the final run through Coleraine. The dream finish for Kennedy and the partisan crowd was not to be, as the Armoy rider limped home, sixteen seconds behind his team mate. The trademark broad grin that beamed through the falling rain from the podium summed up Kennedy's relief after nursing his sick Spartan home.

The 750cc field struggled in nightmare conditions, aquaplaning and fighting wheel spin on the straights at over 150 mph. At the end of lap one, Percy Tait shadowed the Suzuki of Stan Woods, with Mick Grant lacking in practice, on a Kawasaki that was under-geared, languishing outside the top six. Kawasaki teamster Barry Ditchburn lost his own battle with the conditions and a bad case of flu, retiring at the pits after two laps. Tait played a waiting game, aware that Woods had no option but to stop to refuel at some stage. Woods pitted on lap four, hoping that his rivals would follow suit. It was not to be, with Grant's gamble to go the full race distance on one tank paying off, as he claimed third behind Tait and Rutter. Tait's win might not have been pretty, and wrestling the Suzuki in the rain for seven laps is not everyone's idea of fun, but Percy's only victory on the Triangle instantly ranked as a highlight in a career that was long and distinguished.

The increasingly popular 750cc class, elevated to World Championship status at the October congress of the FIM, opened the 1977 race programme and provided its finale.

First race glory would be Grant's, but only after Williams, who had led for virtually the entire six laps, ran out of fuel 400 yards from home. As Grant streaked through the start/finish, the official on the line, expecting Williams' arrival as race winner, held off showing the chequered flag and confusion ensued.

"I crossed the finish line and I expected to see the chequered flag, but I didn't see it. I'd seen the last lap flag, but you only see these things for a fraction of a second, and I thought, have I been mistaken, I daren't stop. I stopped at the hairpin at York and asked a marshal if the race had finished, and he said, 'I think it has, I'm not sure.' I waited for about twenty seconds with the engine running in case someone appeared over the hill, but they didn't. We'd just enough fuel in the tank to do the race so I daren't do a full lap back to the start, so I came round York Hairpin, up the hill and took the first left as a shortcut back to the pits. It was a hot day and my visor was full of flies, and I couldn't see a thing, just a blur. I was just tanking along in first gear doing about 35 mph and I came to a road end with a rope tied across it between two barriers closing it off. I didn't see it. The next thing I know I'm lassoed round the neck by the rope, and I'm sat on top of the bike with two steel barriers on top of me. An old dear came out of one of the houses and asked me if I was all right, and I explained that no, I wasn't all right at all. I've still got a scar on my neck from that."[9]

As the day wore on, Grant's fortunes on the track waned while Williams' soared. The feature race of the day saw Grant lead to Shell Hill before having to stop after fuel poured from the rear breather onto his back tyre, sending the Kawasaki sideways. Grant rejoined, out of contention, and rode bravely to finish fifth, sandwiched between North West 200 newcomers Ron Haslam (fourth) and Dave Potter (sixth). As Williams added the title race 750cc victory to his earlier 500cc win, John Newbold, another rookie to the circuit, pushed the absolute course record to 123.81 mph, and then overhauled Steve Parrish for second place with a last lap of 124.06 mph, in his vain pursuit of Williams.

The 500cc race promised a grandstand finish as Kiwi John Woodley shredded the record books, lap after lap, before stopping with a holed piston on the penultimate

Derek McIntyre

The 350cc grid lines up in glorious sunshine for the start of the 1977 350cc race. They are from left to right: 3 Charlie Williams, Tony Rutter, 53 Bill Simpson, 16 Joey Dunlop, 42 Graham Waring, 51 Alan Stewart, 8 Jim Dunlop, 1 Ray McCullough, 41 Trevor Steele, 65 Bertie Bradford, 14 Neil Tuxworth.

circuit, leaving Williams with a clear run for home. First lap retirements for practice hot-shots Stan Woods, John Newbold and Woodley's fellow countryman, Stu Avant, made life easier for Williams. Woodley's performance was one of the revelations of the meeting, sitting out most of practice after seizing firstly his own Rod Coleman RG500 Suzuki, and then the RG on loan from Avant. While Woodley took consolation in setting a new class record of 120.76 mph, Steve Parrish steered the ex-Barry Sheene Suzuki home ahead of George Fogarty as runner-up.

The partisan crowd's appetite for a home win was whetted when Joey Dunlop led the 250cc race briefly, before Tony Rutter pushed the record to 111.37 mph and inched away for the win. Ray McCullough did well to fight back from an appalling start to claim third, but more than made up for it in a 350cc race that is still talked about as arguably the greatest seen on the Triangle.

After racing shoulder to shoulder for more than sixty-six miles at an average speed of 114.09 mph, the judges could not separate McCullough and Tony Rutter; the only dead heat in the history of the meeting so far.

Both McCullough and Rutter had featured as first-lap leaders, and Alan Stewart had even squeezed into second place ahead of McCullough on lap two. He quickly fell back into the clutches of the chasing trio of Ian Richards, Graham Waring and Neil Tuxworth, as the pair in front set a pace no one could live with. They began lap five side by side. Not even a new record of 116.44 mph made the slightest difference in Rutter's efforts to shake off his rival. The atmosphere around the track crackled with tension as news that McCullough led at Coleraine spread through the 80,000-strong crowd. By Metropole, they were side by side, but nothing could prepare the straining throngs at the pits for the breakneck dash that hurtled over Quarry Hill and across the line in perfect tandem.

"We were together all the race. On the last lap, Ray took the lead coming into Juniper. I was slipstreaming him, and I pulled out to pass him as we went over the line. I went to his left; I thought I'd got it. It was a great race."[10]

"I remember I was leading going into the second last bend of the race, and I decided to go round the outside, went round the outside and got a big slide, almost off it. I got straightened up and going into the next corner, I was on the wrong side of the road and Tony was on the right line. I went up the inside and pushed him out a bit, and the two of us raced to the line. They say it was a dead heat, I couldn't say, I was concentrating too much on getting myself sorted out.

Winner of the 1978 North West 200 superbike and 350cc races, Tony Rutter leads Charlie Williams past the packed railway embankment and into Church Corner.

Rowland White

"I've seen photographs that show Tony in front, and I've seen photographs that show me in front, it depends on the angle they were taken from I suppose. I've always counted myself lucky; Tom Herron and John Newbold aren't around anymore, they both crashed at that last corner. I've always thought myself lucky to get away with that slide."[11]

On the day when Tom Herron returned from the Grands Prix world stage to win the 250cc and superbike races, and set what still remains as the fastest lap ever recorded by any rider on any circuit in the British Isles. Herron leads Grant and Rutter through Primrose Hill, 1978.

Rowland White

Tom Herron returned to the North West 200 in 1978 after a four-year absence from the meeting. His time on the Grand Prix circuit refining and honing his skills to a razor's edge were rewarded with superbike and 250cc victories, and an absolute course record of 127.63 mph; an achievement that still stands as the fastest lap ever recorded by any rider on any circuit in the British Isles.

Herron opened his account with a win in the opening superbike race, setting an absolute course record of 124.14 mph on the way. The pace exacted a heavy toll on the opposition. Clutch trouble sidelined Dave Potter and Kevin Stowe from the action, and Joey Dunlop and John Newbold, who had broken the lap record in practice, toured into the pits at the end of lap one. Mick Grant was down and out first time through Metropole after fuel poured through the breather pipe onto the rear wheel of the Kawasaki. Next time around, Ron Haslam followed suit crashing out of the lead at the same spot. The fans' favourite made it look easy, leading a strung-out procession of Rutter, Charlie Williams and Steve Parrish home.

The 250cc victory came with the same apparent ease. While Ray McCullough disputed second place with Chas Mortimer, Herron simply disappeared, pushing the class record to 113.88 mph.

"He had been away racing on the Continent for a few years. It just showed me how good Tom Herron had become. Before he went away, he never beat me. When he came back home, he was just so much faster.

"Station Corner then was a sharper corner than it is now. I was easing up going through it and he wasn't even getting up off it. I'd been in behind him but he got away from me there. I caught him before Mathers and the same thing happened. I eased it a wee bit and he went through there flat out. That's where he pulled out ground on me. I think he beat me by about seven sec-

onds, I just gave up, he was riding so well."[12]

Another catalogue of retirements saw Dave Potter fade from the 500cc action on lap two, followed by Ron Haslam on lap three. Persistent fuel starvation at the end of the straights frustrated early leader Steve Parrish who settled for fourth place in the end. Whilst John Newbold remained just out of the clutches of George Fogarty for the win, the task of breaking records fell to John G Williams. On a day that set new standards in every class, Williams rejoined the action in fourteenth place after stopping at York on lap one, courtesy of a fuel tap that had been left turned to off, and set off in relentless pursuit. With Herron another retirement, Williams' fastest lap of 122.97 mph was only enough to claim the bottom step on the podium on what would prove to be his final appearance on the Triangle Circuit. John Williams died in hospital after crashing at Wheelers Corner during the Ulster Grand Prix in August 1978.

Tony Rutter added victory in the final superbike race, to his earlier hard-earned 350cc win. As strongly fancied contender Ray McCullough retired his three-cylinder Yamaha at Metropole on lap one, the 350cc race developed into a torrid three-way battle between Rutter, Graham Waring and Steve Tonkin. A seized engine on the final lap dropped Charlie Williams from his race-long position at the head of the chasing pack. Whilst Kevin Stowe just shaded fourth from South African Dudley Crammond and Graham Young, less than a second separated Rutter from Waring and Tonkin at the flag.

Tyre wear had been a major headache for the heavy brigade in the opening six lapper, and as a concession to safety the organisers cut the race distance for the North West 200 feature event from the planned eight laps to five.

"I tested some of the first slick tyres for Dunlop around 1974, when the technology was very much in its infancy.

Esler Crawford

Ron Haslam leads Jeff Sayle , Joey Dunlop, Roger Marshall, 6 Steve Parrish, 8 Tony Rutter, and 67 Alan Jackson towards Ballysally Roundabout as the rest of the 1979 North West 200 superbike field snake-stream out of Shell Hill Bridge, the last race seen on this section of the course.

We were regularly shredding tyres round here, taking the middle out of them. The slightest difference in the suspension set up at the rear could make all the difference. In 1978, we had one shred in practice, and on the second lap, I stopped at Metropole to check it and the bike wouldn't start again. Maybe somebody upstairs was looking after me."[13]

Somebody was certainly looking after Parrish, who somehow stayed on after his handlebars snapped, and Charlie Williams has no doubt that there was an angel on his shoulder on that day in May.

"Now 750s were new to me, so to ride the 750cc Maxton Yamaha around the North West 200 was fantastic. After the first race when I came off the podium I had mentioned to my mechanic, Brian Slack, that I had noticed some oil on the inside of the screen. We thought that it was probably just oil from the petrol, but it was best to check it. As I sat on the grid before the second race, Brian said he had checked it and there was no problem, just a bit of oil out of the petrol.

"Tom led the race in the early stages; Mick and Tony were up there as well. I was involved in a bit of a scrap with Ron Haslam, John Newbold and Kevin Stowe for a couple of laps, with Ron always that little bit in front.

"The three of us were coming down towards Shell from Station, swapping places like we had been doing on the laps before. One place I thought I was pretty good was at the end of the big straight going down towards Shell past the university. The sequence started with a very fast right-hander followed by a left, and then the tight left-hander at Shell Hill. I could go quite deep into the right-hander before I had to start braking. When I came down to Shell Hill on that particular lap, I had slipstreamed Stowe and Newbold and found myself in the lead. We'd probably swapped places two or three times on that lap already.

"Deep into the right-hander, I sat up to brake; no front brake whatsoever. I must have been doing about 170mph. I managed to get round the right-hander, closed my eyes and just leaned the bike over as far as I could going round the left-hander, braking with the rear brake and changing down the whole way, as well as pumping frantically on the front brake to no avail. I thought this is it, your time is up, but somehow I got round. I opened my eyes and everything's fine; I've got a slip road in front of me. But I'd caught Ron Haslam up at an incredible rate of knots, and I could see him going up the right-hand gutter, just starting to peel in.

"I hit his front wheel, doing close to 130 mph. I knocked him clean off, and miraculously I managed to stay on. I got stopped half-way into Coleraine, turned round and came back. Ron was lying on the grass with some marshals looking after him, he was really shaken up. I often think, if Ron Haslam had been three feet further into that corner, I would have hit him side on, and God knows what would have happened.

"The problem was that there was a small fracture on the front brake union. When I applied the front brake it was spraying a very fine mist of hydraulic brake oil onto the inside of the screen; that's why I ended up with no front brake."[14]

With the high-speed dice at the front now between Herron and Rutter with Grant out, Herron, clocked at 179 mph through the speed trap, set his history-making 127.63 mph lap third time around. The frantic pace eventually set his downfall, and as his tyres went off, Herron could only nurse the big Yamaha home in sixth, while Rutter cruised to the win ahead of Stowe and Newbold.

"The only North West I missed between my first in 1974 and my last in 1983 was 1979. I had an invitation to race in Holland in a three-hour race partnering Boet van Dulman on the Gauloises Yamaha. The race was on a Thursday, Boet fell off in practice and I didn't get to ride.

Joey Dunlop's first North West 200 success came in 1979, with wins in the Match race and superbike race, as well as setting a fastest lap of 124.66 mph. Pictured here at Juniper Hill, wheel to wheel with Tony Rutter, one of his toughest rivals.

Jim McBride

"I was riding at Brands Hatch that weekend, before the TT. I phoned my wife from Brands on the Saturday evening to hear how the North West had gone. She told me that Tom had been killed. Well, I lost my closest friend [John Williams] the year before at the Ulster, and then Tom. That was an awful lot to bear. It was at times like that you thought, maybe it's time to stop. You always think it won't happen to you, and thankfully it never did."[15]

Saturday 25 May 1979 marked fifty years since the North West 200 was first held. The day should have been remembered for the golden jubilee celebrations, for Joey Dunlop's double superbike victories, for Mike Hailwood's appearance as VIP guest of honour, for Tony Rutter's stunning 350/500cc double and for Bob Jackson's only North West 200 win in the 250cc race. Instead, the 1979 North West 200 was Irish racing's darkest hour; in an afternoon the golden jubilee became "Black Saturday". At the day's end, the event had claimed the lives of Scottish youngster Brian Hamilton and of Ireland's favourite sporting son, Tom Herron. Dunlop's close friend and fellow Armoy Armada rider, Frank Kennedy, died from his injuries months later. Kevin Stowe and Australian Warren Willing recovered, slowly, but never raced again.

The racing had been straight out of the top drawer, but by Saturday evening as the story of the day's events unfolded, numbed disbelief settled like a black fog across the subdued, silent, thousands straggling home. Suddenly, not a lot made sense or mattered much anymore.

The opening race, the Moran's International Match Race, offered a new format for the racing public. Tom Herron's Select, running with white numbers on red backgrounds and made up of Irish and foreign riders, including Jeff Sayle and Warren Willing, defeated Tony Rutter's Select, black numbers on white, by 193 points to 119.

Grant, Parrish and Sayle made the early pace, riding clear of a first-lap crash near Coleraine University that brought down Willing, Stowe and Kennedy, whose machine burst into flames. Herron had a dramatic escape, riding through a wall of fire at the scene of the accident as Kennedy's bike went airborne and past his head. As Dunlop tracked the top six through Mathers and towards Portrush on lap one, the road behind them burned. Plagued by a slipping clutch from the start, Joey picked off his rivals lap by lap, moving into second, ahead of Parrish on the penultimate lap, and ahead of Grant on the final run from Portrush.

The 350cc race was marred by Brian Hamilton's fatal first-lap crash at Dhu Varren, a section of the course the young Scot had struggled to get right all through practice. Roy Jeffreys was a first-lap faller near the same spot, his Yamaha rebounding into the road and bringing down his brother Mick.

For the third year in a row, Rutter was involved in a race-long, tooth-and-nail, 350cc battle. Steve Tonkin provided the main opposition, after Joey Dunlop dropped from a brief spell at the front on lap two to eventually finish fifth. On the penultimate lap, Tonkin took the advantage at Mathers Cross. Ever the wily campaigner, Rutter remained tucked in his rival's slipstream, saving his final effort for the run to the line before swooping past to win by 0.2 seconds.

Rutter's second win of the day came in the 500cc event. For the first four laps, he stalked Alex George who had looked in charge all the way. On the run from Coleraine, Rutter pulled alongside and pointed to his rival's back wheel. The tyre on George's Suzuki had begun to disintegrate, leaving no option but to ease his pace and fall back into the clutches of Parrish and then Alan Jackson. Mick Grant went down heavily on the approach to York Hairpin after his chain adjuster broke causing the rear wheel to lock and pitch him off.

"I'd just taken the lead before crashing going down into York. The ironic thing was that I'd been round with the safety officials before practice started, and they said, 'Should we put more bales round that telegraph pole,' which was way out of the way, and I said, 'No one's going to hit that.' I hit it and broke my pelvis.

Tom Herron in the fateful 1979 North West 200 superbike race at Metropole. The darkest chapter in the history of the North West 200.

"I knew what had caused the problem. If I hadn't known, if it had been my mistake, then maybe I would have had a problem with it, but we knew exactly what had caused it. I had broken ribs as well which wasn't ideal to go round the TT with, but if you can't take the knocks, don't do it."[16]

The surprise packet of the day came in the form of Cumbrian Bob Jackson stealing the 250cc victory from under the noses of the fancied runners. By lap two, Ian Richards and Rutter had deposed early pacesetter Chas Mortimer and settled into their own private battle.

Clifford McLean

Approaching Portrush, Jackson passed them both to lead by 0.2 seconds going into the third lap. The slender advantage had grown to eight seconds at the flag, with Rutter once again making his move in the final stages to snatch second.

Herron lined up for the final race of the day, Moran's superbike race, carrying injuries sustained after crashing at the Spanish Grand Prix at Jarama the previous week. His damaged right thumb

John Newbold chases Keith Heuwen over Black Hill during their 1980 epic. The 19-year-old newcomer won by one-fifth of a second.

looked cumbersome, unwieldy, and with hindsight, some have expressed the opinion that the injury contributed to the fateful events that were to unfold.

Pole-sitter Ron Haslam led to Portrush on lap two before being sidelined with a rear puncture. New leader Alex George's race was over on lap four, forced from the action with gearbox failure, as Dunlop moved to the front and stayed there. Apart from effecting running repairs on a loose clutch cable in the early stages, Dunlop had a trouble-free run, taking his second win of

PORTRUSH

Clifford McLean

the day despite the attentions of a late-charging Rutter.

The three-man train that crested Quarry Hill in a dog-fight for third place crossed the line headed by Jeff Sayle by inches from Parrish, with Greg Johnstone a further second adrift. Herron had been in the thick of the dice before crashing heavily at Juniper on the last bend of the last lap. He died in Coleraine Hospital that evening.

Further changes to the course in 1980 saw the demise of the Shell Hill section in the interests of safety. Instead, the circuit now turned sharp left onto the short run to Ballysally roundabout, before rejoining the original Triangle. By virtue of the alterations to the circuit, now shortened to 8.9 miles in length, the fastest lap in all four classes would stand as new lap records.

Charlie Williams made it look all too easy with a start-to-finish win in the opening 350cc race. Joey Dunlop had held second place on lap one, but was overhauled by Steve Tonkin and then Tony Rutter as the race progressed. Rutter clocked the fastest lap of the race, 116.57 mph on his final circuit, to finish eight seconds behind Williams.

"I had a very good 350cc Yamaha, and let's be fair, if you have a fast bike at the North West you're going to do well. It wasn't a problem to win that race."[17]

At the end of the 250cc race, comprising a round of the Motor Cycle Racing/Vladivar Vodka 250cc series for the first time, the leader board confirmed a fairy-tale result for the small British Cotton factory, with the Rotax-powered machines filling the first three places.

Tony Rutter's chances of victory slipped from his grasp after leading to the half-way stage, when clutch trouble relegated him to runner-up behind Steven Cull.

"The Cotton was a bit of an unknown quantity, and we had a lot of trouble with it in the beginning. We had trouble in practice and the spares we needed only arrived on the Friday. Mungo, my mechanic, was still building the bike in the paddock on race day. It was amazing that it won the race; I couldn't believe it. That was my first international win, a super race, I really enjoyed it."[18]

Tragedy struck once again when thirty-one-year-old Mervyn Robinson was fatally injured after his Yamaha seized at the notorious Mathers Cross. Robinson was unhappy that he had been allocated the same race number, thirty-one, as his friend and fellow Armoy Armada rider had carried the previous year. On hearing of his brother-in-law's death, Joey Dunlop withdrew from the remainder of the meeting, and in the days that followed, considered quitting the sport. The Armoy Armada Supporters Club met for the final time the following Tuesday evening, after Mervyn Robinson's funeral, and decided to disband the club. In a statement they said:

"The feeling of members is that the club should be buried along with the dead and let them rest in peace."

The race had been a nail-biting affair, with Mick Grant leading from Avant, Newbold, Denis Ireland and Parrish at the end of lap one. Newbold took over at the front until lap four before relinquishing his advantage to Dunlop, who led briefly before grinding to a halt with gearbox failure. Newbold soon joined him as a spectator with a sticking throttle. With his rivals sidelined, Grant had no intention of being caught, and at the end had increased his advantage to fourteen seconds over Avant.

The final race of the day, the Moran's Superbike Race, provided a fitting climax. On his first and only appearance at the meeting, nineteen-year-old Keith Heuwen electrified the 60,000 crowd, setting a fastest lap of 125.01 mph on his way to winning by the width of a tyre from John Newbold.

"The media and the papers at home were full of coverage of the Troubles, and it was quite a big decision for me at nineteen or so to come to race at the North West 200. It's laughable now, but I was a bit concerned about how do they stop someone putting a bomb behind a hedge on the straight when we're all blasting down there. I couldn't believe the difference when I got here.

"I didn't know Northern Ireland or Ulster people at all. I had no Ulster friends apart from Tom Herron who I hadn't known very well. I came here and it was clear from day one, I was going to have a great time. People couldn't do enough, offering to clean the van, polish my boots, people even wanting me to come and stay in their house rather than having me stay in the paddock.

"I hadn't really done any real roads stuff before, and Roger Marshall was very helpful in pointing me in the right direction. I was running a TZ750 Yamaha, quite a good tool; all the quick guys had them. I was amazed how bloody fast it was; in the first practice session, I was forever knocking the throttle off. I just couldn't believe that you could hold something flat out for so long. In those days, TZ750s were throwing out something like 140hp on the dyno, a fair bit for a motorcycle that was quite light. I only weighed ten-and-a-half stone at the time, so the power-to-weight ratio was good, and we had it geared for something like 190 mph, a ridiculous amount of speed. There was nowhere else we went to where the speed was anything like the speeds you'd be doing round here.

"It was almost alien to sit with the throttle flat out for so long, just on the button all the way down the back straight. When you drive along it, it's just straight, but it actually becomes quite undulating when you're approaching 180 mph. You've got to get it white line to white line, you've got to be smooth. The natural tendency is to snap the throttle shut to steer the thing round the corners, when all you need to do is sit in the seat, point very gently, and hold the thing flat out. It's quite a simple process, but having the confidence to do that...

"Mathers Cross and Station Corner have to be the hairiest corners in the world. You approach Station bloody quick, and you go through it bloody quick, and you want to because you've got to carry all that speed down to the university. You've got to have that extra 1 or 2 mph. It's OK if you're behind someone else, then you can get a slingshot effect. People say it's just a triangle and it's all flat out, but the art of drafting is very, very important. You have to be able to get into somebody's slipstream and out of it efficiently to make it work for you.

"The helmet I wore here in 1980, one my brother painted for me, I only wore in that one race. In those days, you didn't have helmets that fitted you as well as they do now. On the straights, the helmet went flat against your face, so when you arrived at Metropole doing 190 mph, you'd been holding your breath for thirty or forty seconds. I had to drill the front mouthpiece so I could breathe.

"In that race, we couldn't be sure we could make the distance with the amount of fuel we could get on board the bike. I had to use tactics, I needed a buddy out there that I could slipstream, not to pass but so that I could use half throttle and just roll behind them on those two big straights.

"I pinched Noddy's [John Newbold] arse going round the Magic Roundabout, slipped up behind him and grabbed him on the arse. He did the same thing back to me, such a good fun race. I knew we were going to pull the pin on it on the last lap, and the ironic thing is that the corner I passed him at to win the race was the corner he was killed at in 1982. It was my first international win, a great race."[19]

For Steve Tonkin, so often the North West 200 "nearly man", it all came good in the 1981 MCR/Vladivar Vodka 250cc championship race. Despite being headed by Charlie Williams early in the race, Tonkin always looked in charge. He had regained the lead before Williams went out when his Yamaha seized, and was never under threat from Pete Wild and Steven Cull, who filled the minor placings.

There was nothing easy about Donny Robinson's 350cc victory, snatching the race from Conor McGinn by one-fifth of a second on the line. Both Robinson and McGinn had taken and retaken the lead on every lap in a race-long struggle. Both were credited with setting the fastest lap, a speed of 116.91 mph, on their final circuit, which bettered Tony Rutter's old record. Third-place finisher Alan Stewart had his own share of excitement in the race after hitting a stray dog at Portrush. Stewart could only speculate that in light of the turn of speed displayed by the unfortunate canine, it had to be a whippet.

Joey Dunlop emerged as the only easy winner of the day, strolling to the chequered flag in the Moran's superbike race on the 1123cc Honda. Complete with streamlined helmet, it was Dunlop's début home appearance in the livery of the Honda works team. As the race progressed, the retirements came thick and fast, with Marshall, Newbold, Grant, George, Robinson and Williams all sidelined with mechanical failure in one form or other.

To the home crowd, it did not really matter as they roared their approval for the local hero. Such was Dunlop's advantage, despite clipping another stray dog wandering in the road at Portrush, that he had the luxury of stopping on the final lap to ask if his old sponsor, John Rea, needed a lift back to the paddock. If Dunlop had an abundance of time, Parrish had none to spare, finally getting the upper hand over Denis Ireland to lead him home by just a second.

There was no time for admiring the scenery in a hectic 500cc race won by Charlie Williams. Unknown to Williams, John Newbold had dropped from the leader board with a four-second lead in hand at half distance when a gearbox bearing broke. Williams, riding the ex-Dave Potter Mitsui Yamaha, headed a four-man battle over the line,

High on the shortlist as one of the best races ever seen on the Triangle circuit, Donny Robinson leads Conor McGinn through Metropole during their 1981 350cc epic. They shared a joint fastest last lap of 116.91 mph, but Robinson got the verdict by a hair's breadth.

Ian Watson

unaware that his efforts would be rewarded with the winner's laurels.

"I didn't think I was leading that race. I'd had a bit of an early tussle with Geoff Johnston on a three-cylinder Yamaha. I managed to see him off, and then caught and passed George Fogarty. I thought John Newbold was leading the race.

"I was on the Mitsui Yamaha, George on a Suzuki. The Suzuki was a lot faster but it wasn't a problem.

I'd got the measure of George and passed him most laps going into Metropole, and was confident that I could beat him. It was just a case of doing him on the brakes and holding him off along the coast road. I was very confident.

"Imagine my amazement as we came down towards Metropole, just going over the hill, long, long before we started to brake, and I felt this little tug on my back. That lets you know there's someone in your slipstream, and it was George. He came past me on the left-hand side. I almost smiled to myself, and thought you might

The Honda Britain works team of Ron Haslam (right) & 1987 500cc World Champion Wayne Gardner (far right) on the grid awaiting the start of practice in 1982.

Clifford McLean

Clifford McLean

think you're going to win this George but you've no chance. Then another bike came past on my right-hand side, it was Steve Parrish. I couldn't believe it, another Suzuki with about 10–15 mph to spare. My mouth fell open. As I looked across at Steve, Alex George came by as well on my left. All of a sudden, I went from certain second place to fourth with three quick bikes in front of me. I saw red; I was so mad that going into Metropole, I outbraked the lot of them. It was a good race, I'd have been upset if I hadn't won that one."[20]

Once again, the word "Tragedy" featured large in the race report headlines, after Suzuki teamster John Newbold sustained fatal injuries, crashing out of the 1982 opening superbike race, yards from the scene of Tom Herron's 1979 accident at Juniper Hill. The scene was a sombre one at the end of an otherwise scintillating day's racing, with the 80,000-strong crowd standing in silent tribute as the Clerk of the Course, Billy Nutt, broke the news over the public address system.

The meeting represented a major coup for the organisers, with the programme opener counting towards the Motor Cycle News Championship; the first time a round had been staged outside England. Newbold's crash came on the second lap as he lay third in a four-strong bunch behind Haslam and Grant, and ahead of Marshall who witnessed the accident.

"John hit my back wheel. I didn't know it was John at the time, and when we came round the next lap, I saw there had been a crash. I couldn't see who it was but you've got to continue. I finished the race and when we came in we got the bad news. John was a great mate; I still keep in touch with his family.

"It may seem very hard from the outside: hard bastard has gone out and not only rode in the next race but also won it. My logic was that John would have wanted me to do that. I could put it out of my mind long enough to get the race over. I was upset. There were something like 80,000 people who had come to see the team race, so you put a show on. Rex White [Suzuki team manager] said we should withdraw, but I said no, we're here to do a job and we'll do it, and we did.

"I felt I was doing more by riding. There's plenty of time to be miserable afterwards. I still think that was the right attitude to have. If you're not going to ride that afternoon, you're never going to ride again."[21]

Unaware of what had happened, the trio carried on and were joined by newcomer Graham Wood, who ghosted his 750cc Yamaha-4 to the front, before spoiling his dream début ride by overshooting at Metropole. It was still wide open as Wood led into the start of the last lap, but it was Marshall ahead at Coleraine and still in front at Portrush. At the flag, it was agonisingly close for Marshall as Haslam drafted him to the line to win by half a bike's length. On hearing of Newbold's accident, neither rider took any further part in the meeting.

In the MCR/EBC championship 250cc race, Donny Robinson displayed an ability to steal victory in the midst of a close-run thing. Robinson emerged as the only Irish winner of the day, in another cliffhanger, sharing a new lap record of 114.74 mph with Pete Wild and Con Law, whose retirement from the top three promoted Steve Tonkin to third.

Tony Rutter's ninth North West 200 victory came in the 350cc race. Newcomer Rob McIlnea had the consolation of sharing a new lap record of 117.51 mph with Rutter, but could only think about what might have been, after a commanding first-lap lead was whittled down by Rutter, Norman Brown and Phil Mellor. Rutter had come from nowhere to hit the front on lap five, while Brown's dream début turned into a nightmare when he was forced to retire on the last lap with carburettor trouble.

His performance in the 500cc race more than made up for the disappointment, pushing eventual winner Stu Avant all the way, raising the lap record to 122.06 mph and then 122.53 mph, before settling for second place, four-fifths of a second behind the New Zealander.

With Haslam and Marshall non-starters in the final race, the North West 200 superbike race came down to a Honda–Suzuki, head-to-head showdown between Dunlop and Grant. As Dunlop floundered on the line, Grant got away cleanly, but by lap two had been caught and passed by the hard-charging Dunlop. As Avant and Wood fought out their own battle, McIlnea set the fastest lap of the race at 123.46 mph to move into and secure third. The race at the

Eventual 500cc winner Stu Avant shadows Norman Brown through Primrose Hill during their 1982 battle.

front was turning into a classic, with both works' runners taking turns at the front. Both led on the final lap, but Grant gained the edge on the brakes last time through Metropole to carry a two-fifths of a second advantage to the line.

It had been another bruising day on the Triangle. For some, the heavy price extracted by the fastest circuit in the British Isles was becoming too much:

"John Newbold was a friend; Cyril, his dad, and his mum were very friendly with Arnold Fletcher, my sponsor at the time. John's death was a real blow. It was bad enough when Tom Herron was killed in 1979, but Tom wasn't a personal friend the way John was. It's not that you're heartless, but you keep it all in the right pigeon-

Clifford McLean

hole when it comes to death in motor-cycle racing, especially when you're a youngster. You're focused on what you do. You don't consider the family implications of people getting hurt, or the loss that those people are suffering when someone gets killed.

"John's death in 1982 was the first time it ever got near to me; I'd never felt it before. I've been very fortunate by not experiencing deaths of family or people close to me, so I don't know what it's like to lose a loved one. John was the first close one."[22]

Without securing an eleventh-hour sponsorship lifeline there would not have been a 1983 North West 200, but Dacia Cars filled the financial void at the last moment, after local company Moran's terminated their long-term involvement with the event.

The introduction of a chicane at Juniper Hill drew opposition from the road-racing purists, but lowered speeds on the frighteningly fast coast road section of the circuit that was so spectacular, but had proved so deadly in recent years.

The meeting was dogged by heavy downpours throughout the day, with the prospect of racing being abandoned a serious option at one point. In the end, the five-race schedule was completed, with Joey Dunlop ending the day with a 500cc/superbike double in a very public, high-profile shakedown of Honda's new RS500 and V4-750 machinery. Mick Grant and Roger Marshall had delivered a double blow to the organisers when both were listed as non-starters on Saturday morning. Grant, carrying heavy strapping on his wrist, the result of an earlier injury, was refused the go-ahead to race by the medics. Marshall, the victim of a mystery bug, was too ill to leave his bed.

Conditions in the opening 500cc event made correct tyre choice crucial. Dunlop took the RS500, shod with inter-mediates front and back, to victory first time out as the opposition floundered in the wet. The Suzuki of Norman Brown led from Graham Wood and Gary Lingham on lap one with Dunlop off the pace and outside the top six. Then the rain came down and Brown's decision to opt for a slick rear/intermediate front combination proved his undoing. As he slipped down the field to fifth, Dunlop's only other real challenger, Brian Reid, edged briefly ahead at Metropole on lap four, before a puncture ended his charge on the following lap. Brown mounted a late rally to set the fastest lap of the race at 111.01 mph and claim fourth place behind Wood and Lingham. Dunlop's victory saw him become the first home-bred 500cc winner since Billy Guthrie in 1973, and the last rider to win a 500cc race on the Triangle; the class was dropped from the programme the following year.

Brown again challenged Dunlop in the opening stages of the final race on the programme, the North West 200 Superbike Race. In response, Dunlop stretched the legs of the sweet-sounding V4 to romp home, nine seconds clear of Brown with Wood completing the podium.

The result gave the Newry rider a brace of superbike runner-up finishes. Wood had disregarded the conditions to deliver an emphatic performance and dominate the earlier Eglinton Hotel superbike race. After a lengthy delay due to heavy rain, Wood hit the front from the flag and was never headed. The expected challenge from Rob McIlnea did not materialise as he retired his Suzuki after a lap, declaring that standing water all around the course made conditions too dangerous for racing. A late charge from Brown brought him to within two seconds of Wood, with Joey's rapid learning curve on the V4 reaping third place.

The 350cc and 250cc events completed a great day for the Irish. The 350cc race ended in a deluge and an elusive victory for Brown. It had been a close-run thing in the early stages with Brown, Donny Robinson and Graham Young all taking spells out in front. By lap three, Brown had edged ahead, and as Robinson slid off at York with two laps remaining, the race as a competition was over. A fastest lap of 107.45 mph took Brown well clear of Young and Courtney Junk at the finish.

Graham Wood at Church Corner on his way to his first superbike victory in 1983. Wood returned to win again in '84 but had to settle for runner-up behind Roger Marshall in '85.

Junk was as surprised as anyone when he claimed his only North West 200 in the 250cc race. A race-long struggle between Con Law and Scot Stewart Cole ended when last-lap mechanical failure brought Law's

campaign to a premature end. With the race in his pocket, Cole threw it all away at the Juniper Chicane, breaking his collarbone in the process. Junk's 250cc Waddon streaked past the flagman unnoticed to begin another lap as the officials awaited the appearance of Law and Cole in vain.

The rain fell again in 1984, bringing with it treacherous conditions that sent first Mick Grant and then Roger Marshall sliding out of the MCN Masters Superbike Race, handing victory on a plate to Joey Dunlop.

Grant was first to go on the second lap at Dhu Varren,

Ian Watson

when his Suzuki slid from under him. Marshall had done everything right up until lap five. As he exited Metropole with a thirteen-second lead, his one mistake was to turn the throttle on his Honda-3 far too early. In an instant, he too was relegated to the role of spectator. Dunlop continued gingerly to win by nine seconds from Steve Parrish. The Honda team had spent a large part of the Friday before the race at the nearby Aghadowey airfield circuit, working on a misfire on the new 750cc Honda that refused to be cured, and which persisted all through the race.

Joey was out of the lead of the North West 200 superbike race, and was reported touring at Ballysally roundabout on lap two. In improving conditions, the race got off to an electrifying start, with three seconds covering Dunlop, Parrish, Graham Wood, Brian Reid, Grant and Gary Lingham. Wood's tyre choice of intermediates front and rear proved an inspired choice with the Scunthorpe rider breaking clear, with a record lap of 115.11 mph third time around, to build a race-winning advantage. Grant, getting to grips with the conditions too late to challenge for the lead, overhauled Barry Woodland and Steve Parrish for second place.

The 350cc and 250cc classes both produced first-time winners. Phil Mellor slid out of contention at Dhu Varren, leaving the way clear for Kevin Mitchell to take the 350cc honours. The lead had see-sawed between the two on each lap until the conditions caught Mellor out. Niall Mackenzie's runner-up finish behind Mitchell and ahead of Johnny Rea was some consolation for his disappointing earlier fifth place in the 250cc race. A holed radiator had ended Joey Dunlop's campaign on lap one. Mackenzie had led the race in the early stages, before being passed by eventual winner Andy Watts on lap two, and then dropping out of contention after his Armstrong slowed and then picked up. Brian Reid secured second place with a fastest lap of 105.09 mph, with Australian newcomer Graeme McGregor completing an all-EMC-mounted top three.

All was right with the world again, as Joey Dunlop obliged the wishes of his legion home support with 250cc and superbike victories in 1985.

After race one, the opening 250cc race, the day seemed to be shaping up as a Dunlop benefit. Andy Watts held off Niall Mackenzie for second place after an electrifying battle behind Dunlop, who reeled off a new class record of 112.21 mph on his final lap to finish two seconds clear. All three had taken turns in front, and Mackenzie still held a real chance of victory until he overshot at Juniper on the frantic last-lap dash.

As the first of the day's two superbike races came to the line, expectations amongst the Dunlop supporters were high. Joey's challenge fizzled out before it had really begun, and he retired the 500cc Honda-3 on lap two. The race quickly developed into an unforgiving head-to-head exchange between Rob McIlnea and Roger Marshall. After eleven years of trying, it finally came good for Marshall, but only after the Skoal Bandit Suzuki stuck in gear and McIlnea was forced to relinquish a hundred-yard lead on the last lap. Marshall's change of luck ended Graham Wood's superbike winning streak, forcing him to settle for second. McIlnea could take solace in the fact that his efforts had been met with some reward in the form of an absolute course record of 119.87 mph. Dunlop would better the achievement before the ink had dried on the record books.

But for Marshall's victory, the day would have ended with Irish riders sweeping the boards. Part one of a Steve Cull double came with a start-to-finish 350cc victory, despite the close attentions of Phil Mellor in the early stages. An oil leak on Mellor's F2 Yamaha saw him drop off the pace and almost into the clutches of third-place man Gene McDonnell.

Part two, the second 250cc race, was a different matter altogether. Again, Dunlop was plagued with mechanical

Photo sequence: Alastair McCook

problems, retiring from the fray with a Honda that refused to fire cleanly. The final standings show that Kimocco-mounted Eddie Roberts led the EMC of Con Law to complete the rostrum behind Cull. The facts and figures do not do justice to the efforts of Andy Watts and Niall McKenzie, who swarmed all over Cull in the early stages. Suddenly Watts' race was over with gearbox failure, while McKenzie dropped from contention when he outbraked himself at Juniper Chicane. He rejoined the race, unaware that his excursion into the greenery had made no difference. The organisers had adjudged that McKenzie and Brian Reid, holding third place on the road, had jumped the start. Both riders were given a one-minute penalty, effectively dropping both to midfield finishes.

The long awaited Dunlop/McIlnea finale materialised in the North West 200 superbike race; it did not fail to deliver. For five laps, McIlnea harassed Dunlop on a machine that was faster in a straight line but not as nimble as the RVF750 Honda. Then, on lap five, the chain jumped the sprocket on the Skoal Bandit Suzuki and McIlnea's race was over. It had been far from an easy victory for Dunlop; McIlnea had pushed him to a new absolute course record of 120.55 mph at the height of the battle. As retirements saw Wood, Mark Salle, Grant and McGregor drop off the leader board, Steve Cull inherited second place, almost a minute behind Dunlop and three seconds ahead of Barry Woodland.

Joey Dunlop's 1985 performance on the Triangle exuded style, class and authority, in contrast to his faltering ride the previous year. It was a time when Joey was arguably at the height of his awesome powers. Two weeks after the North West 200 he not only survived the sinking of the *Tornammona* en route to the Isle of Man TT, but scored a Formula One, Junior and Senior hat trick.

The titanic 1985 250cc battle. Cull, Watts and Mackenzie on the Coast Road approaching Juniper Chicane, three abreast (top). Cull leads into the chicane (middle). Mackenzie rejoins the action after crashing out but the race is already lost (bottom).

Clifford McLean

The works Suzukis of Mick Grant and Graeme McGregor at Metropole in 1985. Grant claimed the team's only finish, third place behind Marshall and Wood in the opening Superbike race.

The year would end with Dunlop crowned Formula One World Champion for the fourth year on the trot, winning all six rounds in the series and amassing a final tally of ninety points to Mick Grant's runner-up total of forty. His sizzling performance that Saturday evening in May in front of his delirious countrymen served warning of what was to come in a season that saw Dunlop run rampage across the roads and tracks of Europe.

The 1986 meeting would see Dunlop Senior sharing the limelight with his younger brother Robert. The trademark battling family trait was there for all to see with Robert claiming the 350cc victory by one-fifth of a second from Gene McDonnell.

McDonnell had built a five-second cushion by the halfway stage. As the race progressed, Dunlop began a tenacious charge that saw him carve chunks off his rival's advantage. He hit the front for the first time at Church

Ian Watson

After years of being the nearly man, it all came good for Roger Marshall in 1985. Pictured at York Corner on his way to his maiden North West 200 win, at last.

Corner, but McDonnell was not finished and led at Juniper Chicane, only to lose the drag to the flag through the last few corners. Dunlop set the fastest lap of the race at 111.78 mph on the hectic final circuit:

"I had an intermediate front and a slick rear, and Eugene had gone for a wet front and an intermediate rear. My dad was saying go for slicks, but I reckoned that three-quarters of the track was wet. As the race progressed, the track was drying out and I was able to pull back the advantage that Eugene had pulled out over the first three laps. It was pretty evenly matched.

"I know that Joey was on top of somebody's motorhome watching the race. He could hear the commentary over the speakers, and he was shouting don't pass him at Metropole; he'll get you back on the coast road. I was thinking the same way, and outbraked him going into Juniper Chicane. I overcooked it, and he got past me and was first out of it. I got a good drive out and was beside him going up Juniper Hill. I knew what tyres he had on and I knew he didn't have the grip on the rear end to take it as quick as me, even though I was on the inside line. I just waited for Eugene to ease off and went through on the inside and that was that. I wasn't going to ease off, I'd made up my mind, even if he'd crashed, I'd have crashed with him. I wasn't even looking at the corner, I was watching Eugene's bike out of the side of my eye, and when I saw him dropping back then I shut off."[23]

The day had got off to the worst possible start for Joey when he crashed out of the opening 250cc race on lap four at Juniper Chicane. In his efforts to reel in eventual race winner Eddie Laycock, Dunlop had touched a white line, made slippery by rain, and his race was over. Whilst Mark Farmer tried everything to get back in touch with Gary Cowan after sliding off and remounting at Metropole, Laycock had the luxury of fifteen seconds to spare over his nearest challenger, Andy Watts. Cowan denied Farmer the third-place slot by fractions of a second, whilst Watts limped home in second on an EMC slowed by suspension problems.

Once again, tragedy overshadowed the event when thirty-year-old Pat McLaughlin was seriously injured after crashing out of the opening race at Mathers Cross. He died from his injuries in hospital three days later.

The second 250cc race of the meeting was almost an action replay of the first, only this time Watts' bike held together and he turned the tables on Laycock. Both Watts and Laycock passed early leader Gary Cowan on the third lap, who responded with the fastest lap of the race at 109.24 mph but could still only finish third, eight-tenths of a second behind Laycock's back wheel. Laycock missed out on sealing a quarter-litre double by less than two seconds.

Even the greatest make mistakes. After touching a white line made slippery by the rain Joey slid off his 250cc Honda at Juniper Chicane in 1986. After receiving stitches he sat out most of the meeting but still managed to win the North West 200 superbike race from Roger Marshall, his Honda team mate.

The distinction of winning the

first superstock race ever included in the programme fell to Trevor Nation. When Phil Mellor retired with a broken battery lead after leading for the first four laps, Nation's race-long battle with Kenny Irons moved up a gear. The timekeepers had been unable to separate them on lap two, and had their work cut out at the end, with Nation having less than a second to spare. Iron's Loctite Yamaha team mate, Steve Parrish, trailed them home in third.

Whilst Dunlop sat out the opening superbike race, recovering from his first race crash, Roger Marshall doubled his tally of North West 200 victories, easing home thirteen seconds clear of Gene McDonnell. Marshall was never headed after deposing Johnny Rea on lap three. Rea's Yamaha cried enough on the following lap; Marshall simply disappeared into the distance. Strong cross-winds had introduced an added element of danger on the long straights, but by the time the grid formed up for the North West 200 Superbike Race, conditions had improved.

Battered and bruised and carrying stitches in his injured knee, Joey took his place on the front row. The prospect of Dunlop on the big 750cc four-stroke versus Marshall on the 500cc two-stroke had been eagerly anticipated by the 80,000-strong crowd; they were not disappointed.

As the race progressed, an epic battle developed. Marshall led by half a second on the opening lap, but on the next circuit, Dunlop and Mark Phillips both moved ahead of the early leader. Marshall was quick to respond too and dispatched Phillips' challenge; but try as he

Alastair McCook

might, Dunlop retained the advantage. With time running out, the battle of nerves reached its climax on the downhill run to Metropole. Neither gave an inch in an outbraking duel that would decide who held the crucial advantage onto the coast road. Dunlop steeled it out by inches, and on the final run across the cliff tops pulled out a winning 1.3-second lead.

A brace of superbike wins combined with a slightly fortuitous 750cc production victory in 1987 saw Joey Dunlop join John Williams and Tony Rutter on the illustrious list of North West 200 hat-trick winners.

Until lap three of the opening superbike race, Phil Mellor looked well on course for his first win on the Triangle. Then a rear-wheel puncture left Mellor battling with the big Suzuki instead of the opposition. He finished fourth in the end, surviving a series of heart-stopping slides on the way, and losing third place to Robert Dunlop on the last lap. The intermediate front/slick rear proved the correct choice of rubber for Joey Dunlop who had galloped the 750cc Honda home eighteen seconds ahead of the 500cc Honda of Alan Irwin.

The superstock race, run alongside the first superbike race, had been a processional business, with Roger Hurst scoring an untroubled win by seventeen seconds from Ray Swann. In sharp contrast, the 1100cc production class was a torrid affair from the start, with never more than inches between Trevor Nation and Geoff Johnston. Both FZR Yamahas were side by side as they flashed through the start/finish at the end of lap two. Both led several times on every lap, but neither could break clear of the other. Nation took the victory by the width of a wheel, with both riders being credited with the same race average of 109.75 mph.

The unmistakable elegant, stylish Joey Dunlop on the Rothmans Honda at Church Corner, on his way to his 1987 hat-trick.

John Tennant

John Lofthouse had the 750cc production class in his pocket until his Suzuki coughed, spluttered and died on the run towards the final corner. Dunlop swept past to take the chequered flag while Lofthouse freewheeled home in second place, robbed of glory by want of a cupful of petrol.

The two 250/350cc races saw honours even with Gary Cowan and Eddie Laycock winning one apiece. Cowan claimed his victory by a bike's length from Brian Reid who lost drive leaving Juniper Chicane for the last time when he missed a gear. It had been far from easy for Cowan who had lost an eternity after overshooting Juniper at the height of his battle with Reid and Steve Cull. Cull settled for third, finishing twelve seconds off the pace and two seconds ahead of Joey Dunlop, who had been last away when his Honda refused to fire. His machine proved more temperamental in race two and Dunlop retired in the early stages. Whilst the Cowan–Reid battle continued, Dubliner Laycock proved a runaway winner, finishing with half a minute to spare over Cowan, who once again just shaded it from Reid.

Dunlop had won the crucial advantage on the grid before a wheel had turned in the day's final superbike race. As conditions improved, the key to success obviously lay in making the correct tyre choice. In the pits, both Joey's 500cc Honda, kitted with slicks, and his 750 shod with intermediates front and back, were warmed up and ready. As the clouds cleared, the 500cc machine was wheeled to the line, only to be replaced minutes later by the 750. With two minutes to go before the race started Dunlop finally elected for his 500cc Honda, throwing those who had followed his lead in making their own tyre choice into disarray.

Dunlop completed his hat-trick with an effortless win,

while behind him the dispute for second between Alan Irwin and Phil Mellor was no place for the faint-hearted. Irwin, riding a 500cc Honda with a gearbox rebuilt by Dunlop after practice, held Mellor off by half a bike's length to complete his own double of superbike runner-up finishes.

If Dunlop's three wins had impressed, Steve Cull's 1988 hat-trick performance was straight out of Boy's Own fiction. Cull, thirty-four years old and unemployed, began his haul by winning an opening superbike race that was high in drama.

As Cull streaked to the front and stayed there on an ex-

Alastair McCook

Dunlop 500cc Honda-triple, Dunlop and Mark Farmer were nose to tail and in his slipstream. Then at the 160-mph sweep through Mathers Cross, Dunlop's 750cc four-stroke cut out without warning. But for Farmer's lightning reactions and a bit of divine intervention the result could have been calamitous, but somehow he hauled his 1100cc Suzuki around

Trevor Nation won three races on the Triangle circuit between 1985 to 1991. Here he leads John Lofthouse though Black Hill in practice for the 1987 1300cc Production race.

the stricken Dunlop. Unaware of the near miss behind him, Cull maintained his relentless pace to win by twenty-five seconds from Eddie Laycock. The familiar North West 200 problems of high speeds, long abrasive straights and racing rubber that did not last relegated Farmer to sixth place in the end. An excursion up a slip road dropped Hislop to fourth, finishing behind Andy McGladdery and ahead of Carl Fogarty.

The opening 250/350cc race exploded into action, and it was clear straightaway there would be no runaway winners in this one. Cull, Fogarty and Brian Reid had all led on lap one, and Woolsey Coulter added another ingredient to the explosive mix when he nosed ahead on lap two. Then Alan Irwin and Eddie Laycock bridged the gap to the leading quartet. Irwin had led on lap four before Reid retired, and the last lap began with any one of five with a shot at victory. Fogarty led them through Metropole, but made one mistake on the run along the coast road. As the Blackburn rider ran wide into the chicane, Cull pounced, squeezing through on the inside to win by three-tenths of a second, with Irwin another two-tenths behind in third.

Clutch problems compounded by one glaring error at the chicane had cost Gary Cowan more time than he could afford in race one. There were no mistakes from the British champion in race two. He posted a record time of 110.14 mph on lap four to break the resolve of Coulter, who had led on lap two, and Joey Dunlop, who settled for third. Carl Fogarty was poised to challenge the leading trio, but a momentary lapse saw his race end in the bales at Juniper, while Robert Dunlop crashed out at Metropole.

The day went from bad to worse for Steve Hislop when he crashed out of the lead on lap five of the production race after hitting neutral. Whilst Hislop could only watch as his Honda burnt itself out at Church Corner, Joey Dunlop took over as Group Two (machines from 400cc to 750cc) leader to cruise home over a minute ahead of Richard Rose.

The final Group One (751cc to 1300cc) standings could only be decided in a last-lap shakedown that ended in favour of Kenny Irons. Whilst 750cc-mounted Hislop had led overall until his spectacular exit, in the early stages there had been nothing in it between Nation, Kevin Mawdsley, Barry Woodland and John Lofthouse. By lap four, Irons had come from nowhere to take the lead from Mawdsley who slid out at Juniper. Irons had little trouble dropping Lofthouse, but Nation stayed with him. The lead switched constantly on the last lap before Irons forced the big Yamaha through at Metropole in what proved to be the decisive move of the race.

Cull's win in the North West 200 superbike race completed his hat-trick, and was by far his most memorable. With less than a lap to complete and victory seemingly assured, Cull slid off at the bottom gear York Hairpin, and in an instant, Dunlop was through and suddenly the tables were turned.

"I won the first superbike race quite easily. The 250cc was a fantastic race to win; any one of five or six could have won it. I was tired after that one and didn't push as hard in the second one. I wanted to save a bit for the last superbike race – I was under pressure – I wanted to win that one.

"I fell asleep a bit on the last lap, and that's how I made a mistake at York Corner. I've looked at the video more times than enough, and I know the front wheel was on the white line and it went when I was braking. I couldn't believe it when I went down. I was calling myself all sorts of names, 'Stupid eejit, how could you fall off on the last lap?' The inside of the helmet was blue.

"I was damn lucky I didn't break the clutch lever or brake lever, but I didn't, got back on it and set after him. I was

Ian Watson

Steve Cull's 1988 hat-trick came the hard way. After sliding off at York on the last lap, he remounted and overtook Joey Dunlop on the final corner. "Joey was always my closest rival... I'm glad I was one of the lucky ones to beat him," he said.

"My luck changed at the TT the next month. I was leading the Senior, set a new lap record of 119.08 mph, when the bike went on fire between Creg na ba and Brandish. The exhaust broke and the petrol pipe was right beside it. You never saw a bike stopping as quick in your life."[24]

Serious injuries sustained in a crash at Brands Hatch in Easter 1989 threatened to end Dunlop's racing career and ruled him out of the North West 200. In his absence, Steve Hislop stole the show, taking both superbike race wins, but was denied a treble by Brian Reid who won the 600cc race by the proverbial hair's breadth.

annoyed with myself because I'd had a good lead. I never went through Mathers Cross as quick, scary. I didn't think I could catch Joey but he didn't expect me to come back, and I think he fell asleep a bit as well.

"He looked behind him going below the railway bridge at Dhu Varren. I'm not joking, he couldn't believe it because I was right up his rear end. I thought, you're beat, it's mine now. That totally destroyed him. I outbraked him going into the chicane on the coast road and that was that. It was a remarkable win; one I'll remember alright.

"Joey was always my closest rival. We got on the very best, and we always gave each other space, no matter where we were. I'm glad I was one of the lucky ones that beat him.

Hislop hit the front on lap three of the King of the Roads superbike race, taking over from Darren Dixon who went out on the following lap with clutch trouble. It could have all been very different if Eddie Laycock's 500cc Honda-3 had run on full power from the start. Ignition trouble had brought Laycock to a standstill at one point. As he resigned himself to the prospect of retirement, the problem cleared and he set off in pursuit. It was a stunning ride from the Dubliner who clawed his way back from tenth place to steal second place from Robert Dunlop on the last lap.

Heavy rain before the final superbike race made no difference to Laycock, who led Hislop by eight seconds after the opening 8.9 miles. Laycock was leaving nothing to chance, and maintained a relentless assault to double his advantage in the space of another lap, and then pushed the gap to twenty seconds after three. On the run into Portrush Laycock's Honda seized, promoting newcomer Steve Spray on the rotary-engined Norton to the head of a charging pack that included Hislop, Jamie Whitham and Dave Leach. The prospect of Norton's first victory in over twenty years ignited the crowd, but it was Hislop who moved ahead on the penultimate lap and led Whitham home by two seconds, with Spray breathing down his neck.

Brian Reid's first North West 200 victory came at the end of a titanic 600cc battle where half a second covered the first three home. The lead had alternated lap by lap between Reid and Hislop. Jim Moodie shadowed Reid and Hislop before moving ahead on lap three. Disaster struck almost immediately when the gritty Scot's steering damper broke as he pulled hard on the brakes at the exit of the start/finish chicane. Reid had lost count of the laps and only realised he was on his home run when the fans began to frantically wave him on along the coast road. With Hislop on his back wheel and Dave Leach too close for comfort, there was no room for error. Reid had no intention of letting the prize slip through his fingers, and held his nerve to triumph in a blanket finish.

Whitham's hour of glory came in a pulsating Suzuki versus Yamaha battle that resulted in a production race win by half a second. The last lap was just like all the others that preceded the grandstand finish. The pair were side by side at Ballysally roundabout,

Leach ahead at Portrush and Whitham leading when it mattered, across the line for the final time. It had been a close-run thing, with Whitham averaging 114.58 mph to Leach's 114.54 mph.

Brian Reid's chance of a second victory disappeared when he overshot at Juniper chicane on lap three of the opening 250/350cc race. Hot-favourite Woolsey Coulter's race was over on the warm-up lap when the handlebar of his Aprillia snapped off, and the potential threat from Eddie Laycock vanished when he retired on lap three. Reid and Johnny Rea had both led on lap one; not even a lap record of 111.42 mph from Kevin Mitchell could shift the ex-Formula Two World Champion from the front. Whilst Reid struggled to regain his rhythm, Mitchell pulled clear to win from Rea with Reid ruing his mistake and finishing third.

Steve Hislop's only North West 200 wins came in 1989 when he won both superbike races.

Mervyn McBride

Reports of rain at Coleraine threw the grid into confusion, but after the pandemonium of last-minute tyre changes, Woolsey Coulter streaked into a race-winning lead in the second 250/350cc race. It was a virtuoso performance from Coulter, who took the field apart on his way to his first pure roads victory and Aprillia's first at the Triangle Circuit. Mitchell, on the wrong tyres, struggled but still finished second ahead of Laycock. All three would play major roles in unimagined dramas yet to unfold in the years that lay ahead in the last decade of the century.

Steve Spray's performance on the rotary-engined Norton had come tantalisingly close to claiming a place in the winners' enclosure in 1989. It had been a rapid comeback curve since Simon Buckmaster's low-key appearance on the Norton in 1988. After the apparent teething problems that dogged Steve Cull's miserable year with the factory, it all came good in 1990.

"I rode the JPS Norton at the North West in 1989. It was desperate to ride; you'd have thought there was a hinge in the middle. It went through the speed trap at 192 mph and it just filled the road. I did a lot of development, and by the end of 1989, they'd got it right, but I went to Ducati, which in retrospect was the wrong move for me. You live and learn from your mistakes. The only decent result I had on it was a third at the Ulster. At all the other races that thing broke my heart."[25]

By 1990, the JPS Norton was breaking the hearts of the opposition. Twenty-five years after Dick Creith scored Norton's last Senior win on the Triangle, Robert Dunlop's emphatic superbike double instantly elevated the all black, silver-trimmed, growling, smoking, flame-spitting Norton to icon status, perhaps the sexiest motor cycle to ever grace the black winding tarmac ribbon by the seaside.

Joey Dunlop had worked to 5 am on the morning of the race preparing his 500cc Honda. The bike developed a water leak on race day and he switched to his 750. Then on lap one approaching Church Corner, Trevor Nation drew alongside him and frantically signalled that the Honda was spewing out oil. The long night's work had been for nothing.

The reigning Formula One World Champion, Carl Fogarty, rode on the limit just to stay in touch with Dunlop's Norton in the opening laps of the first superbike race. At Juniper Chicane on lap one, he went wide onto the grass, sending his Honda sideways. At University on lap two, Fogarty squeezed beneath Dunlop and into the lead, only to trail by three seconds at Metropole. Nation's race ended on lap three; by then Dunlop had the bit firmly between his teeth, streaking to a fourteen-second lead and a new lap record of 120.86 mph. As the race neared its end, Dunlop eased off to win by seven seconds.

Fogarty's determination was obvious as he blitzed off the line in superbike race number two and into a short-lived lead. By lap three, both Fogarty and Nation were out, and Dunlop had hoisted the absolute course record to 121.04 mph. As the diminutive hero played to the crowd, standing the Norton on its back wheel all around the course, Philip McCallan claimed his strongest North West 200 result with a second place ahead of Eddie Laycock.

"I expected to win on the Norton because of the speed of it. They were so quick, but we had a lot of trouble stopping the back tyre from tearing up. The suspension was quite hard and the bike was spinning the back tyre on the straights in top gear and it just overheated the centre of the tyre all the time.

"A lot of people talked about how fast the Norton was, and it was fast surely, but it wasn't the easiest thing to ride. A lot of riders were beat before they started because they knew how quick it was. But I had a Norton to beat as well with Trevor Nation on it.

"It was a great honour for me to be asked to ride for a factory team. They had put their faith in me and it was great to win. I remember flying to Snetterton to race there the next day. Brian Creighton, the Norton designer, was waiting for me. He was crying like a wain, he was so proud."[26]

Dunlop's second superbike win saw him become the third rider in four years to win three races in one day at the meeting. Between his outings on the Norton, Robert had come out on top of a race-long 125cc duel with North West 200 new-comer Alan Patterson. No more than feet had separated them throughout the race despite a new record lap of 103.48 mph from Dunlop. At York Hairpin on the last lap, Patterson lost the tow and the race when he missed a gear, allowing Dunlop to break clear. The family fortunes were reversed when Welsh ace Ian Lougher nipped through Metropole on the last lap to deny elder brother Joey third place.

Dave Leach had been leading the 600cc race from Steve Cull when the red flags came out and the race was stopped after Mark Stirling's spectacular accident at Primrose Hill. Moodie set a new lap record of 113.96 mph when the race was restarted, but could still only manage third. Cull and Leach resumed where they had left off before the enforced delay. Both had led on every lap, and although Cull headed the charge off the round-about for the last time, Leach made the last and decisive move at the Metropole and held Cull at bay on the coast road to take the win.

The 250/350cc race included the North West 200's first

Mervyn McBride

female entrant, Kawasaki-mounted Liz Skinner, in the line-up. While Skinner recorded a DNF in race one and a twenty-seventh place finish in race two, Eddie Laycock notched up two wins from two starts.

The JPS Norton team dominated the superbike class in 1990 and 1991. Only mechanical failure prevented Robert Dunlop from scoring four wins from four starts (top). Trevor Nation maintained the team's perfect record with his victory in the 1991 North West 200 superbike race (above).

His task was made easier in race one when early leader Kevin Mitchell crashed out at Juniper after a coming together with Woolsey Coulter on lap two. A lap later, Coulter slid out entering the start/finish chicane, leaving Laycock free to focus on the task of repelling Philip McCallan's relentless challenge. On the last lap, McCallan ran wide at Metropole, gifting Laycock an opportunity too good to refuse and relegating McCallan to third behind Ian Lougher at the flag.

Laycock's performance was made all the more sensational by the fact that he crashed out at Blackhill in practice, relegating him to start from the fifth row of the grid. It made little difference to Laycock who was challenging Kevin Mitchell for the lead at York on lap one, and was in front four miles later at Coleraine. Half-way through the race, Laycock was five seconds clear of a six-strong chasing pack, an advantage he had extended to eight seconds at the end. The action behind him had been fast and furious with Ian Newton leading Lougher, Rea, McCallan and Rob Orme home in style.

The 1991 meeting was another history-making, action-packed episode, with Robert Dunlop running away with his second hat-trick on the trot, and the JPS Norton team resuming their superbike dominance from the previous year.

The opening lap of superbike race one had an element of déjà vu, with Nation drawing alongside Carl Fogarty on the approach to Church Corner and waving him down. Fogarty's Honda was leaking oil, as was Philip McCallan's works' mount. Niall Mackenzie, Johnny Rea and Dave Leach were all forced to pit after oil sprayed across their visors from McCallan's blown engine.

As he began the run to Portrush on lap two, race leader Joey Dunlop glanced back to see the Nortons in formation and giving chase. On the final lap, the Dunlop brothers were shoulder to shoulder at Ballysally round-

about, but with a mile to go Joey's chain broke, leaving Robert to romp home, thirty-seven seconds clear of his team mate.

Robert notched up the 125cc win with a smooth, assured ride that saw him lead from Juniper on lap one, with Joey making a popular return to the podium in second place, ahead of early leader David Lemon. The 400cc race, run concurrently with the 125s on the road, was decided by half a second in favour of Dave Leach from Steve Ives, after first-lap leader Carl Fogarty ran wide and slid off at Metropole.

Victory in the opening 250/350cc race had been hard earned for Dunlop junior. McCallan had battled to the front of a seven-strong group with a display of focused aggression. Somehow he stayed on board and in front, after clipping the kerb and being thrown out of the saddle at the start of lap two. In an instant, a missed gear change at Coleraine on the final lap dropped McCallan out of contention. Dunlop capitalised on the gifted advantage with a record lap of 114.38 mph, as McCallan and Ian Lougher chased him home.

With three wins under his belt, and two more races to go, Robert Dunlop stood poised on the verge of claiming an unprecedented five wins in a day. The meeting's second 250/350cc race was run at a frantic pace, with Steven Hazlett, Brian Reid, James Courtney and Joey Dunlop swapping places with Lougher and Robert Dunlop throughout the six laps. Ian Lougher's sustained last-lap attack finally paid off when it mattered most – within sight of the chequered flag. On the final corner, he dived underneath Dunlop to steal the win by one-fifth of a second. A new lap record of 114.55 mph was only good enough for bottom step on the rostrum for Reid.

"The first 250cc race had been pretty hot and I had the superbike race to go, which I reckoned I could win. I went out in that race thinking, don't do anything stupid here, take it easy. I ended up leading across the coast road on the last lap. I thought I've only got to ride hard for this bit and I've got it won. I got through the chicane in front and I thought I had it won. You can't pass up there but Ian Lougher came through on the inside. I thought he was going to run wide, but he got round and beat me. Fair enough, it's a very difficult place to pass."[27]

As the first-lap sort-out reached Metropole, Joey Dunlop edged ahead on the brakes to lead the North West 200 superbike race, only for Nation to come straight back and head what was shaping up to be a leading bunch of the usual suspects through Church Corner. Fogarty held second on the entrance to the start/finish chicane on lap two, but led as the race hurtled into lap three. By Ballysally roundabout, Fogarty's Honda was trailing smoke and touring. By Metropole, Nation was out on his own after his team mate's Norton cut out and stopped at Mathers Cross. A delighted Nation crossed the line two seconds clear of a closing Joey Dunlop to claim his first North West 200 superbike success; the JPS team's fourth from four starts.

The 600cc race was an epic, with Philip McCallan, Steve Ives, Bob Jackson, Jim Moodie, Leslie McMaster, Mark Farmer and Dave Leach all fighting for the lead in a race anyone of them could have won. The lead changed at the front of the high-speed train on virtually every corner, but as they swooped on the final run towards Metropole, McCallan went the long way round Bob Jackson to take the lead. As pandemonium broke loose on the final run on the coast road, McCallan remained resolute at the front to head Ives and Jackson across the line as quick as that:

"That race was hard work. There were six or eight of us fighting it out for the lead. It was tough stuff; it wasn't easy."[28]

Philip McCallan returned the following year to succeed where Dunlop had been denied. As the 1992 meeting unfolded, the twenty-eight-year-old Portadown rider ran riot throughout the day's programme, claiming five wins from six starts, and sliding off in the second 250/350cc race.

Win number one came in the opening 250/350cc race. It came the hard way after McCallan outbraked pole-sitter Robert Dunlop on the final run through Metropole. Both were equal in their determination to win, both rode beyond the limit on the dramatic dash on the coast road, with Dunlop losing out by sixteen-hundredths of a second.

"On the first or second lap of that 250cc race after York Hairpin, near where Mill Road roundabout is, there was a building site. At the entrance to it, there were a lot of loose stones, and the bugger went wide and through them and broke my screen. I said right, if that's the way you want to play it, so on the next lap I made sure I was in front of him and did the same back.

"I had been tight behind Philip going up through the railway bridge. Going through the right-hander, just after it, I was right in his slipstream. It's very hard to stay in Philip's slipstream because he goes so close to the edge of the road – he's hard to follow. I was trying to stay tight behind him to get him on the brakes at Juniper Chicane. On the last lap, I couldn't see and moved out a wee bit to see my line, and ran wide and hit the kerb. I had to ease off and he pulled out a few bike lengths and that was it, he's as fast on the coast road as me; I wasn't close enough."[29]

The opening superbike race had already become a ten-wheeled battle as it reached Metropole on lap one, with the Honda Britain RC30s of McCallan, Fogarty and Joey Dunlop line abreast across the road and fending off Yamaha-mounted Mark Farmer and Robert Dunlop's

Alastair McCook

Philip McCallan's history-making five wins in a day in 1992 may never be matched. One of road racing's all-time greats.

earlier when he ran out of brakes and collided with a five-bar gate, Moodie was far from fit, and raced wearing heavy strapping around his damaged ribs. At the end of what had been an action replay of the previous year's cliffhanger, Moodie was helped off his machine, while McCallan proclaimed it, "The hardest race of my life."

The race, restarted after a first-lap crash at Ballysally roundabout had brought out the red flags, was a start-to-finish free-for-all between McCallan, Moodie, Joey Dunlop, Bob Jackson and Mike Edwards. Joey Dunlop had timed his attack to perfection to lead the five-man group for the last time through Metropole. As the thousands on the railway embankment began the celebrations for what would have been Joey's first North West 200 victory since 1988, he missed a gear leaving Church Corner and the race was lost. Mike Edwards' heroics on the grass at Juniper were rewarded with third place, ahead of Dunlop, whose consolation was a new lap record of 115.04 mph.

"You have loads of big moments – you don't remember half of them – but in that 600cc race I had a massive slide at Juniper Hill. Someone had blown up and there was oil all over the road. The bike went completely sideways. I thought I'd lost it but somehow managed to hang onto it, and won."[31]

McCallan's fourth win came at the end of another close-run thing, taking the 400cc race from Johnny Rea by fractions of a second. The race had been a three-way dice throughout, and the last lap typified the action with Steve Lindsell leading at Church, Rea leading going into Juniper and McCallan in front where it counted.

Norton challenge. McCallan was desperate to stay in touch with lap-two leader Fogarty surviving a heart-stopping moment at the start of lap three when he banged off the deep kerbing at Portstewart. On the downhill run into Portrush, Fogarty's Honda cut out without warning, forcing McCallan to take immediate avoiding action. Fogarty's RC30 kicked back into life and he continued to finish fourth, behind Robert Dunlop and Mark Farmer. McCallan had his own worries on the last lap:

"There was oil coming out of the breather and it was running all over the back wheel. My feet kept slipping off the footrests. It was on the back tyre, so you could feel it in every corner. The bike was moving around, and I was covered in oil and couldn't go as fast as I wanted. I still had to win the race."[30]

Jim Moodie's ride to second in the 600cc race, beaten by a tenth of a second, was nothing short of heroic. As the result of an accident at Hengelo in Holland three weeks

The 125cc race, run concurrently with the 400s, brought a win and a new lap record from newcomer Rob Orme. Hot-favourite Robert Dunlop completed a frustrating treble of runner-up finishes, with Joey once again producing a podium finish in the tiddler class.

Robert Dunlop's eighth North West 200 victory came in the second 250/350cc race, after getting the better of Ian Newton's Aprillia on the last lap. McCallan's appetite for mixing it in the thick of the action had not been diminished by his four wins. In the midst of the battle for the lead, McCallan's front wheel gave way under braking at University Corner, and he slid out uninjured.

Joey Dunlop was out of contention, making a mess of his braking after leading the North West 200 superbike race into University on lap one. Fogarty's troubles were clear for all to see as he shook his head in frustration going through the pits on lap three. By then, he was playing catch-up in a game he could not win on a RC30 that refused to perform. Both the factory machines of Fogarty and Joey Dunlop failed to make it to the finish, but the third Honda Britain runner had no worries. McCallan reeled off the fastest lap of the race at 120.94 mph, and broke clear to win from Mark Farmer by two seconds. Again, McCallan's Honda was blowing oil, and Farmer was struggling to see the road ahead after oil coated his visor.

"When you look back on it now, it definitely was some achievement. At the time, you're just so busy you don't have time to think about it; a week later, you're getting ready for the TT. It's such a hectic life you didn't have time to enjoy it really.

"Every one of the five wins was tough – every one. There are places where you can get a win easy, but you don't get a win easy here, you've got to ride for it. It's hard to believe you're going to win five internationals in one day, but you don't think about it. It's just another day's work; a very good day's work. I came here to promote my sponsors, they'd sponsored me to try and win races, so I tried to win races. It's just next day, next race, next job, and try to do the best you can."[32]

Carl Fogarty's run of rotten North West 200 luck changed at last in 1993. Riding the Moto Cinelli 888 Ducati, Fogarty stormed to a double superbike success, and an absolute lap record to boot. Fogarty had almost lost count of the races he had previously led but failed to finish on the Triangle. His celebrations at the end of the first superbike race, fuelled with relief and delight, came after crossing the line seventeen seconds clear of Robert Dunlop. Dunlop had fought back from seventh place at the end of lap one to steal second place from elder brother Joey by just over a second. His battling runner-up performance was enough to place the Italian factory one and two on the podium; their first success at the circuit.

The record lap, at 122.49 mph, came in the second superbike race, with Fogarty once again dominant from the start. Robert Dunlop repeated his earlier second-place finish, but the job this time round was made harder by the attacks waged by McCallan and Holden from lap two onwards. Holden's team had burned the midnight oil sorting out a Yamaha that gave trouble throughout practice. By lap four, Holden had moved ahead of Dunlop, but before the lap was completed, the race was stopped after an accident at Ballysally roundabout. Grand Prix regular Kevin Mitchell's 500cc Harris Yamaha had failed to finish the opening superbike race after his tyres shredded. Exiting the roundabout in race two the tyres lost adhesion, and Mitchell was spat off. The machine burst into flames; moments later an official attending to Mitchell dropped on the track with a heart attack. There was no option but to stop the race, and with time running out, the opportunity for a restart was soon gone. The results were decided on the running order at the end of the previous lap, relegating Holden to fourth, behind Dunlop and McCallan.

Robert Dunlop's third hat-trick of wins more than took his mind off the superbike defeats at the hands of Fogarty. His first win came in the programme opener –

Clifford McLean

the dramatic first 250/350cc race. James Courtney had led from the start before going down heavily at the notorious 140-mph Mathers Cross right-hander. Catch fencing and improvements to the corner saved Courtney from serious injury.

Philip McCallan's erratic progress over the opening three

laps saw him lead on lap one, drop to eight on lap two and climb back to fourth on lap three, before being taken off in a collision with Davy Johnston as they approached Church Corner on lap four.

"I was knocked out for a couple of seconds and had a bit of concussion. I don't really remember much about it. I was a bit dazed after that crash, but I knew what I was doing – just not fit enough to do what I wanted."[33]

With McCallan sidelined, Dunlop set out on his penultimate lap with a twelve-second lead, and cruised to finish well clear of Dave Milling, who claimed second 0.48 seconds ahead of Ian Lougher.

McCallan was fit to resume battle in the second 250/350cc race, after medical opinion had advised against riding in the opening superbike encounter. Despite feeling the affects of his earlier accident, McCallan was Dunlop's only real opposition. He pushed hard for the opening four laps, but dropped off the pace to finish five seconds behind. Woolsey Coulter slipped past a six-strong group locked in a frantic braking duel at Metropole to take third place on the last lap.

Robert Dunlop's third hat-trick included the by now almost obligatory 125cc win. Riding a machine on loan from regular jockey Darren Gawley, Dunlop was pushed all the way by Mick Lofthouse and Rob Orme. All three had led, but Dunlop made experience count nipping ahead at Metropole and snatching victory by 0.27 seconds from Lofthouse.

Like Fogarty, Jim Moodie had waited a long time to taste success. It all finally came together for the tough Glaswegian with a brace of wins, earned from start-to-finish victories in the 600cc and 400cc races.

Moodie streaked away from a six-strong chasing group in the 600cc race and never looked like being caught. A new lap record of 115.61 mph from Dunlop on lap three took him clear of the pack, with only Edwards hanging on to his tow. On the last lap, they were side by side at Coleraine, but Edwards gained the upper hand at Portrush to push Dunlop back to third.

Moodie secured his double in a 400cc race that quickly turned into a high-speed procession. Moodie pushed the lap record to 112.406 mph on his V&M FZR Yamaha to win his second North West 200 by eighteen seconds from Ian Simpson and Brian Reid.

Robert Dunlop's fourth treble North West 200 victory earned credibility at last for the much-maligned RC45, and marked a turning point for Honda early in the 1994 season, in dispelling the machine's reputation as an evil-handling, flawed replacement for the old workhorse, the RC30. A few short weeks further into the 1994 season, the events that would have profound, devastating effects on the life and racing career of Robert Dunlop came suddenly on a sunny Sunday afternoon in June. On the fourth lap of the Formula One TT, delayed to the Sunday due to poor weather, the rear wheel of Robert's North West-winning RC45 collapsed without warning, as he exited Ballaugh village. In an instant, Dunlop was hurled at over 130 mph against a stone wall. The injuries he sustained ended his career as a superbike rider. The pain and sacrifices that Robert Dunlop endured in the years ahead in his indomitable struggle to haul his broken body back onto a motorcycle and come back to racing as a winner are part of a story of ultimate bravery and determination. Very few have given more for their sport than Robert Dunlop.

Those events could not be imagined as the curtain came down on the 1994 North West 200. At the end of the day, Robert Dunlop's tally stood at one 125cc and two superbike victories. Mechanical failure in both 250cc races cheated Dunlop of his best chance of emulating Philip McCallan's achievement of racking up five wins in a day.

In the opening 250cc encounter, pole-sitter Dunlop went out when his Yamaha seized on the warm-up lap. The race will long be remembered for the pulsating last-lap battle that saw Woolsey Coulter steal victory from Ian Newton on the line by a hair's breadth.

Newton had taken the lead with an audacious move around the outside of Coulter at Station Corner on lap one. By lap two, James Courtney was already dropping off the back of the five-man leading group, when he crashed out in spectacular style, exiting Juniper Chicane. On lap four, the sight of Joey Dunlop in front at University Corner raised the volume levels amongst the thronged spectators, but by the following, penultimate, lap, Dunlop lay fourth behind Philip McCallan. Last time through Metropole, Dunlop's Honda ground to a halt, leaving McCallan clear in third place, behind Coulter, who swept through on Newton's inside on

Robert Dunlop sweeps underneath the McCullough Ducati of Michael Rutter on the opening lap of the Alan Hutchinson Tiles N W 200 Superbike race. Dunlop's 1994 treble, his fourth on the Triangle, brought credibility for Honda's troublesome RC 45. Two weeks later Dunlop was lucky to survive a horrendous crash, when the rear wheel of his Medd RC 45 Honda disintegrated during the Formula One TT. The courageous "Micro" fought back from extensive injuries to win again on the Island in the 1998 Ultra Lightweight TT, but only after surviving a spectacular crash in the 1998 North West 200 125cc race.

the last corner to win by the thickness of a coat of paint.

Newton made no mistakes in the second 250cc race, pulling clear of the field by Metropole on lap one and riding to a resounding victory. Jim Moodie had just moved into third place on lap two when the Queen's University Yamaha seized as he tipped it into Juniper Chicane, throwing the luckless Scot into the air and out of the chase. As Coulter made the decisive move in the last-lap sort-out with McCallan for second place, Newton was already celebrating the win.

The opening superbike race had its own dramas from

Alastair McCook

the start, with two riders going down as the second wave of bikes streaked away from the grid. In the ensuing mêlée, Tony Carey's Norton careered off the road and demolished the starter's podium, resulting in race official Mervyn White and a number of race sponsors receiving relatively minor injuries.

The action at the front was fast and furious, with newcomer David Jeffries causing a surprise by challenging for the lead in the early stages. Tyre trouble dropped Jeffries out of contention, whilst Michael Rutter, on board the Ducati that had served Carl Fogarty so well the previous year, retired from the fray on lap two. Joey Dunlop once again retired on the opening lap, and the expected challenge from Philip McCallan, riding a RC45 that was over geared, never came. Whilst McCallan settled for third, Iain Duffus took on the role of challenger and finished one second behind Dunlop's Medd Honda.

In superbike race two, Jeffries and Rutter challenged in the early laps but retired before the race had reached full distance. Once again, Dunlop headed the final leader-board placings, after leading a strung-out field home to complete his hat-trick. The disqualification of Iain Duffus from the runner-up spot as a result of using an oversized engine promoted McCallan and Joey Dunlop to the lower steps of the podium.

"I got great satisfaction from the superbike wins in 1994. From 1990, everybody said that part of the reason I won was because I had better bikes. Things were equal in 1994.

"The RC45s didn't have a great reputation for handling, and I'd had a lot of trouble with mine. I'd fell off it at Mallory Park prior to the North West. We tested at Ballykelly airfield during practice week. The bike was weaving and wobbling when I tried to hold it flat out. I knew I would have to do it on Saturday to be in with a chance of winning. I said to Stuart Medd I was going to

have another run and when she started wobbling, I just shut my eyes and kept her going. Once you've done something once you can do it again, and I had four or five more runs, flat out every time, maybe at 185 mph. Come the race, I was able to do it.

"I remember sitting on the grid before the second superbike race, and Philip coming over and saying to Roger Marshall, the co-ordinator for the Medd team, that he had the wrong gearing in the first race, wait and see what happens in the next one. I just sat below my helmet and I thought you have no chance son, after saying that you definitely have no chance."[34]

The much-anticipated appearance of the New Zealand designed and built Britten V twins had fallen well short of expectations. While David Jeffries, storming début propelled him into the limelight, his uncle Nick's superbike performances on the Britten had failed to impress. The other Britten in the hands of Mark Farmer had been even more low-key, failing to come to the line for superbike two after breaking down in its first outing. Two weeks later during practice for the Isle of Man TT, Farmer lost his life after being thrown from the Britten at the Black Dub.

Dunlop's 125cc victory, sandwiched between his superbike successes, came via an authoritative display that amounted to a total rout of the opposition. Whilst Ian Lougher and Kevin Mawdsley disputed second place with Irish short-circuit champion Phelim Owens, Dunlop disappeared into the distance to win by the proverbial street. Owens' Honda had spluttered throughout practice and had given further trouble on the warm-up lap. The Dungannon rider had expected the machine to cut out at every corner, but still fought gamely to claim second place ahead of Mawdsley. The supermono race, run concurrently with the 125s, brought a win for ex-Grand Prix star Alan Carter on his only visit to the Triangle. Carter's Top Gun Ducati won the meeting's inaugural supermono event easily from Jim Moodie and Mike Edwards.

In the 600cc race, Edwards survived the all-out assault of V&M team mates Ian Simpson and Mark Farmer to take the win in the by now expected 600cc blanket finish. Jim Moodie slid out of the action unhurt first time through Ballysally roundabout. It was one of many dramas in a race that Farmer and Simpson both led. Philip McCallan chased them the whole way, but by midway, the result was in the hands of the three Yamaha riders at the front. On lap three, Edwards slipped from first to third in the run through Juniper Chicane, but pulled out a race-winning lead with new lap record of 117.167 mph on the final circuit, while Simpson held his team mate off by a wheel for second place.

Philip McCallan overcame all the odds to claim 250cc and 600cc wins in 1995. At the start of race week, "Supermac" faced a daunting schedule. His itinerary saw him jet back and forth between practising in Germany for the World Thunderbike Series, run on the Sunday after the North West 200, and practising at Portstewart. Every lap in practice had to count.

"I was under big pressure. The deal with Honda was that I would race the superbike at the North West and the TT, and they'd help me in the Thunderbike Series. That wasn't going well because we didn't have the budget to do it the way we wanted. We were just exhausted all the time doing more than we should have been."[35]

A near disaster in 250cc practice, clouting the kerb heavily and bursting both tyres at Dhu Varren, consigned McCallan to the back row of the grid on race day. It did not stop him winning though; it just made the job harder. By lap two, McCallan was in the midst of a chasing group in pursuit of early leader Ian Newton. McCallan moved ahead for the first time on lap four, but Newton was still right with him as they set out on the final lap. The

Mike Edwards' 1994 600cc win was a close-run thing. The V&M Hondas of Simpson and Farmer were never far away but had to settle for the bottom steps on the rostrum.

Alastair McCook

lead changed at almost every corner, with McCallan making the final decisive move within sight of the finishing line.

"That was a tough, tough race. My bike was so slow, it was unbelievable. I came out of the last chicane on the last lap in the lead, and Ian Newton had passed me by Quarry Hill. He was holding the inside line, making sure I couldn't get in, so I just went round the outside of him and won the race."[36]

McCallan's 600cc win was a much more straightforward affair. He took the race by the scruff of the neck, moving from fifth to first at University Corner on lap one, and from there dictated the pace from the front, set a new lap record of 118.287 mph, and won with ease from Mike Edwards and Bob Jackson.

"One of my easiest North West 200 victories. I just went mad on the first lap, got a couple of seconds lead, and held it from there."[37]

Robert Holden had claimed 600cc pole position in practice, and had held second place for much of the race before his Ducati went off song, dropping him to fourth place in the closing stages. It all came right for the Kiwi in the super-

mono race, run concurrently on the road with the 125s. Holden led from lap two to win from Bob Jackson, with Nick Jeffries overtaking Steve Ruth on the final lap for third place.

The 125cc race was shaping up into a tight, three-cornered battle between Joey Dunlop, Phelim Owens and Ian Lougher, when the race was stopped to allow medical personnel access to a spectator who had become ill. On the restart, he led for the opening two laps, but could not shake off Owens and ex-Grand Prix regular

This near calamity in 1995 250cc practice forced Philip McCallan to start from the back row of the grid. It didn't stop him being first past the chequered flag though.

Alastair McCook

Robin Appleyard. Appleyard had victory in his sights and led through Metropole for the last time. By the finishing line, Appleyard had dropped to third as Owens led Dunlop across the line for the win.

McCallan's back-row position on the 250cc grid proved too big a disadvantage to over-come in race two. The race developed into a dogfight at the front between Newton and Robin Milton, with McCallan holding third by mid-distance. On the penultimate lap, Newton and Milton were together, but as they left the start/finish chicane to begin their last lap, Milton made a crucial error, allowing Newton to leap clear into a winning lead, while Callum Ramsey's last-lap heroics on the brakes demoted McCallan to fourth place.

Alastair McCook

The two superbike races brought

Alastair McCook

Robert Holden's Supermono and superbike wins in 1995 were high points in the popular Kiwi's career.

mixed fortunes for Ian Simpson. The classy Scot set a new absolute course record of 123.53 mph en route to a convincing first-race victory from Michael Rutter. There

Iain Duffus on the Top Gun Ducati leads 1995 superbike race-winner Robert Holden into the start/finish chicane.

was nothing between the Castrol Hondas of Simpson and McCallan, and the charging Ducatis of Rutter and Duffus in the early laps. All four were in contention until Duffus dropped off the pace at mid-distance. Rutter led on the last lap, but at Metropole Simpson nipped past a trio of backmarkers to leave Rutter and McCallan to dispute second place.

Race two ended for Simpson before the flag had dropped when the suspension on his RC45 collapsed on the grid. With clutch failure forcing Rutter out on the warm-up lap, a titanic three-man battle developed from the off between Duffus, McCallan and Holden. Holden had retired from race one with handling problems, but in race two the Ducati was on song and Holden would not be denied. The three-strong pack constantly shuffled positions throughout the six laps, but in a blistering final circuit. Holden moved to the front. McCallan threw everything into his final attack, the RC45 losing drive and squirming beneath him after running onto the grass at Juniper Chicane, while Holden romped home.

Woolsey Coulter annihilated the opposition on the way to winning both 250cc races on the 1996 programme. Coulter rocketed from pole position in race one to hold a nine-second lead by the end of the lap. His only concern came on lap four when he mistakenly misread his pit board showing "P 1" ("P" for place and "1" for first) as "+1", a lead of one second. Coulter's lead at the time was over fourteen seconds, and although he barely needed the extra incentive, he pushed his lead on the next lap to twenty seconds. The real drama in the race lay in an all-guns-blazing dice for second place. Callum Ramsey had done all the hard work, and with only the champagne left to open, it all fell apart when he overshot at Juniper Chicane, leaving Philip McCallan and Gavin Lee to sweep through to complete the top three.

It was a familiar story in race two with Coulter winning as he pleased, while Ramsey continued to make life difficult for himself. After a flying start, Ramsey and his Aprillia ran out of brakes and headlong into the bales at York Hairpin. A gritty comeback ride earned him fifth place and thoughts of what might have been. The loudest cheers of the day came as the 100,000-strong crowd roared their approval for the ageless Joey Dunlop who swept past Phelim Owens at Juniper to claim second place.

With the supermono race dropped by the organisers from the event, the four-lap 125cc runners had the roads to themselves. The eagerly anticipated head-to-head showdown between Phelim Owens and Mick Lofthouse became a non-event, after Owens was hit from behind and brought down by front-row starter Owen McNally

approaching Ballysally roundabout on the warm-up lap. When the flag fell, Joey Dunlop was first off the line, but trailed Lofthouse by Coleraine on lap one. As Lofthouse edged away to lead by four seconds by mid-distance, Dunlop slipped down the field to finish a disappointing ninth place. With memories of how lack of petrol in sight of the flag had denied his brother John victory in the 1987 production race, Lofthouse took nothing for granted until he saw the chequered flag. There was no time to relax in the pulsating three-way battle for rostrum honours behind him. After falling off twice in the previous year's meeting, Denis McCullough made no mistakes, holding off Gavin Lee and Chris Palmer by a whisker at the flag.

The day had got off to a disappointing start by Philip McCallan's high standards. In the opening superbike race, the attrition rate on the high-profile Ducati entries had been high from the start. Robert Holden's Old Spice Ducati failed to make it to the grid, and he was joined on the sidelines by team mate Terry Rymer, whose brakes failed on the run to Metropole on lap one. If Rymer considered himself lucky after his high-speed excursion down the slip road into Portrush, there was no doubt someone was looking after Nick Jeffries who suffered nothing more than bruising after a 150-mph crash at Mathers Cross.

By lap four, the result seemed a foregone conclusion with the yellow McCullough Ducati of Michael Rutter commanding an impressive lead. Suddenly the race was wide open as Rutter retired at Portrush, raising the stakes in Philip McCallan's race-long duel with Ian Simpson. On the final run along the coast road, McCallan seemed to have it all under control, but in a breathtaking move on the final corner, Simpson squeezed his Duckhams Ducati past McCallan's Honda to steal the win.

"I just fell asleep, for the first time in my life, even Simpson couldn't believe he won that one. I had a good

Alastair McCook

lead coming out of the last chicane. The race was wrapped up, and I just dozed off, thinking about the next race. I left the space wide open and he dived through. I couldn't believe it. I was so mad, I had to win the last superbike race to make up for it."[38]

Before winning superbike race number two, McCallan had the small matter of winning the 600cc race to take care of. It was an all-star performance with the Honda star leading from start to finish. The main opposition came in the shape of the V&M Hondas in the hands of Iain Duffus and Ian Simpson standing in as a late replacement for the injured Mike Edwards. McCallan remained only a second clear after two laps, but Duffus' chance

went when he straightlined the new chicane at Magherabuoy on the run to Portrush. He stayed on board to finish third, behind Simpson who in turn finished five seconds behind the Honda-factory rider.

The pack swoop through Primrose Hill on the opening lap of the 1996 125cc race. Michael Wilcox leads Denis McCullough, Gavin Lee (15) eventual winner Mick Lofthouse (8) and Ian Lougher.

McCallan's superbike win came after Michael Rutter's miserable luck continued. As in race one, Rutter streaked away to establish a seemingly decisive advantage. Then on the penultimate lap, as he tipped his Ducati into Metropole, the motor died.

159

"In the first race, I shut off for Metropole on the last lap, and as soon as I opened it up there was nothing there – it was dead. I just rolled to Church Corner and stopped. In the second race, exactly the same thing happened again. Last lap but one, big lead, and I thought I've got this one won, better be careful. As soon as I thought be careful, going into Metropole, the same thing happened at exactly the same place. I tried to get it going but it wouldn't start. I coasted a bit further the second time just to say I'd gone further than the first time. In the first race a fuel pump packed up, in the second it was the quick shift."[39]

After losing part of his gear change at Ballysally roundabout, the best Simpson could manage was to cut his losses and ride shotgun for team mate Jim Moodie, with the Duckhams Ducatis finishing in formation behind the unstoppable McCallan.

The downside of motor-cycle road racing followed quickly after the highs of the 1996 North West 200. Mick Lofthouse and Robert Holden lost their lives in separate accidents in the same early-morning practice session for the 1996 Isle of Man TT.

The 1997 meeting produced a vintage year for lap records and close finishes, with the spoils of victory for the seven-race event spread between six different winners. It was also a day when the new generation came of age, with four new names added to the victors' roll of honour.

Callum Ramsey's first North West 200 win came in the opening 250cc race. John McGuinness, still in search of his first success at the meeting, made Ramsey's task far from easy as he harried him for the five laps. The flying Scot hung on at the finish to edge him out by 0.17 seconds.

The upsets began with hotly tipped contender James

Courtney breaking his wrist and ankle after falling heavily in practice. Ian Lougher crashed out as the entire field bunched behind him on the brakes at York Hairpin on lap one. Philip McCallan lay fifth behind Joey Dunlop first time through Ballysally, but by Portrush, McCallan was touring, his race over. Dunlop finished, but slipped down the rankings to come home in ninth place. After a disastrous practice, Woolsey Coulter started the race from near the back of the grid. By mid-distance, Coulter had made his way through the field and lay fourth behind Phelim Owens at Mathers Cross on lap three, but was forced out with mechanical failure before the lap was over.

McGuinness and Ramsey were clear of the rest by Metropole on lap one, and as the race progressed the advantage swung between them. McGuinness had pulled clear at the front on lap three, only for Ramsey to regain the lead on the following lap. McGuinness came back with an audacious move at Mathers Cross, but on the last-lap run along the coast road they were side by side. Ramsey was first to dive into the left-right-right-left sequence at Juniper to notch up, "The best win I've ever had."

What would prove to be Philip McCallan's last win on the Triangle Circuit came in the day's first superbike race. McCallan had moved into second place behind Michael Rutter by Mathers on lap one, and seized his chance to move ahead when Rutter ran wide and dropped back to third at Metropole. Rutter was back in front of a tight three-cornered battle with McCallan and the Crescent Suzuki of Jim Moodie as they began their fourth lap, but lay second once again behind McCallan as they drove out of York. It was still too close to call on the final run through Juniper, but as Rutter lined up the factory Honda in front for a last shot at glory, the engine on his own RC45 stalled and in an instant fired back in. His back wheel, overburdened with the vicious power delivery, kicked out, sending Rutter high out of the saddle; the race was lost. As McCallan streaked to the flag, Rutter salvaged second place ahead of Moodie.

Luck turned its back on Philip McCallan as the day wore on. The 600cc race shaped up as a minor epic with Rutter, McCallan and Ricky Mitchell heading the charge into Station Corner for the first time. Jim Moodie was a retirement before the first corner, and Ricky Mitchell's race ended exiting Juniper for the first time when he came down with Pete Jennings. By lap two, McCallan had hit the front with the V&M Hondas of Rutter and Ian Simpson swarming all over him. Slowly he edged clear, but Rutter went with him, refusing to be shaken off. Both were inside the lap record on lap four, and Simpson set a new record of 116.459 mph on the last lap but still had to settle for third. On the final lap, Rutter led at Metropole but McCallan passed him at Blackhill only to run wide at Juniper, allowing Rutter through to record his first win at the meeting, fifteen years after his father's last victory there.

"After the year before I thought I was never going to get a win there. The people you were up against around that time, Simpson, Moodie, Duffus and especially Philip, were all hard racers. It was nice to get one over those kind of people. That 600cc race was a fantastic race, elbow to elbow down the straights, fantastic."[40]

The refusal by the organisers to allow Robert Dunlop to race had been the source of controversy in the weeks leading up to the meeting. Dunlop had already raced in a number of Irish national meetings and considered himself more than fit for the task of completing the four high-speed laps of the 125cc race. When the organisers rejected his entry on the grounds that he had not recovered sufficiently from his horrific 1994 TT accident, they were bombarded by letters of protest from race fans. Dunlop and his sponsor P J O'Kane were quick to condemn the actions of some who threatened to disrupt the meeting if Dunlop did not race. Incredibly, the threats were followed through and officials were faced with the task of sweeping nails from the course on race morning.

Phelim Owens had pulled well clear of a chasing pack that included Callum Ramsey on board Robert Dunlop's 125cc Honda by Juniper on lap one but overshot before

Alastair McCook

It takes a lot to beat Philip McCallan but Michael Rutter held off the charging Supermac to win the 600cc race in 1997.

rejoining the race in sixth place. On lap three, Owens set a new lap record of 105.792 mph to reel in Owen McNally and Ramsey who had broken clear. As McNally, Denis McCullough, Ian Lougher and Mark Curtin all broke the old lap record, Owens headed Lougher and McNally home with plenty to spare.

Honda Fireblades dominated the production race entries, but the win went to Ian Simpson riding the Red Bull Ducati. By lap two, Simpson's Ducati was in a four-way scrap with the Fireblades of McCallan and Rutter, and the Suzuki of Jim Moodie. The action was frantic at the front with McCallan leading at York, Simpson at Ballysally and Rutter at Juniper. As Moodie dropped off the pace on lap three, Simpson had an advantage, which he held to win from McCallan with Rutter third.

Handling problems forced Simpson out on the warm-up lap of superbike race two. As the grid thundered towards Portstewart on the warm-up lap, McCallan's pit crew were still working frantically to encourage the RC45 into life. Eventually a trapped fuel pipe was diagnosed, but having missed the warm-up lap, McCallan was forced to start from the pit lane on cold tyres.

"We messed up in that race and had to start from the pit lane. Everyone else had their tyres scrubbed in but I hadn't, so I couldn't push hard on the first lap. If I hadn't overshot at Metropole on lap one, run wide and had to turn the bike around, I'd have been right up there I think.

"The bike had been weaving a little bit in the first race. We had no settings for it; it was all new factory stuff. We thought the ride height was a bit low so we raised it by 6mm and made it worse, we should have lowered it. I didn't care; I was going to ride it anyway. It was a miracle what I did in that race, I'd liked to have done more of course."[41]

McCallan lay fourteenth at the end of the opening lap, as his RC45 skipped and weaved beneath him on the charge in pursuit of a leading bunch of Rutter, Moodie, Simon Beck, Bob Jackson and Woolsey Coulter. McCallan's charge would eventually take him past Coulter, riding the 500cc V-twin Honda, to a fifth-place finish. No one could begrudge Rutter the glory after his

double disappointment from the previous year. He pushed the absolute course record to 122.200 mph on the final lap, but Jim Moodie responded with a lap of 122.320 mph to finish 0.15 seconds in arrears.

The second 250cc race provided a fitting finale for the meeting; with Owen McNally more than making up for his error the previous year, and scoring his first ever road-race win. McNally shrugged off the frustration stemming from a string of runner-up finishes in Irish racing to emerge as a winner on a circuit that ran past his own front door.

Once again, Philip McCallan's Honda let him down, but Woolsey Coulter had his Aprillia flying after his retirement in race one. Coulter, McNally and fourth-place finisher McGuinness all lapped under the lap record, but it was Phelim Owens, whose Aprillia had been fastest through the speed trap at 152 mph, who pushed the lap record to 115.979 mph on his way to third place. When Coulter rounded Metropole for the last time in the lead, it seemed his experience would count and the local man would have to settle for second place again. On the final run along the coast road, McNally seized his chance when Coulter misjudged his braking and led him home to score one of the most popularly received wins seen on the circuit.

"I was well pleased. I always wanted to win a North West since I started racing but I never thought I'd do it. After the first race, I knew my bike was good enough. It was damp in places and I wasn't interested in pushing it too hard. I could see Ramsey and McGuinness were really getting some big slides. I reckoned I had two more races to go in, the roads were drying and I thought there's no point in trying too hard. I just used my head for a change and settled for fifth place in that one. Then we made a few changes for carburation and gearing, got the slick tyres on and it was really flying.

"I think I surprised a lot of people by winning. Coulter's a wily character and after he caught and passed me on the last lap I thought that's it, second place. But he wasn't getting away from me and I began to think I can work with this. In fairness, he made a mistake on the coast road and I got past him and stayed there. It just worked out. He said afterwards that I rode a very smart race, and I was quite pleased with that."[42]

1998 brought further changes to the course in the form of a roundabout on Mill Road, Portstewart. A week before the meeting was due to take place, Joey Dunlop, Owen McNally and John Creith tested the latest change

Alastair McCook

There was no disguising Owen McNally's delight after winning the 250cc race in 1997. Pictured with past winner Ian Newton.

to the course. The general opinion was that the roundabout was a recipe for disaster – an accident waiting to happen. By then, there was little the organisers could do to change things. Come race day, the opinions were proved correct, as a string of accidents at Mill Road resulted in Phelim Owens

and Darren Lindsay being hospitalised with serious injuries, and the racing running hours behind schedule.

In the opening 250cc race, Woolsey Coulter stalled on the grid and came from last place to win on the last lap. The result might have been very different if not for Callum Ramsey virtually throwing the race away on lap three. By then, Coulter had clawed his way up to fifth place behind John Creith, son of 1965 winner Dick, John McGuinness, Ryan Farquhar and Ian Lougher. As Ramsey left Coleraine to begin the second half of the five lapper, he accidentally hit the kill switch on his 250cc Honda Britain machine. By the time Ramsey restarted, his potential winning lead had gone and he languished in eighth place. With a lap to go, only Lougher remained ahead of Coulter. On the last lap, Coulter completed his own mission impossible, sweeping through at Magherabuoy Chicane and then holding off Lougher's last-gasp attack at Juniper to win.

The grid lined up for the opening superbike race with Jim Moodie, a late replacement for the injured Sean Emmet, partnering Matt Llewellyn on the Red Bull Ducatis. The Honda Britain team launched a three-pronged attack in the form of Rutter, Simpson and Duffus riding RC45s, with Joey Dunlop the meeting's most notable absentee after his big crash at the Tandragee 100 the previous weekend. The race quickly developed into a three-way dispute between Rutter, Simpson and Moodie. Rutter threw away his first-lap lead after running wide at Metropole, but came from third to lead again by Magherabuoy on the following lap. As the lead changed constantly throughout the race, the last lap promised a nerve-jangling, grandstand finish. It was not to be. As Moodie held second place at York for the final time, his Ducati slid from beneath him under braking. Rutter following close behind tried to take evasive action, and crashed out as well. While Simpson cruised home

Alastair McCook

In 1998 Joey Dunlop, Owen McNally and John Creith tried the infamous Mill Road roundabout out. They hated it but the roundabout stayed. Joey was injured at the Tandragee 100 and missed the meeting anyway.

all three having spells in front. Things really came to the boil on the last lap. Simpson lay third approaching Ballysally for the final time but led by Mathers. The hard part was holding off Plater who launched attack after attack, almost squeezing through as they crested Blackhill together.

After a three-year absence from the meeting, Robert Dunlop's comeback ride ended in disaster. The race was abandoned after three attempts at running the 125cc class were ended by crashes at different points on the course. The first stoppage came with Dunlop leading after Phelim Owens and Darren Lindsay were both seriously injured in a first-lap calamity at Mill Road. The third and final stoppage came after Dunlop was knocked off his machine on the approach to University Corner. After being thrown in the air like a rag doll, Dunlop smashed upside down and backwards into a heavily baled road sign. Despite breaking a collarbone and ankle, Dunlop showed what resolve really meant by storming to victory two weeks later in the ultra lightweight Isle of Man TT.

"Patsy O'Kane had bought me a bike in 1996 and Billy Nutt [Clerk of the Course] had asked me to do a couple of demonstration laps on it at the North West. I said yes but I wanted to be sure that I was fit to ride it. We took it to Ballykelly to test it and everything was going well until it seized, and bang, I went over the handlebars and broke my arm again in the same bloody place.

"When Billy Nutt turned my entry down in 1997, I could understand his point of view; I'm not stupid. I was disappointed. I have a great admiration for Billy, he's a

untroubled for the win, Rutter remounted to fight off Bob Jackson, John McGuinness and Llewellyn for second place.

Simpson's second win of the day came in a hard-fought 600cc race that went right to the wire. Simpson partnered Rutter on the Motorcycle City Hondas, under the watchful eye of Philip McCallan. After injuring his back in an accident at Thruxton, McCallan was unable to race but assumed the managerial role with his old team.

In true North West 200 600cc tradition the race was a thriller, with Simpson and Rutter being pushed all the way by newcomer Steve Plater on the Sanyo Honda. The race finally got properly underway after being halted twice due to accidents. Plater had been in front when the race was stopped after Mark Rollaston became one of many victims of the already notorious Mill Road roundabout. On the restart the action was hectic, with good man at his job, but equally I do my job well. I thought he might have given me credit for having more intelligence. Perhaps he might have had a change of mind, but then Patsy [O'Kane, ex-sponsor] got on the phone and blew up with him and then everyone dug their heels in.

"I was really up for it in 1998. I was a lot fitter, I had a good bike and I knew for the first time since my accident in 1994 that I wasn't just making up the numbers; I knew I could win.

"After the first crash, I didn't realise that the race had been red-flagged. I didn't realise the seriousness of what had happened with Phelim and Darren; I didn't see their crash.

"It was restarted and we were on the second lap when the race was stopped again. Third time away, I got another good start. Normally going into University, I stay over to the left to stop someone T-boning me. It might not be the fastest line but it's the safest. Then I got my elbow knocked, my hand came off the handlebar, and I think the impact made me hit the thumb-operated front brake, and that made the back wheel kick up. It was luck that there wasn't more off than me."[43]

With the meeting running two hours behind schedule, the production race finally got away with Honda Fireblade-mounted Iain Duffus the early leader. The race soon became a showdown between Honda's established showroom-sales leader ridden by Michael Rutter, and Yamaha's new pretender, the R1, with David Jeffries in the saddle.

By the time Alan Bennallick crashed out of the chasing

Alastair McCook

pack on lap two at Mill Road, Rutter and Jeffries were well clear and locked in combat out in front. Jeffries led for long periods of the race, and

The mighty Honda Britain team of Michael Rutter and Ian Simpson lead Red Bull Ducati rider Jim Moodie through Church Corner during the opening 1998 superbike race.

the straight-line speed of the R1 made life very difficult for Rutter. In the end, Jeffries came within 0.2 seconds of giving Yamaha's new baby its début roads win. Simon Beck threw away a safe third place when he was high-sided from his Kawasaki at Juniper on the last lap, allowing Plater through for his second podium appearance of the day.

"I only rode in the production race in 1998. I thought I had a chance of winning that one, but Michael beat me again. I had only one race all day, and after the long delay, my brain had gone out of gear a bit with the long wait. Michael had already ridden in a couple of races by then and was mentally more up to speed."[44]

Rutter's elusive superbike victory finally came in the final race of the day, the North West 200 superbike race, shortened to four laps. Ian Simpson shadowed him for the entire distance, and led for spells in the early laps, before settling for second place after the rear tyre on the RC45, originally destined to be ridden by Philip McCallan, began to break up in the closing stages.

"My dad loved the North West, I think it was his favourite road race. He always enjoyed racing there and it would mean a lot to me to match him at least. I don't say I want to beat him, but it would be nice to match him."[45]

The 1999 meeting was overshadowed by the death of Donny Robinson. Robinson, a winner at the event in 1981 and 1982, died after coming off his 125cc Honda at Mill Road roundabout during the Tuesday night practice. The session had run in atrocious conditions, and was abandoned shortly after Robinson's accident.

Gary Dickinson leads Robert Dunlop and Owen McNally through Black Hill in the ill-fated 1998 125cc race.

In a fitting gesture, Callum Ramsey dedicated his victories in both 250cc races to Robinson's memory. Ramsey hit the front in race one for the first time at Magherabuoy Chicane, and was soon out of sight of the chasing pack. The only man

The rear tyre of Ian Simpson's RC 45 Honda graphically illustrates why the Triangle circuit has a reputation for shredding racing rubber.

who matched Ramsey's electrifying turn of speed was his Vimto-Honda team mate, John McGuinness. On lap two, McGuinness reclaimed the lead at the 150-mph Station Corner, but trailed Ramsey again by University Corner. Out of sight of the battling Vimto team mates, pole-sitter Owen McNally completed a lonely race-long ride to claim third place, but the story of the race was the tenacious struggle at the front. Lap after lap, Ramsey and McGuinness sat elbow to elbow on the 160-mph straights, and swapped places on virtually every corner. Less than half a bike's length separated them on the line.

Alastair McCook

166

Race two was a much closer affair with the Vimto Hondas battling in the early stages with McNally, Coulter, Lougher and Alan Patterson. Mechanical failure forced Patterson from the action, and a rear puncture halted Coulter's progress. When McNally overshot the start/finish chicane and dropped from the final reckoning, the race came down to a three-man fight between Lougher, McGuinness and Ramsey over the last two laps. Despite setting a new lap record of 116.38 mph, Lougher could only split the Vimto bikes on the road, as Ramsey headed the frantic dash home.

Lougher's consolation came by way of victory in the 125cc class. As the race progressed, Robert Dunlop dropped off the pace and was never really in the hunt for a top-three finish. When Darren Lindsay crashed out at Mill Road for the second year in succession, Lougher was left to fend off the twin challenge of McNally and Phelim Owens. Owens had battled game-ly, holding a loose fuel tank in place with his knees, and led on the final approach to Magherabuoy. Lougher made the passing move that won him the race at the chicane, while McNally pushed the lap record to 105.88 mph to claim second spot.

David Jeffries took the superbike races by the scruff of the neck and made them his own, muscling his V&M R1 Yamaha home in front in both races, and then stole a 600cc race win to seal an historic hat-trick.

Jeffries' win in the opening superbike came in a race that had been stopped on the first lap after Manx rider Paul Dedman was highsided from his Ducati at Juniper Hill. Dedman slammed into two track marshals, John Tweed and his son, John Junior, leaving the organisers with no choice but to stop the race while ambulances rushed all three to hospital.

From the restart, Jeffries made an electrifying start but by lap two, Duffus, his V&M team mate, and Honda teamster Jim Moodie were visibly closing the gap. Duffus led on lap three but could not make the move stick. Even under pressure, Jeffries looked in control. On the final lap at Metropole, the Yorkshire man had it all to do when he slipped back to third, but staged a blistering attack on the run to the line to head Moodie home by the slimmest of margins. Jeffries battled with the opposition as he fought through the pain barrier. At Portrush, an old knee injury flared up, popping his left kneecap out of joint and leaving Jeffries in agony as he chased the two Scots down to claim the biggest win of his career.

The 1999 meeting got off to the worst possible start after the hugely popular Donny Robinson crashed out in truly atrocious conditions during practice. A past winner on the circuit, Donny died in hospital from his injuries. Pictured here during the fateful Tuesday evening practice at Dhu Varren.

Alastair McCook

Alastair McCook

Vimto Honda team mates Ramsey and McGuinness on Juniper Hill, 1999. It was another good day at the office for Ramsey, he won both 250cc races.

"We came here in 1999 with the same shoulder bust again. In 1992, I smashed it up at Daytona; that was the start of it. Then when I crashed at the Ulster Grand Prix at Ireland's Corner in 1992 I hurt it again. Then I hurt it again when I was taken off at Church Corner in 1993. It was just the same shoulder, year after year. We finished up at the TT with all the muscles on the shoulder blade ripped away from my back and that was it. It finished me racing. When you're not physically fit to do what you are mentally fit to do, you're going to get hurt.

"I should have had that 600cc race, but I couldn't stop the bike and turn it. We had a good team and the bikes were superb, I just couldn't ride them the way I wanted to. We had a third in the last superbike race and it was just the ride from hell."[46]

With Ian Simpson missing from the 600cc grid, the result of a broken leg sustained in a crash at Snetterton, Jeffries' main challenge came from Moodie and McCallan. McCallan had his own demons to conquer, and was given pain-deadening injections on the grid for a shoulder injury picked up after a high-speed off at Donington. His discomfort did not show as he fought it out in a hammer-and-tongs sort-out that was impossible to call right to the wire. The last lap produced nine adrenaline-pumping miles with Moodie bravest on the brakes as the leaders approached Mathers Cross three abreast across the road. His advantage lasted to Magherabuoy before McCallan slipped through on the brakes only for Jeffries to pounce at Metropole. While the Yorkshire rider celebrated his second win from two starts and a 600cc lap record of 117.41 mph, McCallan's pain was etched clearly for all to see.

Jeffries' one anxious moment came on the opening lap of superbike two when he led through University Corner but dropped to fifth in an instant after running wide. James Courtney's moment of glory, out in front on the Red Bull Ducati, was short-lived with Jeffries heading the charge by Portrush. The red and yellow V&M Yamaha broke clear of the battle between McCallan, Duffus and Courtney, towing the RC45 of Moodie with him. McCallan took the upper hand to claim third with a do-or-die pass on Duffus last time through Juniper. Moodie pushed hard the whole way, but an absolute course record of 122.26 mph from Jeffries sealed the victory and earned him a place in the history books alongside the greats.

"It's a mega meeting. I like Station Corner; it takes some balls to go round there. It's absolutely flat in fifth on a

Alastair McCook

Philip McCallan fought through the pain barrier to ride in 1999. It was his last competitive appearance in Ireland. At the height of the 1999 600cc battle, Moodie and McCallan chase Jeffries towards York Corner.

600 through there, absolutely awesome. I can go through Mathers pretty quick, but it's downright scary. That roundabout thing [Mill Road], I don't like – it's horrible.

"1999 was the best year I ever had. It didn't really hit me until after I went home. In racing everyone was saying well done, they always do. When you get home and all your mates, who don't really know about racing, are saying brilliant, well done and you go out for a beer, that's when it really hit home. It's going to go down in history, very few people have won three in a day, very few."[47]

The 2000 North West 200 practice week was disrupted by the weather. The organisers waited for swirling mist to clear before the Thursday evening practice got under way, but instead conditions worsened, and with a thick blanket of fog lying around the course, the session was abandoned.

Race day dawned with Joey Dunlop, now forty-eight years old, in pole position for both superbike races. It was a dream come true for John McGuinness, teaming up with Dunlop, his childhood idol, in the Demon Vimto team. For Dunlop, the meeting would provide an invaluable pre-TT race for the SP1 VTR 1000cc Honda. Honda had supplied Dunlop with a tuned Fireblade to use in the major road-race meetings throughout the year. He was far from happy with the machine, and left Honda in no doubt about his thoughts on the matter. In response, Honda offered the thumping V-twin. After finishing fifth in superbike race one, and failing to finish in the next, Joey held little hope of holding off the mighty Yamaha R1s at the TT. In response, Honda pulled out all the stops and finally produced a package that gave the TT legend a fighting chance. In return, he rewarded them with victory in the Formula One TT; one of the sweetest wins of his career.

From the drop of the flag, it quickly became clear that the V&M R1 Yamahas were going to take a lot of beating. By University Corner on lap one of the opening superbike race, Michael Rutter, a late replacement in the team for the injured Ian Simpson, had powered from the third row of the grid to third place. At Metropole

yards from the finishing line. As Donnan lay stunned in the middle of the track, the flag marshal on the final corner had no option but to show a yellow flag, warning riders of the hazard that lay ahead and prohibiting overtaking. Jeffries had no choice but to shelve any plans that he might have had for a last-gasp move and followed his team mate across the line.

Alastair McCook

David Jeffries and the R1 Yamaha were an unstoppable combination in 1999. Here Jeffries muscles the R1 through Portstewart on his way to his first North West 200 victory.

Rutter's performance in the 600cc race was simply stunning. After barely completing a lap in practice, he started from the back row of the grid. While Jim Moodie flew the flag for Honda, doing battle with the R6 Yamaha of David Jeffries at the front, Rutter was carving a path through the field like a hot knife through butter. By the end of the opening lap, Rutter lay well clear at the head of the field behind Moodie and his fellow V&M

Corner, Rutter squeezed past his team mate David Jeffries and into the lead. When a broken gear linkage ended Ian Lougher's race on lap three, Rutter and Jeffries were out in front on their own. The lead swung back and forth between the charging R1s, but on the last lap as Rutter led towards the final corner, John Donnan, almost a lap behind the leaders, was highsided from his machine

riders, Jeffries and Lougher. At the end of lap three, Rutter stalked race leader Jeffries, and on the next led through Portrush. The final frantic circuit built to a pulsating conclusion, with Jeffries breaking the lap record and still finishing in third place. Moodie and Rutter were both on record pace as well, with Moodie ruing being caught behind a back marker, and settling for runner-up, a fifth of a second behind Rutter.

"I'd only done one lap on the bike, and I'd never even sat on it before practice. I started from the back row of the grid and came through. Jim and David had plenty of experience on the bikes they were riding. I knew it was going to be my hardest race, I couldn't believe it when I

His return to ride in front of the 100,000-strong crowd was rewarded with a hat-trick of wins, his best day in a ten-year-long racing career. Win number three came with Rutter finishing strongly out on his own, leading home a strung-out field in the day's second superbike

Alastair McCook

The all-conquering V&M Yamahas of Rutter and Jeffries at Church Corner during the 2000 North West 200 superbike race.

got through the pack. I mean it wasn't easy, there was some late braking but I won it."[48]

Rutter had missed the 1999 North West 200 meeting, and instead had spent a morale-crushing season competing on the world stage in the 500cc Grand Prix class.

race, with Jeffries and Lougher completing the top three.

"No one expected me to do it. A lot of people had David down as having won it before the race started. Everyone thought he would clear off and to be honest I didn't feel that confident myself. It was the first time I had ridden the bikes. When I ended up on the third row of the grid for the superbike races, I thought ah well, just do your best. The R1 was a fantastic bike, it steered real well and the power was there. To be honest my bike and David's were the quickest things out there."[49]

"A friend of mine was at Juniper and he was keeping me informed over his mobile phone. You could hear the tannoy and the bikes going past – it was brilliant. He was shouting, 'Tony your son's coming now', and you could hear the exhaust and everything, and he was telling me, 'He's won, he's won.' Absolutely great that was."[50]

In 2000 Michael Rutter, the latest member of the elite North West 200 hat-trick winners' club. His father Tony is already a long-standing member.

After finishing runner-up to Callum Ramsey in three previous 250cc races, John McGuinness finally added a North West 200

victory to a career tally that already included a British championship, as well as wins at Daytona and the Isle of Man. The early stages of the race had seen McGuinness involved in a tense three-cornered battle with Ramsey and Ian Lougher. With McGuinness already breaking clear, Ramsey was forced to settle for the bottom step on the podium after an excursion up the slip road at Church Corner. McGuinness crossed the line, his arms high in the air in celebration, ten seconds clear of second-place finisher Lougher.

The production race had developed into a tough five-man scrap by Metropole on lap two. Then, in a blink, they were three, after Iain Duffus lost control on the brakes, crashing out and taking race leader David Jeffries with him. On the final time through Ballysally roundabout, Jim Moodie held a ten-yard lead over Richard Britton and Adrian Archibald and seemed to have the race in his pocket. It was not to be. Britton took the lead at Portrush and held off the challenges that came thick and fast on the coast road to score the biggest win of his career.

The 125cc race will live long in the memories of those who

Alastair McCook

were there as an epic four-lapper that any one of four riders could have won right up to the last corner. It also holds a special place in the minds of the road-racing public as the last great shoulder-to-shoulder battle between the Dunlop brothers. The lead changed several times on every lap with all four having spells in front. Paul Robinson, son of Armoy Armada racer Mervyn, seemed headed for a famous win as he headed his two famous uncles and Ian Lougher on the run out of Coleraine for the final time. Lougher made his experience count, moving ahead at Portrush and holding Robinson and Robert Dunlop at bay, to win his second 125cc North West 200 in two years.

"I didn't realise it was the last lap. People may think that's not much of an excuse, but when it's tight at the North West in a race like that, it's won and lost on the coast road. If I'd known it was the last lap, I certainly wouldn't have finished third; I could have ridden more defensively."[51]

The meeting had written another historic episode in the story of the event that came into existence over a lifetime ago. The day had produced new heroes, and in front of his devoted home fans, Joey Dunlop showed flashes of the genius talent that took him to one last great week at the 2000 Isle of Man TT. In the last years of the twentieth century, motor-cycle road racing

Eventual winner Ian Lougher leads the Dunlop family through Black Hill during the hotly disputed 2000 125cc race. Behind Joey 3 (and Robert 2), is their nephew Paul Robinson.

Alastair McCook

had lost some of its finest, most talented riders. The list including Simon Beck, Owen McNally, Donny Robinson and Gary Dynes, all tragically killed in racing accidents, had been body blows to the sport. Joey Dunlop's death, after crashing his little 125cc Honda on a wet Sunday afternoon in the Estonian capital, Tallin, sent shock waves around the world. His fans paid silent tribute in their tens of thousands at what amounted to a state funeral for the greatest sportsman who ever came out of Ireland. Joey Dunlop, as well as being a damn fine motor-cycle road racer, was a hero who did not let you down.

There was no North West 200 in 2001 but a parade of some of the all-time greats on the course in May made the mouth water all the same. Jim Redman leads Giacomo Agostini, Tommy Robb, Ralph Bryans, Robert Dunlop and Brian Reid.

By the time May came round again in 2001, everyday early summer traffic hummed along the coast road. People walked their dogs, ate ice creams, took pictures of each other in the sunshine, and stopped to look at a bunch of exotic-looking motorcycles that wound their way towards Portstewart.

The dreaded plague of foot-and-mouth disease that tore the heart out of the country's rural community in 2001 brought with it restrictions on everyday life events that had come to be taken for granted. As a result, there was no North West 200 to enjoy. Instead, race day was marked with a festival of motor-cycle entertainment that brought some of the great names together to ride in formation on a parade lap along the winding ribbon of road above the cliff tops. Among them were men like Giacomo Agostini, Sammy Millar, Robert Dunlop, Tommy Robb, Jim Redman, Dick Creith and little Ralph Bryans; men who have given us some of our finest memories, who have made the heart beat a little faster, combining grace and danger on a howling racing motor cycle, on the black stuff, between the houses and hedges beside the seaside.

Alastair McCook

There are many more great days to come on the Triangle Circuit in the years that lie ahead. This book tells the story of what has passed up to now, and in that history the name "Dunlop" has featured prominently. In 2002, another generation of Dunlops, William, Gary and Samuel, are all at the beginning of their racing careers, and Robert Dunlop remains a force to be reckoned with in 125cc racing. Do not be surprised if the family's tally of North West 200 wins keeps growing in the not so distant future.

NOTES

1 *Motor Cycle*, May 1973.
2 QUB: Queen's University Belfast.
3 From an interview with Charlie Williams, December 2000.
4 From an interview with Ray McCullough, October 2000.
5 *Motor Cycle*, 24 May 1975.
6 From an interview with Mick Grant, May 2000.
7 Charlie Williams, December 2000.
8 Ray McCullough, October 2000.
9 Mick Grant, May 2000.
10 From an interview with Tony Rutter, October 2000.
11 Ray McCullough, October 2000.
12 Ray McCullough, October 2000.
13 Mick Grant, May 2000.
14 Charlie Williams, December 2000.
15 Charlie Williams, December 2000.
16 Mick Grant, May 2000.
17 Charlie Williams, December 2000.
18 From an interview with Steve Cull, August 2000.
19 From an interview with Keith Heuwen, North West 200, May 2000.
20 Charlie Williams, December 2000.
21 Mick Grant, North West 200, May 2000.
22 Keith Heuwen, May 2000.
23 From an interview with Robert Dunlop, October 2001.
24 Steve Cull, August 2000.
25 Steve Cull, August 2000.
26 Robert Dunlop, October 2001.
27 Robert Dunlop, October 2001.
28 From an interview with Philip McCallan, North West 200, May 2000.
29 Robert Dunlop, October 2001.
30 Philip McCallan, May 2000.
31 Philip McCallan, May 2000.
32 Philip McCallan, May 2000.
33 Philip McCallan, May 2000.
34 Robert Dunlop, October 2001.
35 Philip McCallan, May 2000.
36 Philip McCallan, May 2000.
37 Philip McCallan, May 2000
38 Philip McCallan, May 2000.
39 From an interview with Michael Rutter, October 2000.
40 Michael Rutter, October 2000.
41 Philip McCallan, May 2000.
42 From an interview with the late Owen McNally, August 1997.
43 Robert Dunlop, October 2001.
44 From an interview with David Jeffries, October 2000.
45 Michael Rutter, October 2000.
46 Philip McCallan, May 2000.
47 David Jeffries, October 2000.
48 Michael Rutter, October 2000.
49 Michael Rutter, October 2000.
50 Tony Rutter, October 2000.
51 Robert Dunlop, October 2001.

Clifford McLean

Tony Rutter

Awaiting the start of practice, 1979.

To the road-racing public, Tony Rutter established himself as a huge favourite via a string of wins on the Classic circuits in a career spanning three decades. Rutter began his racing career on a 350cc BSA Gold Star at Brands Hatch in 1962. He made his North West 200 debut in 1970 and scored the first of his ten victories on the track in 1973, with the first of his TT successes coming later that year in the Junior. He makes no secret of his dislike of the chicanes that have been incorporated into the

Triangle Circuit in recent years and his love for the "old" original course.

In the early years, Tony Rutter made the trip across the Irish Sea accompanied by his technical mentor, the renowned engineer Roy Graham. Graham had been a collaborator of Sir Alex Issigonnis, the legendary designer of the Mini. In the late 1960s, Graham and Issigonnis pooled their collective technical know-how to design a frame for Rutter's TDIC Yamaha, after he had constant problems with the factory-designed frame cracking.

An offer of a works ride from the JPS Norton team saw Rutter turn professional in 1972, and over the years his name was synonymous with factories such as Yamaha, Honda and, in the early 1980s, Ducati. After adding the TT Formula Two world title to his c.v., Tony Rutter was seriously injured in an accident at Montjuïc Park, Barcelona, in 1985. Although he raced again, Tony

Rutter never came close to recapturing the glory days. However, he has had the pleasure of witnessing his son Michael's North West 200 and Isle of Man TT successes in recent years.

Rutter shows his trademark style and pace, rounding Black Hill, 1974.

Clifford McLean

Clifford McLean

Tom Herron

Tom Herron had spent years as a highly successful privateer on the Grands Prix circuits before breaking into the big time as 500cc works Suzuki rider in 1979.

The thirty-year-old from Newcastle, Co Down, made his racing début in 1965 and won his first international event, the 350cc race, at the 1970 North West 200. The years of hard work and travelling thousands of miles around the world's Grands Prix circuits on a shoe-string budget with his wife Andrea, sister of works Norton star Peter Williams, paid off with fourth place finishes in the 250cc and 350cc world rankings in 1976. As well as scoring 350cc third-place finishes at the Finnish and Swedish Grands Prix, Herron won the 350cc Isle of Man TT.

The following year, Herron finished runner-up to works Yamaha rider Takazumi Katayama in the 350cc World Championship, and returned to score a 250/350cc double victory on home soil at the 1977 Ulster Grand Prix. Herron delighted the home fans at the 1978 British Grand Prix with runner-up finishes in the 250cc and 350cc classes, but as a privateer was struggling against the works might of Kawasaki's

Leading Grand and Rutter through Primrose Hill, 1978.

Kork Ballington and Kenny Roberts riding the factory Yamahas.

Despite a brace of wins at the 1978 North West 200, Herron will be forever remembered for his absolute course record of 127.63 mph set on the third lap of the superbike race, an achievement that remains the fastest lap ever recorded on any British Isles circuit.

Tom Herron came to race on the Triangle Circuit for the fateful 1979 meeting, holding fourth place in the 500cc World Championship. Injuries that included third-degree burns to his arms and a fractured thumb, sustained during a crash in practice at Jarama, had ruled him out of the Spanish Grand Prix, but he was passed fit to race at the North West 200. His death, after crashing out at the last bend on the last lap of the last race of the day, left a void in racing that has never been filled. His memory lives on, but wherever men gather to talk about or to race motor cycles, Tom Herron is still badly missed.

Alastair McCook

On the grid, 1994.

oey Dunlop

Many thousands of words have been written about Joey Dunlop during his lifetime and since his shocking death on 2 July 2000. Despite them all, he remains an enigma. Where do you begin to describe a career that was so extraordinary, how do you sum up a man who was a legend?

The books will tell you that William Joseph Dunlop began his racing career in 1969 on a Triumph Tiger Cub and that in the years that followed he won twenty-six Isle of Man TT titles, twenty-four victories at the Ulster Grand Prix, thirteen wins at the North West 200, *Motor Cycle News* Man of the Year in 1985 and 2000,

With rival Alan Patterson on Mill Road, 250cc practice, 1999.

Alastair McCook

and was crowned Formula One World Champion five times between 1982 and 1986. In his final season, he started the North West 200 superbike races from pole position, won his third Isle of Man TT hat-trick (Formula One, 125cc and 250cc) and on his final lap recorded the fastest lap, 123.87 mph, of his TT career. He was forty-eight years old at the time.

The statistics on their own are mind-boggling, but they only tell part of the remarkable story. He was a mechanical genius. A humanitarian who risked his own neck and thought nothing of it, making solo trips to bring essential aid to the under-fed and uncared-for children of eastern Europe. No one deserved the MBE, awarded for services to motor cycling in 1985, and the OBE, awarded for his charity work in 1996, more. To the entire nation he was a hero, the people's champion, a down-to-earth superstar who never moved away from or forgot his roots.

Exiting the start/finish chicane on John Harris's 600cc Honda, 2000.

When others wrote him off after he was seriously injured at Brands Hatch in 1989,

Alastair McCook

Alastair McCook

he came back as a winner to prove them wrong. He set a pace in atrocious conditions that no one could live with to win the 1998 Lightweight TT, two weeks after sustaining injuries at the Tandragee 100 that would have kept any other mortal in bed. He did it all with few words and a smile, and backed out of the media spotlight at the first opportunity. He was a one-off, a man blessed with an abundance of talent and a taste for the quiet life. We will never see another like him.

I was privileged to have seen him race, to have stood more times than not, in the incessant Irish rain, watching for a glimpse of the bellowing Honda in full cry, with Dunlop wrapped gracefully around its flowing lines, the long hair trailing from beneath the famous yellow helmet. It was quite simply one of the greatest sights in sport.

With long term friend, mentor and manager Davy Wood.

Alastair McCook

Philip McCallan

*Philip McCallan in 1992
– also see p149.*

The sight of Philip McCallan at full cry on a Honda RC30 or RC45, all elbows and knees, shoulder skimming the grass banks and hedges, rider and machine on the absolute limit, was at once frightening and exhilarating.

The enfant terrible of motor-cycle road racing began his career on a TZ 125cc Yamaha at Aghadowey airfield circuit in August 1984. McCallan's début ended when he slid off in the wet, but the talented beginner persevered, recording his first road-race win riding a 250cc Rotax at the Cookstown 100 in 1987. A brace of wins at the 1988

Manx Grand Prix was followed with three national titles by the end of the year.

The big break came the following year with Honda drafting McCallan into the factory team as a replacement for the injured Joey Dunlop at the Isle of Man TT. In the years that followed, McCallan repaid the Japanese giant's faith with a string of high-profile road-race wins. His achievements are simply unique. No other rider had won more than three races in a day at the North West 200 until Philip racked up five wins from six starts at the

1992 meeting. He followed up his 1993 Ulster Grand Prix hat-trick with five wins at the 1994 meeting, and returned to Dundrod to repeat the achievement in 1996.

Whilst other names may head Philip McCallan on the list of the all-time great TT riders, no one has equalled his 1996 record-breaking performance that took him to four race wins in one week. On the way to notching up eight TT titles, McCallan completed thirty-eight 120+ mph laps around the unforgiving Isle of Man mountain circuit.

The dedication, commitment and spectacular on-the-limit style brought success, but it came at a price. The high-speed crashes, year after year, including two major offs in 1997 at the TT and then the Ulster Grand Prix had taken their toll. Philip sat out the 1998 season, nursing a serious back injury and plotting a comeback. He returned to his home track, the Tandragee 100, at the beginning of the 1999 season to win on the mighty F1 R1 Yamaha. It would be his last win on closed public roads. Still far from fit, he struggled through the North West 200 before taking on the rigorous test of the TT's 37.75 miles. It was simply too much to ask; after finishing third in the Production TT, McCallan withdrew from the Senior race and announced his retirement soon afterwards.

A near calamity in the 1995 250cc practice forced McCallan to start from the back row of the grid, although he still finished first – also see p156.

Alastair McCook

Alastair McCook

Robert Dunlop

Fourteen international North West 200 wins including four hat-tricks earn Robert Dunlop the distinction of being the most successful rider to grace the Triangle Circuit. But for his horrific accident in the Isle of Man in 1994, there is little doubt that Dunlop's tally would be higher. After years spent fighting back to fitness and fighting against officialdom for his right to compete, Robert Dunlop returned to the 125cc podium with a stirring ride to third place in 2000. His story is one of tenacity against all the odds. His struggle to emerge as a star in his own right and not just as the younger brother of a road-racing legend took years, demonstrating the skill and courage that established him at the top of the sport by 1994. His single-minded, never-say-die comeback from injury defied medical expertise and confounded the experts who said he was finished. Robert Dunlop is quite simply one of the bravest sportsmen this island has ever produced.

The first step on the road to success came with a win in the 1983 Manx Grand Prix, Newcomers Junior race. Dunlop headed home an illustrious top three that included Steve Hislop and Ian Lougher to claim one of the few trophies that did not already carry the Dunlop name. His first North West 200 win in 1986 was followed in the years ahead by TT and Ulster Grand Prix success, a British 125cc title and a berth in the JPS works Norton team.

But the glory days came at a high price. A crash at the thirteenth Milestone during the 1986 TT resulted in a catalogue of injuries that included a punctured lung, broken ribs, a broken shoulder blade, cheek and jaw. A major off at Monza in 1992 was followed the following year by another TT prang in practice at Waterworks. The accident in the 1994 TT, exiting Ballaugh village during the Formula One race, robbed Dunlop of the chance to move onto the world stage as a superbike rider. It very nearly cost him his life.

There are those who suggest that Robert Dunlop's true vocation was as a 125cc rider, and that if he had concentrated on the class, a career in Grand Prix racing would surely have lay ahead. It is exclusively on the smaller 125cc machinery that he now plies his trade, notching up an emotional victory in the 1998 Ultra Lightweight TT as well as returning to Dundrod as a winner. It would be a foolish man who would bet against the prospect of Robert Dunlop standing on top of the North West 200 rostrum, at least one more time.

ORGANISATION OF THE NORTH WEST 200

Each year's North West 200 – bigger, better and faster than the one before – is the end product of twelve months' hard work. A small band of members from the Coleraine and District Motor Club, all unpaid volunteers, ensure that Ireland's biggest sporting event runs like clockwork.

Annually a crowd of between 100,000 and 150,000 spectators travel from corners of the British Isles and beyond to line the 8.9-mile circuit, many only feet from the 190 mph superbikes. On the day, the North West 200 draws a crowd three times greater than that attending the Isle of Man TT festival. Every vantage point is taken up hours before the action begins.

Weeks before the event takes place a band of hard-working club members begin the task of preparing the course, painting braking lines on the road, painting the kerbs at the edge of the road, erecting corner boards, ensuring bales and air fencing are in place; the task is never ending. It is a logistical nightmare co-ordinating volunteers, the DOE who do their utmost to ensure that the public roads circuit is in first-class condition for racing, the police, the local council, and the Northern Ireland Tourist Board. On race day over 700 marshals are on duty as well as medical personnel, fire control and communications workers.

The cost of running one of Europe's biggest motorcycle events doesn't come cheap. No one pays to watch the awesome spectacle, and the money generated from programme sales and car parking charges falls well short of the conservative estimate of £200,000 needed to put on one of the greatest shows on the planet. The key to underwriting the hefty bill is to find a generous sponsor. Over the years sponsorship has come from a variety of local businesses who helped the organisers make ends meet. In 1993 Coca Cola signed up as the North West 200's main sponsor, injecting a much-needed cash boost that guaranteed the entries have continued to flood in from the World's top road racers.

The North West 200 is undoubtedly the result of a team effort, but if one individual were to take their share of credit it has to be Billy Nutt MBE. Nutt's efforts as Clerk of the Course, a position he relinquished in 2000, have made his name synonymous with the meeting. His reputation for professionalism and getting things done, sometimes in very tough circumstances, is built on his years of devotion and dedication to the sport. Without the efforts of Billy Nutt and the Coleraine and District Motor Club it is unlikely that the North West 200 would have grown and developed to its place as one of the great races in the international road-racing calendar.

MOST SUCCESSFUL MANUFACTURERS

Manufacturer	Number of Wins	Years
Yamaha	66	1968–2000
Honda	62	1964–2000
Norton	38	1930–91
Excelsior	10	1930–49
Suzuki	10	1970–89
Rudge	8	1929–34
Ducati	8	1959–97
Aprillia	7	1989–97
AJS	7	1938–62
Velocette	5	1934–52

MOST SUCCESSFUL RIDERS

Rider Name	Number of Wins	Years
Robert Dunlop	14	1986–94
Joey Dunlop	13	1979–88
Philip McCallan	11	1991–97
Tony Rutter	10	1973–82
Michael Rutter	7	1999–2000
Steve Cull	6	1980–88
Woolsey Coulter	5	1989–98
Mick Grant	5	1978–82
John Williams	5	1974–77
Tommy Robb	5	1959–65
Ian Simpson	5	1995–98
Arthur Wheeler	5	1951–62

RESULTS *1929–2000*

Results given in the following sequence: rider name, machine, handicap and actual time.
Where information is not given it is unknown.
No races were held in 1940–46, 1948, 1963, 1972 and 2001.

1929

1. W J McCracken - 348cc Velocette - 27 Minutes - 3 Hr 8 Min 35 Sec
North West 200 Perpetual Trophy and £20
2. M McQuigg - 246cc Zenith - 51 Minutes - 3 Hr 39 Min 50 Sec
3. W H T Meageen - 346 cc JAP - 18 Minutes - 3 Hr 7 Min 12 Sec
4. J W Shaw - 349cc Norton - 19 Minutes - 3 Hr 10 Min 14 Sec
5. E G Lamney - 346 Rex Acme - 38 Minutes - 3 Hr 33Min 4 Sec
6. A McIntyre - 174cc Abingdon K D - Two laps and 53 Minutes - 4 Hr 49 Min 6 Sec
7. G E Nott - 499cc Rudge - 30 Seconds - 2 Hrs 58 Min 41 Sec
8. J G Burney - 346cc Royal Enfield - 22 Minutes - 3 Hr 29 Min 25 Sec

Fastest time in 250cc class M McQuigg   3 Hr 39 Min 50 Sec
Portstewart Cup and £2

Fastest time in 350cc class W H T Meageen 3 Hr 7 Min 12 Sec
Portrush Cup and £2

Fastest time in 500cc class G E Nott 2 Hr 58 Min 41 Sec
Coleraine Cup and £2

Fastest Lap Percy "Tim" Hunt 490cc Norton 9 min 23 sec 70.53 mph

1930

500cc

1. G E Nott - 499cc Rudge - 2Hr 55 Min 55 Sec - 67.98 mph
2. P Walls - 499cc Rudge - 3 Hr 0 Min 53 Sec - 66.12 mph
3. S Woods - 490cc Norton - 3 Hr 2 Min 27 Sec - 65.55 mph
Fastest Lap H G Tyrell Smith 499cc Rudge 74.1 mph

350cc

1. P Hunt - 350cc Norton - 3 Hr 0 Min 12 Sec - 66.37 mph
2. J W Shaw - 350cc Velocette - 3 Hr 3 Min 24 Sec - 65.21 mph
3. J G Burney - 346cc Royal Enfield - 3 Hr 12 Min 20 Sec - 62.1 mph
Fastest Lap   P Hunt 350cc Norton   72.48 mph

250cc

1. E Fernihough - 172c Excelsior - 3 Hr 42 Min 27 Sec - 53.76 mph
2. M McQuigg - 246 Zeneith Jap - 3 Hr 49 Min 55 Sec - 52.01 mph
Fastest Lap   W A Drummond O K Supreme 59.25 mph

HANDICAP

500cc

1. P Walls - Rudge - 20 Min
2. G E Nott - Rudge - Scratch
3. S Woods - Norton - Scratch

350cc

1. T Creighton - Excelsior - 20 Min
2. P Hunt - Norton - Scratch
3. J W Shaw - Velocette - 3 Min

250cc

1. E Fernohough - Excelsior
2. M McQuigg - Zeneith
No other finishers

1931

500cc

1. G E Nott - Rudge - 2Hrs 43 Min 53 Sec - 72.97 mph
2. S Woods - Norton - 2 Hrs 48 Min 27 Sec - 71.04 mph
3. W H T Meagen - Norton - 2 Hrs 49 Min 10 Sec - 70.70 mph
Fastest Lap S Woods Norton 8 Min 49 Sec 75.36 mph

350cc

1. G W Walker - Rudge - 2 Hrs 57 Min 28 Sec - 67.39 mph
2. H Taggart - Rudge - 3 Hrs 1 Min 57 Sec - 65.55 mph
3. E Brooks - Raleigh - 3 Hrs 3 Min 46 Sec - 65.08 mph
Fastest Lap G W Walker Rudge   9 Min 37 Sec 69.09 mph

250cc

1. E C Fernihough - Excelsior - 3 Hrs 20 Min 48 Sec - 59.56 mph
2. C Taylor - O K Supreme - 3 Hrs 25 Min 1 Sec - 58.88 mph
No other finishers
Fastest Lap H G T Smith Rudge 9 Min 56 Sec 66.89 mph

HANDICAP

500cc

1. W J McCracken - Norton - 10 Min
2. G E Nott - Rudge - Scratch
3. W H T Meagen - Norton - 4 Min

350cc

1. E Brooks - Raleigh - 14 Min
2. H Taggart - Rudge - 12 Min
3. G W Walker - Rudge - Scratch

250cc

1. E C Fernihough - Excelsior - 5 Min
2. C Taylor - O K Supreme - 6 Min

1932

500cc

1. G E Nott - Rudge - 2 Hrs 37 Min 41 Sec - 75.84 mph
2. F J Drummond - Norton - 2 Hrs 46 Min 1 Sec - 72.03 mph
3. S Woods - Norton - 2 Hrs 46 Min 47 Sec - 71.75 mph
Fastest Lap G E Nott Rudge   8 Min 31 Sec 78.01 mph

350cc

1. W L Handley - Rudge - 2 Hrs 53 Min 45 Sec - 68.83 mph
2. H Pinnington - A J S - 2 Hrs 56 Min 27 Sec - 67.77 mph
3. R J Gray - Velocette - 3 Hrs 16 Min 46 Sec - 60.78 mph
Fastest Lap H G T Smith Rudge 9 Min 13 Sec 72.01 mph

250cc

E Fernihough - Excelsior - 3 Hrs 14 Min 10 Sec
No other finishers
Fastest Lap C H Manders 9 Min 56 Sec 66.89mph

HANDICAP

Open

1. H Pinnington - 32 Min
2. R J Gray - 40 Min
3. G E Nott - Scratch

500cc

F J Drummond - Norton - 8 Min

350cc

H Pinnington - A J S - 32 Min

250cc

E Fernihough - Excelsior - 30 Min

1933

500cc

1. S Woods - Norton - 2 Hrs 42 Min 27 Sec - 73.62 mph
2. M Mahoney - Rudge - 3 Hrs 9 Min 59 Sec - 62.95 mph
No other finishers
Fastest Lap S Woods Norton 8 Min 33 Sec 77.71 mph

350cc

1. P Hunt - Norton - 2 Hrs 47 Min 30 Sec - 71.4 mph
2. H Pinnington - A JS - 3 Hrs 0 Min 12 Sec - 66.37 mph
3. W Shaw - Norton - 3 Hrs 8 Min 10 Sec
Fastest Lap P Hunt Norton 8 Min 47 Sec 75.64 mph

250cc

1. J Woodside - Rudge - 3 Hrs 5 Min 12 Sec - 64.58 mph
2. E C Fernihough - Excelsior - 3 Hrs 28 Min 5 Sec - 57.48 mph
3. N A Robson O K - Supreme - 3 Hrs 32 Min 31 Sec - 56.2 mph
Fastest Lap C H Manders Rudge 9 Min 37 Sec 69.09 mph

HANDICAP

Open

1. P Hunt - 12 Min

2. J Woodside - 27 Min

3. M Mahoney - 31 Min

500cc

M Mahoney - 31 Min

350cc

H Pinnington

250cc

E Fernihough

1934

500cc

1. J Guthrie - Norton - 2 Hrs 28 Min 49 Sec - 80.37 mph
2. G E Nott - Rudge - 2 Hrs 35 Min 50 Sec - 76.75 mph
3. J H White - Norton - 2 Hrs 39 Min 41 Sec - 74.89 mph
Fastest Lap J Guthrie Norton   8 Min 5 Sec 82.16 mph

350cc

1. W F Rusk - Velocette - 2 Hrs 42 Min 25 Sec - 73.66 mph
2. J J O'Neill - Velocette - 2 Hrs 46 Min 11 Sec - 71.97 mph
3. H Pinnington - Norton - 2 Hrs 48 Min 9 Sec - 71.13 mph
Fastest Lap   W F Rusk Velocette   8 Min 47 Sec 75.68 mph

250cc

1. M McSorley - Rudge - 2 Hrs 59 Min 21 Sec - 66.69 mph
2. N Robson - Dunelt - 3 Hrs 4 Min 0 Sec - 65.0 mph
3. J Duncan - New Imperial - 3 Hrs 4 Min 5 Sec - 64.97 mph
Fastest Lap   G Burney Moto Guzzi   9 Min 28 Sec 70.19 mph

HANDICAP

Open

1. N Robson - 47 Min
2. J J O'Neill - 19 Min
3. J Guthrie - Scratch

500cc

J H White - 7 Min

350cc

J J O'Neill - 19 Min

250cc

J Duncan - 26 Min

1935

500cc

1. J Guthrie - Norton - 2 Hrs 31 Min 25 Sec - 78.99 mph
2. S B Darbishire - Norton - 2 Hrs 36 Min 17 Sec - 76.53 mph
3. H G T Smith - A J S - 2 Hrs 46 Min 5 Sec - 72.01 mph
Fastest Lap   J Guthrie Norton 8 Min 9 Sec 81.53 mph

350cc

1. W F Rusk - Norton - 2 Hrs 36 Min 55 Sec - 76.22 mph
2. H Taggart - Norton - 2 Hrs 45 Min 37 Sec - 72.21 mph
3. J Chambers - Norton - 2 Hrs 49 Min 35 Sec - 70.52 mph
Fastest Lap   W F Rusk Norton 8 Min 27 S sec 78.63 mph

250cc

1. C H Manders - Excelsior - 2 Hrs 56 Min 40 Sec - 67.69 mph
2. M McSorley - Rudge - 3 Hrs 0 Min 35 Sec - 66.23 mph
3. L G Martin - Python - 3 Hrs 17 Min 6 Sec - 60.68 mph
Fastest Lap C H Manders Excelsior and J G Burney Moto Guzzi 9 Min 31 Sec 69.82 mph

HANDICAP

Open

1. S B Darbishire - 15 Min
2. W F Rusk - 12 Min
3. H Taggart - 18 Min

500cc

J W Beevers - 15 Min

350cc

H Taggart - 18 Min

250cc

M McSorley - 29 Min

1936

500cc

1. J Guthrie - Norton - 2 Hrs 27 Min 9 Sec - 81.28 mph
2. J W Beevers - Norton - 2 Hrs 47 Min 52 Sec - 71.24 mph
Fastest Lap J Guthrie Norton 7 Min 53 Sec 84.28 mph

350cc

1. J H White - Norton - 2 Hrs 35Min 53 Sec - 76.73 mph
2. E R Thomas - Velocette - 2 Hrs 38 Min 20 Sec - 75.51 mph
3. H G T Smith - Excelsior - 2 Hrs 45 Min 52 Sec - 72.11 mph
Fastest Lap J H White Norton 8 Min 27 Sec 78.63 mph

250cc

1. C H Manders - Excelsior - 2 Hrs 57 Min 7 Sec - 67.52 mph
2. H Pinnington - Excelsior - 2 Hrs 59 Min 5 Sec - 66.78 mph
3. R Harris - Rudge - 3 Hrs 0 Min 13 Sec - 66.36 mph
Fastest Lap C H Manders Excelsior 9 Min 27 Sec 70.31 mph

HANDICAP

Open

1. J E Little
2. N B Pope
3. R Harris

500cc

J W Beevers

350cc

J E Little
250cc

R Harris

1937

500cc

1. J Guthrie - Norton - 2 Hrs 25 Min 32 Sec - 82.17 mph
2. F L Frith - Norton - 2 Hrs 27 Min 13 Sec - 81.24 mph
3. J McCreadie - Rudge - 2 Hrs 56 Min 11 Sec - 67.88 mph
Fastest Lap J Guthrie Norton 7 Min 54 Sec 84. 106 mph

350cc

1. J H White - Norton - 2 Hrs 36 Min 33 Sec - 76.47 mph
2. S Wood - Excelsior - 2 Hrs 39Min 11 Sec - 75.13 mph
3. H G T Smith - Excelsior - 2Hrs 40 Min 53 Sec - 74.45 mph
Fastest Lap J H White Norton 8 Min 25 Sec 78.94 mph

250cc

1. S V Smith - Excelsior - 3 Hrs 2Min 57 Sec - 65.37 mph
2. G McAdam - New Imperial - 3 Hrs 3 Min 9 Sec - 65.3 mph
Fastest Lap C H Manders Excelsior 9 Min 17 Sec   71.57 mph

HANDICAP

Open

1. J E Little - 23 Min
2. G McAdam - 41 Min
3. R Pennycock Norton - 27 Min

500cc

J McCreadie Rudge

350cc

J F R Martin

250cc

G McAdam

1938

500cc

1. J Moore - Norton - 2 Hrs 45Min 56 Sec - 71.22 mph
2. E Lyons - Triumph - 2 Hrs 52 Min 11 Sec - 69.46 mph
3. C D Foord - Norton - 3 Hrs 5 Min 2 Sec - 64.64 mph
Fastest Lap S Woods Velocette 8 Min 50 Sec 75.22 mph

350cc

1. R Foster - A J S - 2 Hrs 42 Min 37 Sec - 69.46 mph
2. A J Bell - Norton - 2 Hrs 50 Min 10 Sec - 66.38 mph
3. J B Moss - Norton - 2 Hrs 50 Min 16 Sec - 66.34 mph
Fastest Lap A R Foster A J S 9 Min 5 Sec 73.14 mph

250cc

1. H G T Smith - Excelsior - 2 Hrs 44 Min 57 Sec - 64.54 mph
2. D Parkinson - Excelsior - 2 Hrs 44 Min 57 Sec - 62.6 mph
3. H Hartley - Rudge - 2 Hrs 52 Min 42 Sec - 61.56 mph
Fastest Lap H Hartley Rudge 10 Min 3 Sec 66.11 mph

HANDICAP

Open

1. A E Moule - Norton - 22 Min
2. E Lyons - unknown - 22 Min
3. H Carter - Norton - 20 Min

500cc

E Lyons

350cc

A E Moule

250cc

H Hartley

1939

500cc

E Lyons - Triumph - 2 Hrs 39 Min 34 Sec - 74.95 mph
Fastest Lap S Woods Velocette 8 Min 1 Sec 82.88 mph

350cc

1. J E Little - Velocette - 2 Hrs 30 Min 20 Sec - 75.14 mph
2. L D Gilbert - Norton - 2 Hrs 47 Min 6 Sec - 67.6 mph
3. C R Clarke - Norton - 2 Hrs 51 Min 35 Sec - 65.83 mph
Fastest Lap W F Rusk Velocette and J E Little Velocette 8 Min 33 Sec 77.71 mph

250cc

1. D Parkinson - Excelsior - 2 Hrs 37 Min 44 Sec - 67.4 mph
2. C Tattersall - C T S - 2 Hrs 38 Min 49 Sec - 66.94 mph
3. A Glendinning - Excelsior - 2 Hrs 43 Min 58 Sec - 64.84 mph
Fastest Lap D Parkinson 9 Min 22 Sec 70.93 mph

HANDICAP

Open

1. I Drysdale - Rudge - 28 Min
2. L D Gilbert - 26 Min
3. L E Little - 6 Min

500cc

E Lyons

350cc

L D Gilbert

250cc

I Drysdale

1947

500cc

1. A J Bell - Norton - 2 Hrs 42 Min 17 Sec - 73.96 mph
2. R McCandless - Norton - 2 Hrs 50 Min 23 Sec - 70.19 mph
3. B Meli - Norton - 2 Hrs 50 Min25 Sec - 70.18 mph
Fastest Lap A J Bell Norton 8 Min 22 Sec 79.41 mph

350cc

1. M Templeton - Norton - 2 Hrs 46 Min 3 Sec - 68.03 mph
2. J E C Purnell - Norton - 2 Hrs 47 Min 13 Sec - 67.55 mph
3. A E Moule - Norton - 2 Hrs 47 Min 14 Sec - 67.54 mph
Fastest Lap E Lyons Norton 8 Min 43 Sec 76.226 mph

250cc

1. P Gill - Excelsior - 2 Hrs 41 Min 32 Sec - 65.81 mph
2. R J B Drinkwater - Excelsior - 2 Hrs 51 Min 8 Sec - 62.12 mph
3. J A Dickson - Excelsior - 2 Hrs 59 Min 55 Sec - 59.75 mph
Fastest Lap P Gill Excelsior 9 Min 36 Sec 69.212 mph

HANDICAP

Open

1. B Meli - 21 Min
2. M Templeton - 16 Min
3. P Gill - 11 Min

500cc

B Meli 21 - Min

350cc

T H Turner

250cc

J A Dickson

1949

500cc

1. A J Bell - Norton - 2 Hrs 23 Min 53 Sec - 83.12 mph
2. J Lockett - Norton - 2 Hrs 24 Min 47 Sec - 82.6 mph
3. R McCandless - Norton - 2Hrs 36 Min 0 Sec - 76.66 mph
Fastest Lap A J Bell Norton 7 Min 46 Sec 85.55 mph

350cc

1. H L Daniell - Norton - 2 Hrs 20 Min 25 Sec - 80.44 mph
2. F L Frith - Velocette - 2 Hrs 20 Min 25.5 Sec - 80.45 mph
3. G E Duke - Norton - 2 Hrs 23 Min 47 Sec - 78.56 mph
Fastest Lap F L Frith Velocette 8 Min 8 Sec 81.69 mph

250cc

1. H Kirby - Excelsior - 2 Hrs 40 Min - 52 Sec
2. C Tattersall - C T S - 2Hrs 42 Min 15 Sec - 66.51 mph
3. W G Dehaney - Excelsior - 2 Hrs 44 Min 35 Sec - 64.59 mph
Fastest Lap J McKimm Excelsior 9 Min 29 Sec 70.06 mph

HANDICAP

Open

1. A J Glazebrook - 17 Min
2. H L Daniell - Scratch
3. F L Frith - Scratch

500cc

R Knox - 17 Min

350cc

G E Duke - 3Min

250cc

C Tattersall - 9.5 Min

1950

500cc

1. A J Bell - Norton - 2Hrs 19 Min 31 Sec - 85.723 mph
2. J Lockett - Norton - 2 Hrs 19 Min 31.2 Sec - 85.722 mph
3. H Hinton - Norton - 2 Hrs 24 Min 33 Sec - 82.74 mph
Fastest Lap A J Bell Norton 7 Min 30 Sec 88.59 mph

350cc

1. G E Duke - Norton - 2 Hrs 16 Min 51 Sec - 82.54 mph
2. A F Wheeler - Velocette - 2 Hrs 23 Min 51 Sec - 78.52 mph
3. A J Glazebrook - A J S - 2 Hrs 26 Min 18 Sec - 77.21 mph
Fastest Lap G E Duke Norton7 Min 58 Sec 83.4 mph

250cc

1. R A Mead - Velocette - 2 Hrs 26 Min 58 Sec - 72.34 mph
2. A E Shaw - Norton - 2 Hrs 34 Min 4 Sec - 69.0 mph
3. J McKimm - Excelsior - 2 Hrs 37 Min 25 Sec - 67.53 mph
Fastest Lap R A Mead Velocette 8 Min 57 Sec 74.23 mph

HANDICAP

Open

1. W A Whitehead
2. A W McGaffin
3. R T Matthews

500cc

A J Bell - 1 Min

350cc

W A Whitehead - 21 Min

250cc

R A Mead - 11.5 Min

1951

500cc

1. G E Duke - Norton - 2 Hrs 14 Min 49 Sec - 88.71 mph
2. J Lockett Norton - 2 Hrs 19 Min 47 Sec - 85.56 mph
3. R Dale - Norton - 2 Hrs 25 Min 46 Sec
Fastest Lap G E Duke Norton 7 Min 12 Sec

350cc

1. R Dale - Norton - 2 Hrs 22 Min 53 Sec - 83.7 mph
2. J Lockett - Norton - 2 Hrs 22 Min 54 Sec - 83.69 mph
3. R H Sherry - AJS - 2 Hrs 29 Min 5 Sec - 80.22 mph
Fastest Lap G E Duke Norton 7 Min 27 Sec 89.19 mph

250cc

1. A Wheeler - Velocette - 2 Hrs 27 Min 50 Sec - 71.91 mph
2. D Andrews - Velocette - 2 Hrs 34 Min 39 Sec - 68.74 mph
3. F Purslow - Norton - 2 Hrs 38 Min 1 Sec - 67.28 mph
Fastest Lap A Wheeler Velocette 8 Min 55 Sec

HANDICAP

Open (500cc & 250cc)

1. G Proctor - Norton
2. J Hayes - 348cc AJS
3. R H Sherry - 348ccc AJS

Open (350cc)

1. R H Sherry - AJS
2. C G Griffiths - AJS
3. S Anderton - AJS

500cc

1. G Proctor - Norton
2. J Hayes - 348cc AJS
3. R H Sherry - 348cc AJS

350cc

1. R H Sherry - AJS
2. C G Griffiths - AJS
3. S Anderton - AJS

250cc

1. D Andrews - Velocette
2. A Wheeler - Velocette
3. W Dehaney - Excelsior

1952

500cc

1. K Arber - Norton - 2 Hrs 21 Min 10 Sec - 84.72 mph
2. W A C McCandless - Norton - 2Hrs 24 Min 47 Sec - 82.61 mph
3. H Clark - Norton - 2 Hrs 31 Min 0 Sec - 79.2 mph
Fastest Lap I K Arber Norton 7 Min 26 Sec 89.38 mph

350cc

1. H A Pearce - Velocette - 2 Hrs 20 Min 0 Sec - 80.68 mph
2. A E Moule - Norton - 2 Hrs 21 Min 39 Sec
3. A C Taylor - Norton - 2 Hrs 23 Min 55 Sec - 78.49 mph
Fastest Lap H A Pearce Velocette 7 Min 56 Sec 83.573 mph

250cc

1. A Wheeler - Moto Guzzi - 2 Hrs 24 Min 7 Sec - 73.77 mph
2. D G Andrews - Excelsior - 2 Hrs 33 Min 28 Sec - 69.27 mph
3. J McCreadie - Excelsior - 2 Hrs 36 Min 2 Sec - 68.13 mph
Fastest Lap A Wheeler Moto Guzzi 8 Min 38 Sec 76.96 mph

HANDICAP

Open

1. I K Arber Norton - 10 Min
2. D C Birrell - 12 Min
3. H A Pearce - 7 Min

500cc

1. K Arber - Norton - 10 Min
2. W A C McCandless - Norton - 3.5 Min
3. H M Tonge - 12 Min

350cc

1. D C Birrell - 12 Min
2. H A Pearce - 7 Min
3. U S Gate

250cc

1. D G Andrews - 14 Min
2. J McCreadie - 16 Min
3. A Wheeler - 1 Min

1953

500cc

1. S Lawton - Norton - 2 Hrs 8 Min 27 Sec - 93.01 mph
2. K Kavanagh - Norton - 2 Hrs 8 Min 35 Sec - 92.92 mph
3. R Armstrong - Gilera - 2 Hrs 11 Min 32 Sec - 90.83 mph
Fastest Lap S Lawton Norton 6 Min 54 Sec 96.2 mph

350cc

1. R McIntyre - AJS - 2 Hrs 9 Min 54 Sec - 86.86 mph
2. H A Pearce - Velocette - 2 Hrs 10 Min 41 Sec - 86.34 mph
3. G L Patterson - AJS - 2 Hrs 15 Min 58 Sec - 82.99 mph
Fastest Lap Ray Amm Norton 7 Min 30 Sec 88.5 mph

250cc

1. A Wheeler - Moto Guzzi - 2 Hrs 19 Min 7 Sec - 76.34 mph
2. D G Andrews - Excelsior - 2 Hrs 21Min 45 Sec - 74.92 mph
3. F Purslow - Velocette - 2 Hrs 22Min 10 Sec - 74.7 mph
Fastest Lap A Wheeler Moto Guzzi 8Min 29 Sec 78.24 mph

HANDICAP

Open

1. R McIntyre - 5 Min
2. T H Turner - 19.5 Min
3. H A Pearce - 5 Min

500cc

1. T H Turner - 19.5 Min
2. R Knox - 18 Min
3. T B N Smith - 21 Min

350cc

1. R McIntyre - 5 Min
2. H A Pearce - 5 Min
3. G L Patterson - 6 Min

250cc

1. D G Andrews - 16 Min
2. F Purslow - 16 Min
3. W Billington - 19 Min

1954

500

1. R Armstrong - Gilera - 2 Hrs 8 Min 44 Sec - 92.81 mph
2. R McIntyre - Matchless - 2 Hrs 10 Min 47 Sec - 91.35 mph
3. L Carter - Norton - 2 Hrs 8 Min 58 Sec - 87.49 mph*
*Completed 17 laps
Fastest Lap G E Duke Gilera 6 Min 49 Sec 97.37 mph

350cc

1. D Ennett - AJS - 2 Hrs 10 Min 51 Sec - 86.23 mph
2. H A Pearce - Velocette - 2 Hrs 12 Min 23 Sec - 85.23 mph
3. R Allison - Norton - 2 Hrs 12 Min 54 Sec - 84.9 mph
Fastest Lap R Allison Norton 7 Min 34 Sec 87.72 mph

250cc

1. A Wheeler - Moto Guzzi - 2 Hrs 14 Min 22 Sec - 79.04 mph
2. W J Maddrick - Moto Guzzi - 2 Hrs 18 Min 39 Sec - 71.81 mph*
3. W Ferguson - Excelsior - 2 Hrs 18 Min 40 Sec - 71.8 mph*
*Completed 15 laps
Fastest Lap A Wheeler Moto Guzzi 8 Min 6 Sec 81.94 mph

HANDICAP

Open

1. V T Williams - 19Min
2. R B Rensen - 17 Min
3. J M Bowen - 14 Min

500cc

1. J J Wood - 15 Min
2. K W Swallow - 19 Min
3. E W L Hunt - 16 Min

350cc

1. V T Williams - 19 Min
2. R B Rensen - 17 Min
3. J M Bowen - 14 Min

250cc

1. W A Martin - 30 Min
2. W Ferguson - 15 Min

1955

500cc

1. G E Duke - Gilera - 2 Hrs 2 Min 26 Sec - 97.6 mph
2. H R Armstrong - Gilera - 2 Hrs 4 Min 39 Sec - 95.85 mph
3. J Brett - Norton - 2 Hrs 7 Min 40 Sec - 93.58 mph
Fastest Lap G E Duke Gilera 6 Min 39 Sec 99.98 mph

350cc

1. J J Wood - BSA - 2 Hrs 11 Min 2 Sec - 86.11 mph
2. R Brown - AJS - 2 Hrs 13 Min 42 Sec - 84.40 mph
3. R W Herron - BSA - 2Hrs 15 Min 55 Sec - 83.02 mph
Fastest Lap JJ Wood BSA 7 Min 34 Sec 87.72 mph

250cc

1. A Lyons - NSU - 2 Hrs 18 Min 6 Sec - 76.9 mph
2. H Kirby - Velocette - 2 Hrs 21 Min 12 Sec - 75.21 mph
3. J E Herron - BSA - 2 Hrs 19 Min 23 Sec - 71.43 mph*
*Completed 15 laps
Fastest Lap A Lyons NSU 8 Min 20 Sec 79.65 mph

HANDICAP

Open

1. D May - BSA
2. M E Low - 499cc BSA
3. J Woods - Norton

500cc

1. M E Low 499cc - BSA
2. A R Sutherland - BSA
3. M P Roche - Norton

350cc

1. S Murray - AJS
2. R W Herron - BSA
3. R Brown - AJS

250cc

1. H Kirby - Velocette
2. J E Herron - BSA
3. W G Dehaney - Velocette

1956

500cc

1. R Anderson - Norton - 2 Hrs 9 Min 37 Sec - 92.18 mph
2. G B Tanner - Norton - 2 Hrs 12 Min 5 Sec - 90.45 mph
3. D G Chapman - Norton - 2 Hrs 14 Min 42 Sec - 88.70 mph
Fastest Lap R McIntyre Norton 6 Min 58 Sec 95.25 mph

350cc

1. D Ennett AJS - 2 Hrs 7 Min 13 Sec - 88.70 mph
2. R B Rensen - Norton - 2 Hrs 8 Min 4 Sec - 88.11 mph
3. A King - AJS - 2 Hrs 8 Min 5 Sec - 88.09 mph
Fastest Lap A King AJS 7 Min 19 Sec90.72 mph

250cc

1. S H Millar - NSU - 2 Hrs 1 Min 8 Sec - 87.67 mph
2. E Hinton - NSU - 2Hrs 1 Min 39 Sec - 87.30 mph
3. J E Herron - Norton - 2 Hrs 7 Min 3 Sec - 73.14 mph*
Completed 14 laps
Fastest Lap E Hinton NSU 7 Min 17 Sec 91.13 mph

HANDICAP

Open

1. R Anderson - 499cc Norton
2. J E Herron - 248cc Norton
3. E Hinton - 248cc NSU

500cc

1. R Anderson
2. W A Holmes - Norton
3. B Purslow - Norton

350cc

1. R B Rensen - Norton
2. A King - AJS
3. V T Williams - Norton

250cc

1. J E Herron - Norton
2. E Hinton - NSU

1957

500cc

1. J Brett - Norton - 2 Hrs 2 Min 58 Sec - 96.88 mph
2. K H Patrick - Norton - 2 Hrs 10 Min - 91.48 mph
3. J J Wood - Norton - 2 Hrs 3 Min 20 Sec - 91.23 mph*
Completed 17 laps
Fastest Lap J Brett Norton 6 Min 37 Sec 100.03 mph

350cc

1. R Anderson - Norton - 2 Hrs 1 Min 49 Sec - 93.13 mph
2. W A Holmes - Norton - 2 Hrs 6 Min 27 Sec - 88.98 mph
3. J Buchan - Norton - 2 Hrs 8 Min 13 Sec - 87.76 mph
Fastest Lap R Anderson Norton 6 Min 55 Sec 95.96 mph

250cc

1. S H Millar - NSU - 2 Hrs 1 Min 18 Sec - 87.30 mph
2. F Purslow - NSU - 2 Hrs 6 Min 32 Sec - 78.46 mph
3. H Kirby - Velocette - 2 Hrs 7 Min 37 Sec - 77.79 mph
Fastest Lap S H Millar NSU 7 Min 24 Sec 89.44 mph

HANDICAP

Open

1. R Anderson - Norton
2. W A Holmes - Norton
3. H Kirby - Velocette

500cc

1. K Patrick - Norton
2. A E Sutherland - BSA
3. W E Herron - Norton

350cc

1. W A Holmes - Norton
2. J Buchan - Norton
3. M T Brooks - Norton

250cc

1. H Kirby - Velocette
2. W G Dehaney - Velocette
3. I F Telfer - Norton

1958

500cc

1. J Brett - Norton - 2 Hrs 1 Min 20 Sec - 98.4 mph
2. R N Brown - Norton - 2 Hrs 7 Min 44 Sec - 93.47 mph
3. B J Daniels - Norton - 2 Hrs 1 Min 41 Sec - 92.66 mph*
*Completed 17 laps
Fastest Lap R McIntyre Norton 6 Min 30 Sec 102.04 mph

350cc

1. A King - Norton - 2 Hrs 1 Min 0 Sec - 93.19 mph
2. K Patrick - Norton - 2 Hrs 2 Min 2 Sec - 92.40 mph
3. W A Holmes - Norton - 2 Hrs 2 Min 26 Sec - 92.10 mph
Fastest Lap K Patrick Norton and W A Holmes Norton 6 Min 59 Sec 94.98 mph

250cc

1. S H Millar - NSU - 2 Hrs 1 Min 51 Sec - 87.09 mph
2. M Hailwood - NSU - 2Hrs 1 Min 52 Sec - 87.08 mph
3. T H Robb - NSU - 2 Hrs 2 Min 21 Sec - 86.74 mph
Fastest Lap T H Robb NSU 7Min 22 Sec 90.04 mph

HANDICAP

Open

1. B J Daniels - Norton
2. P D Chatterton - 348cc Norton
3. W J Sawford - 499cc Norton

500cc

1. B J Daniels - Norton
2. W J Sawford - 499cc Norton
3. J R Hurlstone - Norton

350cc

1. P D Chatterton - 348cc Norton
2. K H Patrick - Norton
3. W A Holmes - Norton

250cc

1. M Hailwood - NSU
2. R Gray Moto - Guzzi
3. D Pratt - GMV

1959

500cc

1. R McIntyre - Norton - 1 Hr 3 Min 59 Sec - 101.21 mph
2. P Middleton - Norton - 1 Hr 5 Min 45 Sec - 98.26 mph
3. J R Holder - Norton - 1 Hr 5 Min 46 Sec - 98.24 mph
Fastest Lap R McIntyre Norton 6 Min 28 Sec 102.56 mph

350cc

1. A King - Norton - 1 Hr 1 Min 32 Sec - 97.01 mph
2. A Shepherd - AJS - 1 Hr 2 Min 37 Sec
3. T H Thorp - Norton - 1 Hr 3 Min 35 Sec - 93.58 mph
Fastest Lap A King 6 Min 45 Sec 98.26 mph

250cc

1. T H Robb - GMS - 53 Min 45 Sec - 86.38 mph
2. N Orr - NSU - 55 Min 27 Sec - 83.73 mph
3. J W Dickson - NSU - 55 Min 35 Sec - 83.48 mph
Fastest Lap T H Robb GMS 7 Min 40 Sec 86.55 mph

125cc

1. T H Robb - Ducati - 43 Min 47 Sec - 75.72 mph
2. F Purslow - Ducati - 43 Min 48 Sec - 75.71 mph
3. W M Webster - M V Agusta - 45 min 47 - Sec 72.44 mph
Fastest Lap T H Robb Ducati 8 Min 29 Sec 78.18 mph

HANDICAP

500cc

1. P Middleton - Norton
2. F Gordon - Norton
3. J Robertson - Norton

350cc

1. J Adam - Norton
2. E Mayhew - AJS
3. A King - Norton

250cc

1. J Dixon - NSU
2. T H Robb - NSU
3. N Orr - NSU

1960

500cc

1. D W Minter - Norton - 99.32 mph
2. T H Robb - Matchless
3. A Shepherd - Matchless
Fastest Lap D W Minter Norton and T H Robb Matchless 102.3 mph

350cc

1. A Shepherd - AJS - 91.82 mph
2. R McIntyre - AJS
3. M T Brooks - Norton
Fastest Lap R McIntyre AJS and A Shepherd AJS 93.64 mph

250cc

1. T H Robb - GMS - 85.45 mph
2. T H Thorp - TTS
3. J W Dixon - Adler
Fastest Lap T H Robb GMS 87.85 mph

HANDICAP

500cc

1. R Spence - Norton
2. R C Rowe - Norton
3. T H Robb - Matchless

350cc

1. F A Neville - Nortton
2. J L Payne - Norton
3. A Shepherd - Matchless

250cc

1. T H Robb - GMS
2. T H Thorp - TTS
3. J W Dixon - Adler

1961

500cc

1. R McIntyre - Norton - 56 Min 39 Sec - 105.44 mph
2. P Read - Norton - 58 Min 4 Sec - mph
3. F Neville - Matchless - 58 Min 21 Sec - 102.30 mph
Fastest Lap R McIntyre Norton 106.86 mph

350cc

1. R McIntyre - AJS - 46 Min 29 Sec - 100.15 mph
2. P Read - Norton - 46 Min 33 Sec - 99.74 mph
3. F Neville - AJS - 46 Min37 Sec - 99.60 mph
Fastest Lap P Read Norton101.78 mph

250cc

1. T H Robb - GMS - 36 Min 26 Sec - 91.92 mph
2. G Carter - NSU - 36 Min 34 Sec - 90.69 mph
3. A Wheeler - Moto Guzzi - 36 Min 46 Sec - 90.2 mph
Fastest Lap T H Robb GMS 7 Min 8 Sec 92.982 mph

HANDICAP

500cc

1. F Neville - Matchless
2. P D Chatterton - Norton
3. S G Purvis - Matchless

350cc

1. J T Griffiths - AJS
2. F Neville - AJS
3. N Lindsay - Norton

250cc

1. J Pinckney - Norton-Velo
2. G Carter - NSU
3. A Wheeler - Moto Guzzi

1962

500cc

1. A Shepherd - Matchless - 57 Min - 44.8 Sec
2. R Spence - Norton - 58 Min 2 Sec - 102.86 mph
3. W McCosh - Matchless - 59 Min 14.6 Sec - 100.76 mph
Fastest Lap A Shepherd Matchless 6 Min 23 Sec 103.91 mph

350cc

1. A Shepherd - AJS - 45 Min 33.8 Sec - 101.90 mph
2. P Middleton - Norton - 45 Min 55.2 Sec - 1011.11 mph
3. R Bryans - Norton - 46 Min 40.2 Sec - 99.48 mph
Fastest Lap A Shepherd AJS 6 Min 24 Sec 103.64 mph

250cc

1. A Wheeler - Moto Guzzi - 94.10 mph
2. A Shepherd - Aermacchi - 93.78 mph
3. G Carter - NSU - 92.99 mph
Fastest Lap A Wheeler Moto Guzzi 6 Min 58 Sec 95.206 mph

HANDICAP

500cc

1. A E Shaw - Norton
2. W Evans - Norton
3. R Spence - Norton

350cc

1. R Bryans - Norton
2. F Fisher - Norton
3. E Oliver - AJS

250cc

1. A Wheeler - Moto Guzz
2. T W Findlay - Norton
3. A Shepherd - Aermacchi

1964

500cc

1. R Creith - Norton - 58 Min 23.4 Sec - 102.23 mph
2. J Findlay - Matchless
3. J Wilkinson - Norton
Fastest Lap J Findlay Matchless 6 Min24.4 Sec 103.53 mph

350cc

1. R Bryans - Honda - 46 Min 0.6 Sec - 100.91 mph
2. W McCosh - AJS - 47Min 31.2 Sec - 97.70 mph
3. J Findlay - AJS - 47Min 31.4 Sec - 97.69 mph
Fastest Lap R Bryans Honda 6 Min 29.6 Sec 102.14 mph

250cc

1. R Bryans - Honda - 34 Min 22.2 Sec - 96.49 mph
2. G Purvis - Mondial - 35 Min 57 Sec - 92.27 mph
3. J Isherwood - Honda - 36 Min 21.2 Sec - 91.22 mph
Fastest Lap R Bryans 6 Min 46.8 Sec 97.83 mph

HANDICAP

500cc

1. A E Shaw - Norton
2. R Creith - Norton
3. W Scott - Matchless

350cc

1. A Jardin - Norton
2. B J Davies - AJS
3. W McCosh - AJS

250cc

1. J Isherwood - Honda
2. G Purvis - Mondial
3. R Bryans - Honda

1965

500cc

1. R Creith - Norton - 57 Min 24.6 Sec - 103.97 mph
2. G Buchan - Norton - 58 Min 45.4 Sec - 100.59 mph
3. D F Shorey - Norton - 59 Min 30.6 Sec - 100.31 mph
Fastest Lap R Creith Norton 6 Min 14 .6 Sec 106.23 mph

350cc

1. I McGregor - Norton - 47 Min 8.6 Sec - 98.48 mph
2. J H Cooper - Norton - 47 Min 10.2 Sec - 98.42 mph
3. R L Ireland - Norton - 47 Min11.4 Sec - 98.34 mph
Fastest Lap I McGregor Norton 6 Min 35.4 Sec

250cc

1. T H Robb - Bultaco - 34 Min 48 Sec - 95.28 mph
2. R L Ireland - Honda - 34 Min 49 Sec - 95.22 mph
3. J Blanchard - Aermacchi - 35 Min 29.2 Sec - 93.45 mph
Fastest Lap R L Ireland 6 Min49 Sec 97.30 mph

HANDICAP

500cc

1. R N Steel - Matchless
2. A C Wilmott - Norton
3. R Creith - Norton

350cc

1. C Watts - Norton
2. J Clark - AJS
3. A T Lawton - Norton

250cc

1. R McCullough - Greeves
2. T Barnes Moto - Guzzi
3. R L Ireland - Honda

1966

500cc

1. P J Williams - Matchless - 1 Hr 0 Min 53.8 Sec - 98.03 mph
2. G Buchan - Norton - 1 Hr 0 Min 56.8 Sec - 97.95 mph
3. R N Steele - Matchless - 1 Hr 3 Min 3 Sec - 94.68 mph
Fastest Lap I McGregor Norton 6 Min 32 Sec 101.52 mph

350cc

1. G Buchan - Norton - 47 Min35.4 Sec - 97.56 mph
2. J Blanchard - Norton - 48 Min 11.8 Sec - 96.33 mph
3. R Steele - AJS - 48 Min 17.4 Sec - 96.15 mph
Fastest Lap T H Robb Bultaco 6 Min 39.4 Sec 99.64 mph

250cc

1. J Blanchard - Bultaco - 34 Min 31.6 Sec - 96.05 mph
2. P J Williams - Greeves - 35 Min 8.4 Sec - 94.37 mph
3. R McCullough - Bultaco - 35 Min 45.8 Sec - 92.73 mph
Fastest Lap J Blanchard Bultaco 6 Min 40.9 Sec 99.29 mph

HANDICAP

500cc

1. R Flack - Norton
2. G Buchan - Norton
3. R Steele - Matchless

350cc

1. T Lawton - Norton
2. G Mateer - Norton
3. D Gallagher - AJS

250CC

1. J Blanchard - Bultaco
2. W Jones - Yamaha
3. P J Williams - Greves

1967

500cc

1. F Stevens - Hannah Paton - 56 Min 44.8 Sec - 105.19 mph
2. J Blanchard - Matchless - 58 Min 12 Sec - 102.57 mph
3. M Uphill - Norton - 58 Min 36.6 Sec - 101.84 mph
Fastest Lap F Stevens Hannah Paton 6 Min 13 Sec 106.66 mph

350cc

1. F Stevens - Hannah Paton - 45 Min 57 Sec - 101.04 mph
2. M Uphill - Norton - 48 Min 37 Sec - 95.48 mph
3. R L Ireland - Norton - 49 Min 22 Sec - 94.05 mph
Fastest Lap F Stevens Hannah Paton 6 Min 27 Sec 102.38 mph

250cc

1. S Murray - Bultaco - 35 Min 34.6 Sec - 93.22 mph
2. P McGarrity - Honda - 35 Min 39 Sec - 92.59 mph
3. D Chatterton - Yamaha - 36 Min 2.8 Sec - 92 mph
Fastest Lap P McGarrity Honda 6 Min 56.6 Sec 95.52 mph

HANDICAP

500cc

F Stevens - Hannah Paton
350cc

J Ogle Norton

250cc

T Wilmott - Royal Enfield

1968

500cc

1. J Cooper - Matchless - 54 Min 22.5 Sec - 105.44 mph
2. R Nelson - Hannah Paton - 54 Min 35.6 Sec - 105.2 mph
3. R Gould - Norton - 54 Min 52.8 Sec - 104.66 mph
Fastest Lap J Cooper Matchless 107.45 mph

350cc

1. B Smith - Honda - 43 Min 37.2 Sec - 102.42 mph
2. B Steenson - Aermacchi - 43 Min 41 Sec - 102.25 mph
3. J Hartle - Aermacchi - 44 Min 18.6 Sec - 100.83 mph
Fastest Lap B Steenson Aermacchi 104.23 mph

250cc

1. R Gould - Yamaha - 30 Min 57.4 Sec - 103.08 mph
2. B Steenson - Aermacchi - 32 Min 2 Sec - 99.54 mph
3. J Findlay - Bultaco - 32 Min 30 Sec - 98.19 mph
Fastest Lap R Bryans Honda 109.23 mph

1969

500cc

1. J Blanchard - Seeley - 54 Min 3.8 Sec -106.26 mph
2. B Steenson - Seeley - 54 Min 43.6 Sec -104.98 mph
3. T H Robb - Norton - 55 Min 25.6 Sec -103.64 mph
Fastest Lap J Blanchard Seeley 107.69 mph

350cc

1. R Gould - Yamaha - 41 Min 25 Sec - 107.87 mph
2. P Read - Yamaha - 41 Min 54.8 Sec - 106.57 mph
3. J Findlay - Yamaha - 43 Min 5.8 Sec - 103.66 mph
Fastest Lap R Gould Yamaha 108.61 mph

250cc

1. R Gould - Yamaha - 30 Min 50 Sec - 103.50 mph
2. T H Robb - Yamaha - 32 Min 24.2 Sec - 98.59 mph
3. M Uphill - Crooks Suzuki - 32 Min 29.6 Sec - 98.44 mph
Fastest Lap R Gould Yamaha 104.63 mph

1970

500cc

1. P J Williams - Matchless - 53 Min 57.2 Sec - 106.46 mph
2. J Cooper - Seeley - 55 Min 43.4 Sec - 103.7 mph
3. B Nelson - Hannah Paton - 55 Min 44 Sec - 103.03 mph
Fastest Lap B Steenson Seeley 5 Min 52.2 Sec 108.73 mph

350 cc

1. T Herron - Yamaha - 41 Min 54.6 Sec - 106.61 mph
2. J Cooper - Yamsel - 42 Min 37.4 Sec - 104.83 mph
3. C Crawford - Aermacchi - 44 Min 2.8 Sec - 101.44 mph
Fastest Lap T H Robb Yamaha 5 Min 52.6 Sec 108.61 mph

250cc

1. R Bryans - Honda - 31 Min 12.8 Sec - 101.95 mph
2. M Uphill Crooks - Suzuki - 31 Min 29.6 Sec - 101.33 mph
3. T Rutter - Yamaha - 31 Min 31.4 Sec - 101.23 mph
Fastest Lap R Bryans Honda 103.16 mph

750cc Production

1. M Uphill - 650 Triumph - 48 Min 3 Sec - 106.25 mph
2. P Tait - 750 Triumph - 48 Min 11.6 Sec - 105.96 mph
3. P J Williams - 750 Norton Commando - 48 Min 31 Sec - 104.83 mph

500cc Production

1. S Graham - Suzuki - 48 Min 14.6 Sec - 94.58 mph
2. J Williams - Honda - 49 Min 45.4 Sec - 91.50 mph
3. H Robertson - Triumph - 50 Min 35.2 Sec - 88.32 mph

250cc Production

1. C Carr - Ossa - 52 Min 26.4 Sec - 88.58 mph
2. R Bryans - Suzuki - 53 Min 33.6 Sec - 86.64 mph
3. S Woods - Suzuki - 53 Min 40 Sec - 88.25 mph

1971

500cc

1. J Cooper - Seeley - 40 Min 41.2 Sec - 93.52 mph
2. G Barry - Matchless - 40 Min 43.4 Sec - 93.43 mph
3. J Williams - Matchless - 43 Min 15.4 Sec - 90.05 mph
Fastest Lap J Cooper Seeley 6 Min 40.2 Sec 95.07 mph

350cc

1. P Smart - Yamaha - 44 Min 16.4 Sec - 100.25 mph
2. J Cooper - Yamsel - 44 Min 42.4 Sec - 99.28 mph
3. T Rutter - Yamaha - 44 Min 51.8 Sec - 98.94 mph
Fastest Lap P Read Yamaha 6 Min 9.4 Sec 102.99 mph

250cc

1. D Chatterton - Yamaha - 35 Min 10.6 Sec - 90.13 mph
2. J Cooper - Yamaha - 89.54 mph
3. R McCullough - Yamsel - 35 Min 40.4 Sec - 88.87 mph
Fastest Lap P Smart Yamaha 6 Min 25 Sec 98.82 mph

1973

200cc

1. Jackie Robinson - Honda - 19 min 19 sec - 90.55mph
2. S Dempster - Honda
3. C Junk - Honda
Fastest Lap J Robinson 91.69mph

250cc

1. T Rutter - Yamaha - 39 min - 6.8 sec - 104.32 mph
2. J Williams - Yamaha
3. T Herron - Yamaha
Fastest Lap T Rutter 105.97 mph

350cc

1. T Rutter - Yamaha - 36 min 54.4 sec - 110.56 mph
2. J Williams - Yamaha
3. B Randle - Yamaha
Fastest Lap T Rutter 112.44 mph

500cc

1. B Guthrie - Yamaha - 39 min 46.6 sec - 102.58 mph
2. S McClements - Ryan Norton
3. D Shimmin - Suzuki
Fastest Lap W McCosh 104.96 mph

750cc

1. G Barry Norton - 38 min 15 sec - 106.52 mph
2. W Herron - Norton
3. J Cooper - BSA
Fastest Lap J Cooper 108.20 mph

1974

250cc

1. R McCullough - Yamsel - 37 min 51.4 sec - 107.77 mph
2. J Williams - Yamaha
3. M Grant - Yamaha
Fastest Lap R McCullough 109.70 mph (Record)

350cc

1. J Williams - Yamaha - 39 min 36.4 sec - 102.17 mph
2. T Rutter - Yamaha
3. W Guthrie - Yamaha
Fastest Lap J Williams 104.70 mph

500cc

1. J Williams - Yamaha - 38 min 44.2 sec - 105.38 mph
2. C Williams - Yamaha
3. G Mateer - Yamaha
Fastest Lap J Williams 106 36 mph

750cc

1. J Willliams - Yamaha - 51 Min 38.6 sec - 112.88 mph
2. B Randle - Yamaha
3. W Guthrie - Yamaha
Fastest Lap J Williams 115.80 mph (Course Record)

1975

250cc

1. D Chatterton - Yamaha - 37 min 59 sec - 110.57 mph
2. M Sharpe - Yamaha
3. C Carr - Yamaha
Fastest Lap   D Chatterton   111.66 mph (Record)

350cc

1. C Williams - Yamaha - 36 min 50.4 sec - 114.01 mph
2. B Heath - Yamaha
3. N Tuxworth - Yamaha
Fastest Lap   N Tuxworth   115.83 mph (Record)

500cc

1. M Grant - Kawasaki - 36 min 11.2 sec - 116.06 mph
2. T Rutter - Yamaha
3. B Heath - Yamaha
Fastest Lap   M Grant 117.49 mph (Record)

750cc

1. M Grant - Kawasaki - 40 min 0.6 sec - 119.96 mph
2. B Ditchburn - Kawasaki
3. A North - Yamaha
Fastest Lap   M Grant   122.62 mph (Course Record)

1976

250cc

1. I Richards - Yamaha - 44 min 59.8 sec - 94.33 mph
2. T Rutter - Yamaha
3. J Dunlop - Yamaha
Fastest Lap   I Richards 96.90 mph

350cc

1. R McCullough - Yamaha - 42 min 54.6 sec - 98.90 mph
2. T Rutter - Yamaha
3. S McClements - Yamaha
Fastest Lap T Rutter 102.87 mph

500cc

1. M Sharpe - Spartan - 42 min 18.4 sec - 100.31 mph
2. F Kennedy - Spartan
3. P Tait - Suzuki
Fastest Lap F Kennedy 102.29 mph

750cc

1. P Tait - Suzuki - 46 min 20.4 sec - 104.66 mph
2. T Rutter - Yamaha
3. M Grant - Kawasaki
Fastest Lap T Rutter 106.86 mph

1977

250cc

1. T Rutter - Yamaha - 32 min 56 sec - 110.45 mph
2. J Dunlop - Yamaha
3. R McCullough - Yamaha
Fastest Lap T Rutter 111.37 mph (Record)

350cc

1. R McCullough - Yamaha & T Rutter Yamaha - 31 min 53 sec - 114.09 mph
3. I Richards - Yamaha
Fastest Lap   T Rutter 116.44 mph (Record)

500cc

1. J Williams - Suzuki - 30 min 50 sec - 117.79 mph
2. S Parrish - Suzuki
3. G Fogarty - Suzuki
Fastest Lap   J Woodley 120.76 mph (Record)

750cc

1. M Grant - Kawasaki - 30min 23.4 sec - 119.69 mph
2. G Barry - Yamaha
3. N Tuxworth - Yamaha
Fastest Lap J Williams 122.97 mph (Record)

NW 200 Superbike Race

1. J Williams - Yamaha - 24 min 53.8 sec - 121.75 mph
2. J Newbold - Yamaha
3. S Parrish - Suzuki
Fastest Lap J Newbold 124.06 mph (Course Record)

1978

250cc

1. T Herron - Yamaha - 32 min 24.6 sec - 112.23 mph
2. R McCullough - Yamaha
3. C Mortimer - Yamaha
Fastest Lap T Herron 113.88 mph

350cc

1. T Rutter - Yamaha - 31 min 29 sec - 115.54 mph
2. G Waring - Yamaha
3. S Tonkin - Yamaha
Fastest Lap T Rutter 117.19 mph

500cc

1. J Newbold - Suzuki - 30 min 27.8 sec - 119.40 mph
2. G Fogarty - Suzuki
3. J Williams - Suzuki
Fastest Lap J Williams 122.97 mph

750cc

1. T Herron - Yamaha - 29 min 39 sec - 122.68 mph
2. T Rutter - Yamaha
3. C Williams - Yamaha
Fastest Lap T Herron 124.14 mph

NW 200 Superbike Race

1. T Rutter - Yamaha 24 min 17.8 sec - 124.76 mph
2. K Stowe - Yamaha
3. J Newbold - Yamaha
Fastest Lap T Herron 127.63 mph

1979

250cc

1. B Jackson - Yamaha - 33 min 1 sec - 110.17 mph
2. T Rutter - Yamaha
3. I Richards - Yamaha
Fastest Lap   B Jackson 111.78 mph

350cc

1. T Rutter - Yamaha - 31 min 46.4 sec - 114.48 mph
2. S Tonkin - Yamaha
3. D Huxley - Yamaha
Fastest Lap   D Huxley 116.58 mph

500cc

1. T Rutter - Yamaha - 30 min 16.4 sec - 120.15 mph
2. S Parrish - Suzuki
3. A Jackson - Suzuki
Fastest Lap   M Grant 122.47 mph

Match Race

Tom Herron Select 193 points
Tony Rutter Select 119 points
1. J Dunlop - Yamaha - 30 min 18.6 sec - 120.01 mph
2. M Grant - Suzuki
3. J Sayle - Yamaha
Fastest Lap J Dunlop 124.66 mph

1000cc

1. J Dunlop - Yamaha - 30 min 13.6 sec - 120.34 mph
2. T Rutter - Suzuki
3. J Sayle - Yamaha
Fastest Lap J Dunlop 123.81 mph

1980

250cc

1. S Cull - Cotton - 33 min 46.6 sec - 110.97 mph
2. T Rutter - Cotton
3. C Mortimer - Rotax
Fastest Lap S Cull 112.57 mph

350cc

1. C Williams - Yamaha - 32 min 35.4 sec - 115.01 mph
2. T Rutter - Yamaha
3. S Tonkin - Yamaha
Fastest Lap   C Williams 116.40 mph

500cc

1. M Grant - Suzuki - 31 min 23.2 sec - 119.42 mph
2. S Avant - Suzuki
3. D Ireland - Suzuki
Fastest Lap J Dunlop 121.97 mph

1000cc NW 200 Superbike Race

1. K Heuwen - Yamaha - 34 min 56.2 sec - 122.61 mph
2. J Newbold - Yamaha
3. D Ireland - Suzuki
Fastest Lap   K Heuwen 125.01 mph (Record)

1981

250cc

1. S Tonkin - Armstrong - 33 min 26.6 sec - 112.07 mph
2. P Wild - Yamaha
3. S Cull - Yamaha
Fastest Lap   C Williams 113.52 mph(Record)

350cc

1. D Robinson - Yamaha - 32 min 25.4 sec - 115.6 mph
2. C McGinn - Yamaha
3. A Stewart - Yamaha
Fastest Lap   D Robinson & C McGinn 116.91 mph

500cc

1. C Williams - Yamaha - 31 min 56 sec - 117.37 mph
2. G Fogarty - Suzuki
3. A George - Suzuki
Fastest Lap   J Newbold 119.87 mph

NW 200 1300cc Race

1. J Dunlop - Honda - 35 min 44.8 sec - 119.83 mph
2. S Parrish - Yamaha
3. D Ireland - Yamaha
Fastest Lap J Dunlop 121.06 mph

1982

250cc

1. D Robinson - Yamaha - 28 min 23.2 sec - 113.17 mph
2. P Wild - Yamaha
3. S Tonkin - Armstrong
Fastest Lap   Robinson, Wild, & C Law 114.74 mph

350cc

1. T Rutter - Yamaha - 27 min 51.2 sec - 114.93 mph
2. P Mellor - Yamaha
3. R McIlnea - Yamaha
Fastest Lap   R McIlnea & T Rutter 117.51 mph

500cc

1. S Avant - Suzuki - 26 min 35 sec - 120.85 mph
2. N Brown - Suzuki
3. C Williams - Yamaha
Fastest Lap   N Brown 122.53 mph

Superbike Race One

1. R Haslam - Honda - 26 min 21.6 sec - 121.88 mph
2. R Marshall - Suzuki
3. G Wood - Yamaha
Fastest Lap   R Haslam & R Marshall 123.47 mph

NW 200 Superbike Race

1. M Grant - Suzuki
2. J Dunlop - Honda
3. R McIlnea - Yamaha
Fastest Lap   R McIlnea 123.46 mph

1983

250cc Race

1. C Junk - Waddon - 101.92 mph
2. N Tuxworth - British Wicks
3. D Robinson - Yamaha

Fastest Lap   C Junk & S Cole 103.90 mph

350cc

1. N Brown - Yamaha - 104.67 mph
2. G Young - Yamaha
3. C Junk - Yamaha
Fastest Lap   N Brown 107.45 mph

500cc

1. J Dunlop - Honda - 106.05 mph
2. G Wood - Yamaha
3. G Lingham - Suzuki
Fastest Lap   N Brown 111.01 mph

Superbike Race One

1. G Wood - Yamaha - 104.46 mph
2. N Brown - Suzuki
3. J Dunlop - Honda
Fastest Lap   N Brown 107.53 mph

NW 200 Superbike Race

1. J Dunlop - Honda - 105.64 mph
2. N Brown - Suzuki
3. G Wood - Yamaha
Fastest Lap   S McClements 108.24 mph

1984

250cc

1. A Watts - EMC - 36 min 25.7 mph - 102.89 mph
2. B Reid - EMC
3. G McGregor - EMC
Fastest Lap   B Reid 105.09 mph

350cc

1. K Mitchell - Yamaha - 36 min 9.5 sec - 103.66 mph
2. N Mackenzie - Armstrong
3. J Rea - Yamaha
Fastest Lap   K Mitchell 105.99 mph

MCN Masters Superbike Race

1. J Dunlop - Honda - 35 min 1.3 sec - 107.02 mph
2. S Parrish - Yamaha
3. G Wood - Yamaha
Fastest Lap   R Marshall 109.27 mph

NW 200 Superbike Race

1. G Wood - Yamaha - 42 min 30.4 sec - 113.37 mph
2. M Grant - Suzuki
3. B Woodland - Suzuki
Fastest Lap   G Wood 115.11 mph

1985

250cc Race One

1. J Dunlop - Honda - 28 min 57.3 sec - 110.95 mph
2. A Watts - EMC
3. N Mackenzie - Armstrong
Fastest Lap   J Dunlop 112.21 mph

250 Race Two

1. S Cull - Honda - 28 min 49.4 sec
2. E Roberts - Kimocco
3. C Law - EMC
Fastest Lap   N Mackenzie 113 mph (Record)

350cc

1. S Cull - Yamaha - 33 min 38 .7 sec - 111.4 mph
2. P Mellor - Yamaha
3. G McDonnell - Yamaha
Fastest Lap S Cull 112.21 mph (Record)

Superbike Race One

1. R Marshall - Honda - 27 min 4 sec - 118.69 mph
2. G Wood - Yamaha
3. M Grant - Suzuki
Fastest Lap   R McIlnea 119.87 mph

NW 200 Superbike Race

1. J Dunlop - Honda - 31 min 36.3 sec - 118.59 mph
2. S Cull - Suzuki
3. B Woodland - Suzuki
Fastest Lap   J Dunlop 120.55 mph (Record)

1986

250cc Race One

1. E Laycock - EMC - 30 min 7.1 sec - 106.67 mph
2. A Watts - EMC
3. G Cowan - Honda
Fastest Lap   J Dunlop 108.87 mph

350cc

1. R Dunlop - Yamaha - 29 min 29.4 sec - 108.94 mph
2. G McDonnell - Yamaha
3. N Tuxworth - Yamaha
Fastest Lap   R Dunlop 111.78 mph

Superstock Race

1. T Nation - Suzuki - 29 min 8 sec - 110.27 mph
2. K Irons - Yamaha
3. S Parrish - Yamaha
Fastest Lap   T Nation 112.57 mph

Superbike Race One

1. R Marshall - Honda - 28 min 15.4 sec - 113.69 mph
2. G McDonnell - Suzuki
3. M Phillips - Suzuki
Fastest Lap   R Marshall 115.27 mph

NW 200 Superbike Race
1. J Dunlop - Honda - 29 min 43.9 sec - 108.05 mph
2. R Marshall - Honda
3. S Cull - Suzuki
Fastest Lap J Dunlop 110.74 mph

250cc Race Two

1. A Watts - EMC - 29 min 56.3 sec - 107.31 mph
2. E Laycock - EMC
3. G Cowan - Honda
Fastest Lap   G Cowan 109.24 mph

1987

250cc/350cc Race One

1. G Cowan - Honda 29 min 3.4 sec - 110.56 mph
2. B Reid - EMC
3. S Cull - Honda
Fastest Lap   B Reid 112.45 mph

Superstock Race

1. R Hurst - Yamaha - 29 min 16.2 sec - 109.75 mph
2. R Swann - Suzuki
3. G Lingham - Kawasaki
Fastest Lap   R Hurst 112.09 mph

1300cc Production Race

1. T Nation Yamaha - 27 min 46.1 sec - 115.69 mph
2. G Johnston - Yamaha
3. B Morrison - Suzuki
Fastest Lap   G Johnston 117.16 mph

Superbike Race One

1. J Dunlop - Honda - 28 min 21.4 sec - 113.29 mph
2. A Irwin - Honda
3. R Dunlop - Suzuki
Fastest Lap J Dunlop 115.6 mph

North West 200 Superbike Race

1. J Dunlop - Honda - 27 min 5.2 sec - 118.61 mph
2. A Irwin - Honda
3. P Mellor - Suzuki
Fastest Lap J Dunlop 119.83 mph

250cc Race Two

1. E Laycock - Yamaha - 29 min 30.3 sec - 108.88 mph
2. G Cowan - Honda
3. B Reid - EMC
Fastest Lap B Reid & E Laycock 111.94 mph

750cc Production Race

1. J Dunlop - Honda - 29 min 32.2 sec - 108.77 mph
2. J Lofthouse - Suzuki
3. S Cull - Suzuki
Fastest Lap J Lofthouse 110.17 mph

1988

250cc/350cc Race One

1. S Cull - Honda - 29 min 31.2 sec - 108.54 mph
2. C Fogarty - Honda
3. A Irwin - Yamaha
Fastest Lap S Cull 109.28 mph

1300cc Production Race

1. K Irons - Yamaha - 28 min 59.8 sec - 110.5 mph
2. T Nation - Suzuki
3. J Lofthouse - Suzuki
Fastest Lap T Nation 111.95 mph

750cc Production Race

1. J Dunlop - Honda - 29 min 22.4 sec - 109.08 mph
2. R Rose - Suzuki
3. I Newton - Suzuki
Fastest Lap   S Hislop 111.4 mph

Superbike Race One

1. S Cull - Honda - 27 min 28.5 sec - 116.62 mph
2. E Laycock - Honda
3. A McGladdery - Suzuki
Fastest Lap   S Cull 117.28 mph

NW 200 Superbike Race

1. S Cull - Honda - 27 min 33.5 sec - 116.26 mph
2. J Dunlop - Honda
3. K Irons - Honda
Fastest Lap   S Cull 117.28 mph

250cc/350cc Race Two

1. G Cowan - Yamaha - 29 min 15.3 sec - 109.52 mph
2. W Coulter - Honda
3. J Dunlop - Honda
Fastest Lap   G Cowan 110.22 mph (Record)

1989

250cc/350cc Race One

1. K Mitchell - Yamaha - 29 min 6.17 sec - 111.329 mph
2. B Reid - Yamaha
3. J Rea - Yamaha
Fastest Lap   K Mitchell 112.007 mph (Record)

600cc

1. B Reid - Yamaha - 24 min 28.05 sec - 110.35 mph
2. S Hislop - Honda
3. D Leach - Yamaha
Fastest Lap   S Hislop 111.371 mph

Production Race

1. J Whitham - Suzuki - 23 min 33.8 sec - 114.585 mph
2. D Leach - Yamaha
3. G Johnston - Yamaha
Fastest Lap   J Whitham 115.992 mph (Record)

750cc King of the Roads Race

1. S Hislop - Honda - 27 min 37.75 sec - 117.267 mph
2. E Laycock - Honda
3. R Dunlop - Honda
Fastest Lap   E Laycock 118.335 mph (Record)

NW200 Superbike Race

1. S Hislop - Honda - 29 min 50.49 sec - 108.574 mph
2. J Whitham - Suzuki
3. S Spray - Norton
Fastest Lap   S Hislop 113.608 mph

250cc/350cc Race Two

1. W Coulter - Aprillia - 29 min 57.99 sec - 108.121 mph
2. K Mitchell - Yamaha
3. E Laycock - Yamaha
Fastest Lap W Coulter 109.804 mph

1990

125cc

1. R Dunlop - Honda - 20 min 58.01 sec - 103.03 mph
2. A Patterson - Honda
3. I Lougher - Honda
Fastest Lap   R Dunlop 103.48 mph

250cc Race One

1. E Laycock - Yamaha - 28 min 46.89 sec - 112.57 mph
2. I Lougher - Yamaha
3. P McCallan - Honda
Fastest Lap   I Lougher 113.64 mph (Record)

250cc Race Two

1. E Laycock - Yamaha - 28 min 40 31 sec - 113 mph
2. I Newton - Yamaha
3. I Lougher - Yamaha
Fastest Lap   E Laycock 113.51 mph

Superbike Race One

1. R Dunlop - Norton - 26 min 55.46 sec - 120.337 mph
2. C Fogarty - Honda
3. E Laycock - Honda
Fastest Lap   R Dunlop 120.58 mph

NW 200 Superbike Race

1. R Dunlop - Norton - 27 min 17.58 mph - 119.075 mph
2. P McCallan - Honda
3. E Laycock - Honda
Fastest Lap   R Dunlop 121.04 mph (Record)

1991

125cc

1. R Dunlop - Honda - 21min 0.54 sec - 102.81 mph
2. J Dunlop - Honda
3. D Lemon - Honda
Fastest Lap   J Courtney 103.03 mph

250cc/350cc Race One

1. R Dunlop - Yamaha - 28 min 40.82 sec - 112.97 mph
2. P McCallan - Honda
3. I Lougher - Yamaha
Fastest Lap   R Dunlop 114.38 mph

600cc

1. P McCallan - Honda - 23 min 44.44 sec - 113.73 mph
2. S Ives - Yamaha
3. B Jackson
Fastest Lap   P McCallan 114.49 mph

750cc

1. R Dunlop - Norton - 26 min 55.48 sec - 120.34 mph
2. T Nation - Norton
3. I Simpson - Yamaha
Fastest Lap   R Dunlop 121.73 mph

NW 200 Superbike Race

1. T Nation - Norton - 26 min 51.86 sec - 120.61 mph
2. J Dunlop
3. I Simpson - Yamaha
Fastest Lap   T Nation 121.92 mph

250cc/350cc Race Two

1. I Lougher - 28 min 31.46 sec - 114.38 mph
2. R Dunlop - Yamaha
3. B Reid - Yamaha
Fastest   B Reid 114.55 mph

400cc

1. D Leach - Yamaha - 19 min 58 sec - 108.18 mph
2. S Ives - Yamaha
3. B Reid - Yamaha
Fastest Lap   S Ives 108.87 mph

1992

125cc

1. R Orme - Honda - 20 min 25.26 sec - 105.77 mph
2. R Dunlop - Honda
3. J Dunlop - Honda
Fastest Lap   R Orme 106.47 mph (Record)

250cc/350cc Race One

1. P McCallan - Honda - 28 min 27.09 sec - 113.88 mph
2. R Dunlop - Yamaha
3. A Irwin - Honda
Fastest Lap   P McCallan 115.47 mph

600cc

1. P McCallan - Honda - 23 min 33.63 sec - 114.6 mph
2. J Moodie - Honda
3. M Edwards - Honda
Fastest Lap   J Dunlop 115.04 mph (Record)

Superbike Race

1. P McCallan - Honda - 26 min 52.24 sec - 120.58 mph
2. R Dunlop - Norton
3. M Farmer - Yamaha
Fastest Lap   R Dunlop 121.62 mph

NW 200 Superbike Race

1. P McCallan - Honda - 26 min 52.26 sec - 120.57 mph
2. M Farmer - Yamaha
3. I Simpson - Kawasaki
Fastest Lap   P McCallan 120.94 mph

250cc/350cc Race Two

1. R Dunlop - Yamaha - 28 min 7.12 sec - 115.23 mph
2. I Newton - Aprillia
3. W Coulter - Honda
Fastest Lap   I Newton 115.86 mph

400cc

1. P McCallan - Honda - 20 min 1.58 sec - 107.86 mph
2. J Rea - Yamaha
3. S Lindsell - Yamaha
Fastest Lap   J Rea 108.49 mph

1993

125cc

1. R Dunlop - Honda - 20 min 35.8 sec - 104.87 mph
2. M Lofthouse - Honda
3. R Orme - Honda
Fastest Lap   R Dunlop 105.89 mph

250cc/350cc Race One

1. R Dunlop - Yamaha - 28 min 45.68 sec - 112.65 mph
2. D Milling - Yamaha
3. I Lougher - Yamaha
Fastest Lap   R Dunlop 113.64 mph

600cc

1. J Moodie - Honda - 23 min 27.05 sec - 115.13 mph
2. M Edwards - Honda
3. J Dunlop - Honda
Fastest Lap   J Dunlop 115.62 mph

Superbike Race One

1. C Fogarty - Ducati - 26 min 41.83 sec - 121.86 mph
2. R Dunlop - Ducati
3. J Dunlop - Honda
Fastest Lap C Fogarty 121.86 mph

NW 200 Superbike Race

1. C Fogarty Ducati - 13 min 11.95 sec - 122.76 mph
2. R Dunlop - Ducati
3. P McCallan - Honda
Fastest Lap   C Fogarty 122.49 mph (Record)

250cc/350cc Race Two

1. R Dunlop - Yamaha - 28 min 8.72 sec - 115.12 mph
2. P McCallan - Honda
3. W Coulter - Yamaha
Fastest Lap   P McCallan 115.45 mph

400cc

1. J Moodie - Yamaha - 19 min 29.4 sec - 110.83 mph
2. B Reid - Yamaha
3. I Simpson
Fastest Lap   J Moodie 112.41 mph (Record)

1994

125cc

1. R Dunlop - Honda - 20 min 24.54 sec - 105.84 mph
2. P Owens - Honda
3. K Mawdsley - Honda
Fastest Lap   R Dunlop 106.37 mph

250cc/400cc Race One

1. W Coulter - Aprillia - 28 min 20.53 sec 114.32 mph
2. I Newton - Aprillia
3. P McCallan - Honda
Fastest Lap   P McCallan 115.13 mph

600cc

1. M Edwards - Yamaha - 23 min 22.64 sec - 117.17 mph
2. I Simpson - Yamaha
3. M Farmer - Yamaha
Fastest Lap   M Edwards 117.37 mph (Record)

Superbike Race One

1. R Dunlop - Honda - 26 min 47.33 sec - 120.95 mph
2. I Duffus - Yamaha
3. P McCallan - Honda
Fastest Lap   P McCallan 121.85 mph

NW 200 Superbike Race

1. R Dunlop - Honda - 26 min 51.47 sec - 120.64 mph
2. P McCallan - Honda
3. J Dunlop - Honda
Fastest Lap   R Dunlop 121.21 mph

250cc/400cc Race Two

1. I Newton - Aprillia - 28 min 18.71sec - 114.44 mph
2. W Coulter - Aprillia
3. P McCallan
Fastest Lap   I Newton 115.12 mph

Supermono Race

1. A Carter - Ducati - 20 min 24.01 sec - 105.88 mph
2. J Moodie - Harris Yamaha
3.M Edwards - MZ
Fastest Lap   A Carter 109.45 mph

1995

125cc

1. P Owens Honda - 15 min 16.73 sec - 106.03 mph
2. J Dunlop - Honda
3. R Appleyard - Honda
Fastest Lap P Owens 106.35 mph

250cc/400cc Race One

1. P McCallan - Honda - 27 min 59.39 sec - 115.76 mph
2. I Newton - Aprillia
3. C Ramsey - Yamaha
Fastest Lap   P McCallan 116.57 mph (Record)

600cc

1. P McCallan - Honda - 22min 49.85 sec - 118.26 mph
2. M Edwards - Honda
3. B Jackson - Honda
Fastest Lap   P McCallan 118.29 mph (Record)

Superbike Race One

1. I Simpson - Honda - 26 min 29.77 sec - 122.28 mph
2. M Rutter - Ducati
3. P McCallan - Honda
Fastest Lap   I Simpson 123.53 mph (Record).

NW 200 Superbike Race

1. R Holden - Ducati - 26 min 40.5 sec - 121.46 mph
2. P McCallan - Honda
3. I Duffus - Ducati
Fastest Lap   I Duffus 122.36 mph

Supermono Race

1. R Holden - Ducati - 14 min 52.16 sec - 108.95 mph
2. B Jackson - MHD
3. N Jeffries - Hornet
Fastest Lap   R Holden 108.99 mph

250cc/400cc Race Two

1. I Newton - Aprillia - 27 min 56.5 sec - 115.96 mph
2. R Milton - Honda
3. C Ramsey - Honda
Fastest Lap   I Newton 116.32 mph

1996

125cc

1. M Lofthouse - Honda - 20 min 37.96 sec - 104.688 mph
2. D McCullough - Honda
3. G Lee - Honda
Fastest Lap   M Lofthouse 104.902 mph

250cc/400cc Race One

1. W Coulter - Aprillia - 28 min 27.83 sec - 113.829 mph
2. P McCallan - Honda
3. G Lee - Honda
Fastest Lap   W Coulter 115.16 mph

600cc

1. P McCallan - Honda - 23 min 20.68 sec - 115.658 mph
2. I Simpson - Honda
3. I Duffus - Honda
Fastest Lap   P McCallan 115.59 mph

Superbike Race One

1. I Simpson - Ducati - 26 min 59.58 sec - 120.03 mph
2. P McCallan - Honda
3. I Duffus - Honda
Fastest Lap   P McCallan 120.38 mph

NW 200 Superbike Race

1. P McCallan - Honda - 27 min 6.47 sec - 119.52 mph
2. J Moodie - Ducati
3. I Simpson - Ducati
Fastest Lap   M Rutter 120.92 mph (Record)

250cc/400cc Race Two

1. W Coulter - Aprillia - 28 min 31.98 sec - 113.553 mph
2. J Dunlop - Honda
3. P Owens - Honda
Fastest Lap   C Ramsey 114.358 mph

1997

125cc

1. P Owens - Aprillia - 20 min 34.17 sec - 104.613 mph
2. C Ramsey - Honda
3. I Lougher - Honda
Fastest Lap   P Owens 105.792 mph (Record)

250cc/400cc Race One

1. C Ramsey - Honda - 24 min 11.56 sec - 104.61 mph
2. J McGuinness - Aprillia
3. P Owens - Aprillia
Fastest Lap   P Owens 113.05 mph

600cc

1. M Rutter - Honda - 23 min 15.67 sec - 115.72 mph
2. P McCallan - Honda
3. I Simpson - Honda
Fastest Lap   I Simpson 116.46 mph (Record)

Superbike Race One

1. P McCallan - Honda - 22 min 30.3 sec - 119.61 mph
2. M Rutter - Honda
3. J Moodie - Suzuki
Fastest Lap   P McCallan 120.43 mph

NW 200 Superbike

1. M Rutter - Honda - 26 min 32.92 mph - 121.73 mph
2. J Moodie - Suzuki
3. B Jackson - Kawasaki
Fastest Lap   J Moodie 122.32 mph (Record)

250cc/400cc Race Two

1. O McNally - Aprillia - 23 min 23.65 sec - 115.06 mph
2. W Coulter - Aprillia
3. P Owens - Aprillia
Fastest Lap   P Owens 115.98 mph (Record)

Production Race

1. I Simpson - Ducati - 23 min 8.01 sec - 116.36 mph
2. P McCallan - Honda
3. M Rutter - Honda
Fastest Lap   P McCallan 117.59 mph (Record)

1998

250cc/400cc

1. W Coulter - Honda - 23 min 53.93 sec - 112.21 mph
2. I Lougher - Honda
3. R Farquhar - Honda
Fastest Lap   C Ramsey 113.91 mph

600cc

1. I Simpson - Honds - 23 min 37.04 sec - 113.54 mph
2. S Plater - Honda
3. M Rutter - Honda
Fastest Lap   B Jackson 114.41 mph

1998 Production Race

1. M Rutter - Honda - 18 min 42.58 sec - 114.57 mph
2. D Jeffries - Yamaha
3. S Plater - Honda
Fastest Lap   D Jeffries 115.17 mph

Superbike Race One

1. I Simpson - Honda - 22 min 41.94 sec - 118.13 mph
2. M Rutter - Honda
3. B Jackson - Kawasaki
Fastest Lap   M Rutter 118.91 mph

NW 200 Superbike Race

1. M Rutter - Honda - 18 min 5.46 sec - 118.49 mph
2. I Simpson - Honda
3. I Duffus - Honda
Fastest Lap   M Rutter 119.13 mph

125cc

Race Abandoned

1999

125cc

1. I Lougher - Honda - 20 min 22.91 sec - 105.141 mph
2. O McNally - Honda
3. P Owens - Honda
Fastest Lap   O McNally 105.883 mph (Record)

250cc/400cc Race One

1. C Ramsey - Honda - 27 min 57.82 sec - 115.09 mph
2. J McGuinness - Honda
3. O McNally - Aprillia
Fastest Lap   C Ramsey 115.718 mph

600cc

1. D Jeffries - Yamaha - 22 min 58.07 sec - 116.71 mph
2. P McCallan - Yamaha
3. J Moodie - Honda
Fastest Lap   D Jeffries 117.40 mph (Record)

Superbike Race One

1. D Jeffries - Yamaha - 22 min 15.14 sec - 120.470 mph
2. J Moodie - Honda
3. I Duffus - Honda
Fastest Lap I Duffus 121.40 mph

NW 200 Superbike Race

1. D Jeffries - Yamaha - 26 min 26.46 sec - 121.72 mph
2. J Moodie - Honda
3. P McCallan - Yamaha
Fastest Lap   D Jeffries 122.26 mph (Record)

250cc/400cc Race Two

1. C Ramsey - Honda - 27 min 54.16 sec - 115.348 mph
2. I Lougher - Honda
3. J McGuinness - Honda
Fastest Lap   I Lougher 116.38 mph (Record)

2000

125cc

1. I Lougher - Honda - 21 min 17.84 sec - 100.65 mph
2. P Robinson - Honda
3. R Dunlop - Honda
Fastest Lap   M Wilcox 101.54 mph

250cc/400cc

1. J McGuinness - Honda - 28 min 56.65 sec 111.23 mph
2. I Lougher - Honda
3. C Ramsey - Yamaha
Fastest Lap   J McGuinness 112.96 mph

600cc

1. M Rutter - Yamaha - 23 min 34.00 sec - 113.79 mph
2. J Moodie - Honda
3. D Jeffries - Yamaha
Fastest Lap   J Moodie 114.89 mph (Record)

Production Race

1. R Britton - Yamaha - 23 min 30.24 sec - 114.09 mph
2. J Moodie - Honda
3. A Archibald - Honda
Fastest Lap   J Moodie 114.59 mph

Superbike Race One

1. M Rutter - Yamaha - 27 min 32.45 sec - 116.903 mph
2. D Jeffries - Yamaha
3. I Duffus - Honda
Fastest Lap   M Rutter 118.35 mph

NW 200 Superbike Race

1. M Rutter - Yamaha - 27 min 09.29 sec - 118.56 mph
2. D Jeffries - Yamaha
3. I Lougher - Yamaha
Fastest Lap   M Rutter 119.547 mph (Record)

INDEX

ACKNOWLEDGEMENTS

This book would not have been possible without the help of the following people: Irene Ackerman, Keith Beattie, Liam Beckett, John Blanchard, Ralph Bryans, Eddie Cambell, Malcolm Carling, Richard Creith, Steve Cull, Robert Dunlop, Geoff Duke, Victor Freeman, Jimmy Geddis, Mick Grant, Paul Harron (Commissioning Editor), Keith Heuwen, David Jeffries, Ernie Lyons, Jim McBride, Mervyn McBride, Philip McCallan, Nigel McClatchey, Glenn McGivern, Derek McIntyre, Clifford McLean, the late Owen McNally, Michael McSorley, Eddie Mateer, Wayne Matier (Designer), Don May, Sammy Millar, Steve Murry, Phil Read, Tommy Robb, Michel Rutter, Tony Rutter, Simon Thomas, Steven Wilson and Rowland White.